WEST'S LAW SCHOOL ADVISORY BOARD

JESSE H. CHOPER
Professor of Law,
University of California, Berkeley

JOSHUA DRESSLER
Professor of Law, Michael E. Moritz College of Law,
The Ohio State University

YALE KAMISAR
Professor of Law, University of San Diego
Professor of Law, University of Michigan

MARY KAY KANE
Professor of Law, Chancellor and Dean Emeritus,
University of California,
Hastings College of the Law

LARRY D. KRAMER
Dean and Professor of Law, Stanford Law School

JONATHAN R. MACEY
Professor of Law, Yale Law School

ARTHUR R. MILLER
University Professor, New York University
Professor of Law Emeritus, Harvard University

GRANT S. NELSON
Professor of Law, Pepperdine University
Professor of Law Emeritus, University of California, Los Angeles

A. BENJAMIN SPENCER
Associate Professor of Law,
Washington & Lee University School of Law

JAMES J. WHITE
Professor of Law, University of Michigan

INTERNATIONAL TRADE and ECONOMIC RELATIONS

IN A NUTSHELL

Fourth Edition

By

RALPH H. FOLSOM
Professor of Law
University of San Diego

MICHAEL WALLACE GORDON
John & Mary Lou Dasburg Professor of Law
University of Florida

JOHN A. SPANOGLE
William Wallace Kirkpatrick Professor of Law
The George Washington University

Mat #40756907

HUDSON VALLEY COMMUNITY COLLEGE LIBRARY

Thomson/Reuters have created this publication to provide you with accurate and authoritative information concerning the subject matter covered. However, this publication was not necessarily prepared by persons licensed to practice law in a particular jurisdiction. Thomson/Reuters are not engaged in rendering legal or other professional advice, and this publication is not a substitute for the advice of an attorney. If you require legal or other expert advice, you should seek the services of a competent attorney or other professional.

Nutshell Series, In a Nutshell, the Nutshell Logo and West Group are trademarks registered in the U.S. Patent and Trademark Office.

COPYRIGHT © 1996 WEST PUBLISHING CO.
© West, a Thomson business, 2000, 2004
© 2009 Thomson/Reuters
      610 Opperman Drive
      St. Paul, MN 55123
      1-800-313-9378

Printed in the United States of America

ISBN: 978-0-314-19520-3

We dedicate this book to those who teach international trade and economic relations in all of its various forms, and especially to the many faculty who have so thoughtfully helped us over the years to improve the successive editions of our problem-oriented *International Business Transactions* coursebook.

*

PREFACE

The authors have completed the eighth edition of *International Business Transactions in a Nutshell*. This fourth edition of *International Trade and Economic Relations in a Nutshell* was previously titled *International Trade and Investment in a Nutshell*. Coverage of foreign investment law is now located in the *IBT Nutshell*. Together, these Nutshells cover all significant areas of international business, from selling goods across borders to foreign direct investments abroad, plus the role of nations in regulating trade and economic relations, both unilaterally and by participation in bilateral and multilateral agreements.

International Business Transactions in a Nutshell focuses principally on international commercial transactions, letters of credit, E-commerce, transfers of technology, foreign investment, expropriations, extraterritorial antitrust, and international business litigation and arbitration. *International Trade and Economic Relations in a Nutshell* focuses on controls on imports and exports, customs unions and free trade agreements, and the law and economic relations of the World Trade Organization, the European Union and NAFTA.

The allocation of chapters between the two Nutshells required some value judgments, as did the decisions on what to include in each chapter. These judgments will be familiar to those who have read or adopted our *International Business Transactions: A Problem-Oriented Coursebook*, originally published in 1986, with many new editions since then. For detailed, footnoted professional coverage of the area, please see our *Hornbook on International Business Transactions* (Second Edition, 2001) or its concise student version, *Principles of International Business Transactions* (2005).

We have been aided by colleagues at our own law schools and others both in this country and abroad, by student research assistants and by persons in practice. We welcome continued suggestions for the next edition.

>RALPH H. FOLSOM
>RFOLSOM@SANDIEGO.EDU
>MICHAEL W. GORDON
>GORDON@LAW.UFL.EDU
>JOHN A. SPANOGLE
>ASPANOGLE@LAW.GWU.EDU

October 2008

OUTLINE

	Page
PREFACE	V
TABLE OF CASES	XV

Introduction. From Brockton and Burbank to Brasilia, Bombay, Brussels and British Columbia 1

The Boston Client 1
The Bartow Client 3
United States Import Remedies 4
Global Trade Law 6
Economic Status 8
Export Controls 9
Regional and Bilateral Trade Law 12

Chapter One. World Trade and Multinational Enterprises 14

Patterns of World Trade and Economic Relations 16
Services Trade 17
The Rise of Asia 18
Nontariff Trade Barriers 19
Trade Incentives 20
The Legal Framework of Trade 22
The Multinational Enterprise (MNE) 23
MNE Financial Practices: Transfer Pricing 25
The Role of Corporate Counsel to a MNE 28

OUTLINE

	Page
A Hypothetical Day for MNE Corporate Counsel	30

Chapter Two. The World Trade Organization (WTO) and International Monetary Fund (IMF) ... 32

The GATT (1947): History and Provisions ... 34
Trade in Goods: Core GATT Principles ... 36
GATT Procedures ... 37
The GATT Multinational Trade Negotiations (Rounds) ... 39
The USTR, Fast Track and Bilateral Trade Agreements ... 41
The World Trade Organization (WTO) and GATT 1994 ... 44
WTO Agreements and U.S. Law ... 46
GATT/WTO Nontariff Trade Barrier Codes ... 48
The WTO Agreement on Agriculture ... 51
The General Agreement on Trade in Services (GATS) ... 53
WTO Decision–Making ... 55
Consensus Rules ... 57
Admission to the WTO ... 58
Dispute Settlement Under WTO ... 59
Phase 1: Consultation ... 62
Phase 2: Panel establishment, investigation and report ... 63
Phase 3: Appellate review of the panel report ... 66
Phase 4: Adoption of the panel or Appellate Body decision ... 67
Phase 5: Implementation of the decision adopted ... 67
Phase 6: Compensation Option ... 68
Phase 7: Authorized Retaliation ... 68
Retaliation in Action ... 70

OUTLINE

	Page
U.S. Involvement in WTO Dispute Resolution	72
The International Monetary Fund (IMF)	78
IMF Operations	79
Special Drawing Rights (SDRs)	81
The EURO Zone	82

Chapter Three. Restrictions on Imports — 85

United States Trade Laws	85
U.S. Import Laws	87
The Origins of United States Tariffs	91
United States Tariff Rates	92
Column 1 Tariffs and the GATT	94
Foreign Trade Zones	95
Customs Classification	96
Customs Valuation	98
Rules of Origin	99
Generalized Tariff Preferences for Developing Nations	100
Caribbean Basin, Andean and African Trade Preferences	103
Goods Incorporating United States Components	106
Duty Free Access to the United States	107
U.S. Import Quotas	108
U.S. Public Procurement	111
Buy American	111
GATT Code and U.S. Response	114
WTO Procurement Code	116
U.S. Product Standards	117
WTO Product Standards Law	119
Tuna, Shrimp and Beef Disputes	120
Responses of Domestic Producers to Import Competition	122
Dumping and Antidumping Duties	124
U.S. Antidumping Law	126

OUTLINE

	Page
Market Economy Dumping Determinations	128
Nonmarket Economy Dumping Determinations	130
U.S. Implementation of the WTO Antidumping Code	131
Interpretation of the WTO Antidumping Code	134
Subsidies and Countervailing Duties	135
WTO Subsidies Code	137
U.S. Countervailing Duty Law	139
Red, Yellow, Amber and Green Light Subsidies	140
Enforcement Procedures	142
U.S. Escape Clause (Safeguard) Proceedings	143
Protective Relief	145
Adjustment Assistance	146
The WTO Safeguards Agreement	147
Interpretation	148
U.S. Steel Tariffs	149
U.S. Court of International Trade	150
Chapter Four. Controls on Exports	152
U.S. Export Policy	154
The Export Administration Act and Regulations	156
The Process of Licensing Exports	158
Commerce Control List	159
Licensed Exports	160
Licensing Timetable	161
Sanctions for EAA Violations	163
Boycott Provisions and U.S. Export Laws	164
Antiboycott Provisions of U.S. Export Laws	166
Sanctions	167
Foreign Corrupt Practices Act	168
1988 Amendments	169
OECD Code	171
Section 301 and Super 301	171
Section 301 Procedures	172

OUTLINE

	Page
Super 301	174
Effect of WTO Dispute Settlement	176

Chapter Five. Free Trade Agreements and Customs Unions 177
GATT Article 24 179
GATS Integrated Services' Agreements 181
Developing World Integration 182
Africa 183
Islamic World 185
Latin America and Caribbean 186
A Case Study: The Association of Southeast Asian Nations (ASEAN) 188
Declarations and Summits 190
ASEAN Trade Rules and Industrial Projects 192
Freer Trade 192
International Impact 194
ASEAN Complementation Schemes and Joint Ventures 196
Complementation Schemes 196
Joint Ventures 197
East Asian Integration 199

Chapter Six. The European Union 201
Three Communities 202
Multiple Official Languages 204
Europe Without Internal Frontiers 205
Free Movement 205
EU Citizenship—Rights of Residence 207
Treaty On European Union (1993) 208
Amsterdam Treaty (1999) 209
Treaty of Nice (2003) 210
Defeat of a Constitution for Europe (2005) 212
The Proposed Reform Treaty 213
Governance: The Council of Ministers 215

OUTLINE

	Page
Governance: The Commission and Law–Making	217
Powers of the Commission	218
Legislative Involvement	219
Governance: The European Parliament	220
Diverse Legislative Roles	221
Budgetary Powers	223
The European Court of Justice and Court of First Instance	224
ECJ Procedures	224
Linkage with National Courts	226
Power Struggles and Member State Prosecutions	227
Court of First Instance	228
The Nature of European Law	229
Regulations and Directives	230
Doctrine of Direct Effect	230
National Legal Remedies for Directly Effective Law	232
EU Law Enforcement	234
Grounds for Appeal	234
Supremacy	235
Free Movement of Goods	237
Cassis Formula	238
Exceptions to Free Movement	240
Intellectual Property	240
Exhaustion Doctrine	241
Computer Software, Databases and Data Privacy	242
Free Movement of Workers	244
Right of Establishment	245
Freedom to Provide Services	246
Legal Profession	246
Broadcasting	248
Free Movement of Capital	249

OUTLINE

	Page
Common Transport Policy	250
Common Agricultural Policy	251
Environmental Policy	253
Taxation	254
Trade Relations	255
Jurisdiction and Enforcement of Judgments	257
Business Organizations Law	257
Social Policy	260
Equal Pay and Equal Treatment	263
A Timeline of European Integration	265

Chapter Seven. NAFTA and Free Trade in the Americas 268
CANADA–U.S. Free Trade 268
The CUSFTA Agreement in Outline 269
Trade in Goods 269
Rules of Origin 273
Services and Investment 274
Dispute Settlement Under CUSFTA 277
Antidumping and Subsidy Disputes 278
Extraordinary Challenges 278
North American Free Trade 280
Fast Track Negotiations 281
The NAFTA Agreement in Outline 282
Trade in Goods 283
Rules of Origin 284
Energy 286
Food Products 286
Product Standards 287
Safeguards (Escape Clause Proceedings) 288
Procurement 289
Trade in Services 290
Transport 291
Telecommunications 292

OUTLINE

	Page
Cross–Border Investment and Investor–State Arbitrations	293
Investor Rights	293
Investor–State Arbitrations	295
Exclusions	296
Financial Services	297
National Commitments	297
Intellectual Property	299
Other NAFTA Provisions	300
Business Visas	300
State Monopolies and Antitrust	300
Miscellaneous Provisions	301
Right of Withdrawal	302
Dispute Settlement Under NAFTA	302
Forum Selection: NAFTA or WTO	303
Chapter 20	303
Antidumping or Subsidy Disputes	305
The Side Agreements on Labor and the Environment	306
Environmental Disputes	306
Labor Disputes	307
Comparison with the European Union	308
Free Trade and the Americas	309
Fast Track Delayed	310
Fast Track Arrives	310
U.S. Free Trade Agreements—NAFTA Plus	312
Quebec and NAFTA	314
Conclusion	316
A NAFTA/Free Trade in the Americas Timeline	317
INDEX	319

TABLE OF CASES

References are to Pages

Centrafarm BV v Sterling Drug Inc (C–15/74), 1974 WL 41529 (ECJ 1974), *241*

Georgetown Steel Corp. v. United States, 801 F.2d 1308 (Fed.Cir. 1986), *142*

Mead Corp., United States v., 533 U.S. 218, 121 S.Ct. 2164, 150 L.Ed.2d 292 (2001), *97*

United States v. _____ (see opposing party)

*

INTERNATIONAL TRADE and ECONOMIC RELATIONS
IN A NUTSHELL

Fourth Edition

*

INTRODUCTION

FROM BROCKTON AND BURBANK TO BRASILIA, BOMBAY, BRUSSELS AND BRITISH COLUMBIA

The Boston Client

Representing a Boston client who (1) manufactures goods, for example children's clothing and knapsacks, for sale to numerous retail store buyers in the United States, for example in Brockton and Burbank, and who (2) purchases the parts for such products from U.S. sellers, for example in Salem and San Francisco, usually does not involve the application of U.S. trade law governing imports and exports. But our Boston client is an "international" company—it sells and buys where it can obtain the best price. That means it sells to and buys from parties in foreign nations as well as in the United States. Consequently, U.S. trade law affecting *exports* is applicable when our Boston client sells the goods abroad, for example to buyers in Brasilia and Bombay. U.S. trade law affecting *imports* is applicable when our Boston client purchases parts for the manufacture of its products from Singapore or Sao Paulo.

In each case, importing or exporting, our client must be familiar with the characteristics of competition on an international scale. The client assumes different risks and becomes subject to different laws. Those laws are not only U.S. laws but the laws affecting imports and exports of the foreign nations in which our client does business. Such foreign laws may include rules which appear to exist solely to protect domestic industries. There may be high tariffs, or quotas, or a vast array of nontariff barriers affecting our client's exports, such as packaging or labeling requirements, safety certification or compliance with health standards. But that also may be how the foreign buyer or seller views the laws of the United States. The United States is not exempt from creating nontariff barriers. The Boston client's importers (buyers) in Brasilia or Bombay may be charged with dumping the Boston sourced goods on the local market, or benefitting from U.S. subsidies. The Boston client may not believe it is acting unfairly in selling to buyers in Brasilia or Bombay, but it has become subject to protective legislation in these foreign nations.

Just as it may be the target in one case, our client may shoot the arrows in another. If the Boston client is unable to sell to its old buyers in Brockton or Burbank, because Singapore or Sao Paulo sellers are not only selling parts to our client, but also selling finished products in competition directly to the Brockton or Burbank buyers, the U.S. trade laws may help our client. This is not because our client is an international trader, but because it is a *domestic* entity which is part of an industry injured or threatened with injury by the foreign goods. The same laws might help a U.S. company which has never engaged and has no intention of engaging in international trade.

The Bartow Client

Assume that in the small town of Bartow, Florida, a company employs about thirty people and for decades has manufactured a variety of textile products for sale solely in Florida from material produced in North Carolina. It makes children's clothing and knapsacks, just as does the Boston entity described above. But unlike our Boston client, the Bartow company does not sell abroad. It does not even sell in Georgia! Its owners and employees work hard in meeting the demand for its products in Florida. It pays fair, but not excessive wages. Management is very cost conscious, but believes the company can compete with anything produced by companies subject to the same rules of minimum wages, pollution controls, workshop safety, social security, etc.

Two problems have arisen in the past few months, however, which have involuntarily thrust this small town enterprise into being a participant in international trade. A large Florida department store chain which had bought its clothing for years from the Bartow entity informed the company that it was dropping its line of products and replacing them with nearly identical products manufactured by parties in Singapore and Sao Paulo. These are the same foreign sellers that the Boston client has claimed are causing it harm. The foreign made clothing costs the Florida retail chain 40 percent less than they had been paying the Bartow manufacturer. The second concern arose when the company was asked by a local tourist attraction to bid on the manufacture of 1,000 children's knapsacks in the form of dolphins. The company wanted the job and cut its profit to a narrower margin than it normally accepted. When it presented the design and the bid to the buyer it was told the same knapsacks could be had for half the price in Singapore or Sao Paulo.

United States Import Remedies

Why is it possible that the prices could be so low? Both the Boston and the Bartow companies are clearly being injured by these imports. Further inquiry may disclose similar injury to the U.S. children's clothing and knapsack industries as a whole, rather than to just these two domestic companies. Perhaps the products were being subsidized by the foreign governments. That may allow the Boston or Bartow company to request that the U.S. government commence an investigation under U.S. trade laws which may end in the conclusion that subsidies were present and there was material injury, or a threat of such injury, consequently calling for the imposition of countervailing tariff duties.

Or the foreign companies may be dumping (in contrast to the foreign governments providing subsidies) the products on the U.S. market. If they are doing so, meaning selling their products for "less than fair value", i.e., the price for which they are sold in the foreign domestic market where they are manufactured, the U.S. government may begin an investigation. If it is concluded that dumping was present and there was material injury, or a threat of such injury, there may be an imposition of antidumping duties. If the source of the foreign goods were Shanghai, where there may be an inadequate market economy cost analysis, it may be very difficult to establish the presence of subsidies, or sales at less than fair value to establish dumping. If China is defined as a nonmarket economy, and that seems less likely with each passing year of its drive to establishing a market economy in most sectors, another section of the U.S. trade laws may allow the Boston or Bartow companies to challenge the Shanghai products without proof of dumping or subsidies, essentially because they come from a nation with a political system we do not regard with favor. This action, called a "market disruption" or Section 406 action, has been used infrequently in the past for foreign policy reasons. It will diminish in use even more as nonmarket nations move along the path towards market economies with democratic governments.

If the foreign goods are from the vast majority of market economy nations, and if they cause or threaten *serious* as opposed to *material* injury to the U.S. industry, the Boston or Bartow company may make use of the U.S. safeguard or Section 201 "escape clause" action provision to limit their entry. But how the U.S. government responds to a domestic company's claim of injury from foreign competition may be based more on political relations with the foreign nation than an accurate interpretation of the U.S. law. The Boston or Bartow company may correctly feel more a pawn in international politics than a player in international business. For example, the United States may not wish to irritate the government of Singapore if it is helping the United States open more air routes in Asia to American carriers, or to irritate the government of Brazil if the two nations are close to a settlement of a longstanding dispute over intellectual property protection, or to irritate the government of China if there are sensitive negotiations over the use of prison labor or freeing a political dissident.

The Bartow company never intended to engage in international trade. It has not. It still sells nothing abroad. But it is fearful that soon it will sell nothing in Florida as well. Its officials and lawyers must learn about international business and trade law if the company is to survive, or even if it is not to survive, to provide its former employees with U.S. trade adjustment assistance made available to companies which lose out to foreign competition.

Global Trade Law

Although there are significant variations in the trade laws and economic relations of different nations, for most nations there are some accepted norms. Roughly 150 trading nations are members of the World Trade Organization (WTO), the successor to the General Agreement on Tariffs and Trade (GATT). Since its formation at the end of World War II, the GATT/WTO has grown in membership, in reducing tariffs, and in successfully abolishing many nontariff trade barriers. The rules noted above of various nations which allow countervailing duty, dumping and safeguard (escape clause) actions all have some of their roots in the GATT/WTO. Hence, exports by either of the U.S. companies may encounter exactly the same international trade remedies in, say, Brazil or India. Beyond these areas, the WTO "package" of 1994 agreements covers many relevant issues: Customs law, trade quotas, agricultural products, health regulation of foods, textiles and clothing (hello Boston and Bartow!), technical product regulations, trade in services, trade-related intellectual property rights and dispute settlement. These agreements are reviewed in Chapter 2.

Our client, whether it is the Boston or Bartow entity, is likely to be more interested in stopping the foreign competition or foreign application of trade remedies than in how it is stopped. Domestically, it may make little difference whether the action chosen is against foreign subsidies, dumping, surges of imports, market disruption, or any other actionable activity under any part of U.S. trade law. It is the end result the client wishes to achieve, a reduction or elimination of the allegedly "unfair" foreign competition. The path to that result will be the recommended course of action suggested by the client's counsel. Thus counsel must know about the full array of choices available under the U.S. trade laws, and (if U.S. exports are involved) how to defend against trade remedies in foreign jurisdictions.

Economic Status

Regarding U.S. imports, the choice may differ depending on the nature of the foreign nation's economic and political characterization. *Developed* nations do use barriers to imports and offer subsidies to exports. They tend to be fewer in number and often are more sophisticated than barriers or subsidies in developing nations. *Developing* nations may use a greater variety of trade barriers, and justify them because they are developing economically. Trade organizations such as the WTO may grant developing nations special rights to impose barriers against imports, or assist exports. *Nonmarket economy* nations (NMEs) by definition lack market economy characteristics and may substantially subsidize industry. The United States does not allow countervailing duty actions to be brought against imports from a nonmarket economy nation because the subsidies of those nations are not bounties or grants within the meaning and purpose of the countervailing duty law, because of the nature of nonmarket economy nations, and because Congress has provided for dealing with such nations under other trade law provisions. The identity of the foreign country as developed or developing, and as market or nonmarket, is thus important to the application of the appropriate trade law provisions. China's economic status is especially controversial.

There are fewer nonmarket economies today than a decade ago, and many nonmarket economies are in a stage of transition to market economies. Thus there may be a question regarding the nature of the foreign economy. It may be both a developing and a nonmarket economy. It may be an advanced developing country (ADC) or newly industrializing country (NIC), but still be a nonmarket economy. It may be a nonmarket economy trying to become a market economy, but having difficulty overcoming decades of state central planning and government involvement in the production and distribution of goods. Or it may be a nonmarket economy which prefers to remain a nonmarket economy, but which finds it necessary to do business with market economies and opens the door to market economy characteristics only enough to achieve specific goals.

Export Controls

Most of these comments have involved restrictions on imports. U.S. restrictions on imports would help our Boston client in so far as it is a seller of its products within the United States to buyers in Brockton or Burbank, but might hurt that client if the imports of components for its production from Singapore or Sao Paulo are restricted and cause it to buy higher priced domestic components in the United States from Salem or San Francisco. Some reference has also been made to controls on exports. To the extent that such controls exist in the United

States, and limit our Boston client from exporting to buyers in Brasilia or Bombay, our client would be harmed. If export controls are imposed by the governments in Singapore or Sao Paulo on the components our client needs, it may have to buy them at higher prices from Salem or San Francisco. Unlike import trade remedies, which have been harmonized through the WTO, export control laws tend to be uniquely national in character.

Export controls usually are not imposed for the same reasons as import controls, with the exception that some nations, mainly developing countries, may tax both imports and exports as a revenue raising device. But the United States, and many other nations, usually limit exports for such reasons as national security, foreign policy goals, or scarcity of certain domestic resources. Most nations encourage exports, often providing incentives, and often engaging in assistance which may constitute unfair trade such as subsidies. Because export controls often are intended to serve political goals, the executive may be given considerable discretion in imposing export limitations to certain nations. In the United States, conflict between the Congress, which believes it has authority over all aspects of foreign commerce, and the President, who believes the executive has control over all aspects of foreign policy, has led to frequent conflict and inability to enact new export laws.

Our Boston client may be prohibited from exporting some or all of its products to all nations, or may be prohibited from exporting anything to specific nations. Export controls are thus designed to limit certain goods to any nation, or limit any goods to certain nations, or certain goods to certain nations. To assure compliance, exports may have to have a license. The export rules in the United States long divided licenses for the most part between *general* and *validated* licenses. General licenses did not require an application to and approval by the government, only furnishing certain information upon export which was useful for compiling trade statistics. Validated licenses required an application to and permission from the Department of Commerce, often with the scrutiny of and sometimes inordinate delay of approval by, the Department of Defense. This complex matrix of licenses was replaced in 1996 by a scheme intended to be more exporter-friendly. The end of the Cold War, the movement of many nonmarket economy nations towards democracy and market economics, and the realization by many developing nations that joining the developed world was more promising than leading the third world, has encouraged the United States to adopt a simpler export control scheme.

As we have noted, governments participate in regulating the transfer of goods across borders—imports and exports, covered in Chapters 3 and 4. Our Boston client may have decided that the maze of laws and regulations in those areas where it has sold its products, such as Brasilia and Bombay, or perhaps Beijing, is so extensive that the only way to penetrate that market is to establish a direct foreign investment. It might also choose to transfer technology to a domestic manufacturer in one or more of those areas, but it may feel that to control the technology, and to maximize profits, direct foreign investment is the best alternative. These alternative transactions are covered in our *IBT Nutshell*.

Regional and Bilateral Trade Law

Suppose your Boston client gets an order to ship its goods to Brussels, and your Bartow client to British Columbia. The domestic laws of Belgium and Canada will affect such trading, and so will the laws of the European Union and the NAFTA. Preferential trade agreements are rapidly expanding around the globe. Did we mention that Brazil belongs to the MERCOSUR customs union and Singapore now has free trade agreements with the United States, Japan and others? And India is pushing ahead inside the South Asian Free Trade Area. The range of laws and economic relations you must consider in advising your clients just expanded beyond domestic and international law to include regional law, the framework within which free trade agreements and customs unions frequently operate. Naturally there are variations on the theme of regional trade law, with the European Union and NAFTA serving as prototypes. We will introduce you to this regional trade law phenomenon in Chapters 5, 6 and 7.

What follows in the material ahead is an introduction to the laws and policies, the organizations and entities, and the people involved in international trade and economic relations. This Nutshell will cover government imposed restrictions on imports and exports; the GATT and the WTO; free trade agreements and customs unions; and regional economic integration with an emphasis on the European Union and the North American Free Trade Agreement. The authors' *International Business Transactions in a Nutshell* complements this Nutshell. It covers such issues as the documentary sale and use of letters of credit, technology transfers, foreign investment, expropriations, extraterritorial antitrust, and international business litigation and arbitration. The two Nutshells are intended to provide a broad introduction to the people and institutions who practice international business law, and the government and multilateral organizations which both encourage and restrict international trade and economic relations.

CHAPTER ONE

WORLD TRADE AND MULTINATIONAL ENTERPRISES

The United States is one of a few central players in the world in international trade and economic relations. It has engaged in foreign trade from the moment of its independence over two centuries ago. One of the reasons independence was sought was England's imposition of severe restrictions on trade between the colonies and foreign nations. In less than two centuries from achieving independence, the United States became the leading trade power in the world. For over a decade after World War II, the United States was in the envious and economically advantageous position of being the major center of production of finished goods for export. But with extraordinary economic growth in Japan and Europe, by the 1980s the United States no longer dominated world trade. It had to compete for sales abroad, and also in the domestic market within the United States. Traditional surpluses in the balance of trade with most nations in some cases began to be reversed. The United States had to deal with increasingly large trade deficits with Japan. But Japan was only the beginning, China has emerged as the most formidable single nation trading partner in the world, and India is increasingly a major trading force in the world economy. Both played major roles in the difficult trade debates in the recent Doha WTO negotiations, which ended without reaching any significant agreements.

The deficit status of U.S. international trade in the past two decades has caused trade to be a topic of common conversation, often because of perceived threats to jobs for the American worker and the quality of life of the American people. The trade surplus of earlier decades has become a trade deficit of disturbing proportions. This has generated annual Congressional proposals of an increasingly restrictive nature, drawing comparisons with the depression inducing Smoot–Hawley law of 1930. U.S. exports have continued to grow, but imports have grown more rapidly. Even the significant fall of the dollar in the first decade of the new century against U.K. Sterling and the Euro has not reversed the deficit.

The importance of trade and its underlying economic relations should be apparent. But the huge capacity of the United States to consume foreign products is out of balance with its ability to find reciprocal consumption for its products abroad. That is due to many reasons, problems of quality, real and perceived, problems of barriers to trade imposed by every nation, and problems of government leadership. Those who view the United States from abroad continually point to excessive consumption and inadequate savings, and to the budget deficit, as the principal reasons for the deteriorating

U.S. trade position. Washington hears the complaints, but makes few corrections. It is easier to blame other nations. After all, the United States still generates a formidable share of world trade and will continue to do so.

Even individual states have remarkable trade statistics. California alone generates billions of dollars of U.S. world trade, making its "gross state product" greater than the gross national products of all but a few nations of the world. In the last few years, however, the per capita standard of living of several other nations has reached and exceeded that in the United States. The periodic issuance of impressive aggregate trade figures from Washington tends to mask an ebbing and equalizing status and role in the world community. Status as an economic power is gained slowly when the nation's energy is directed towards the production and distribution of goods and services, but is lost quickly when that energy is directed more to consumption than production, more to producing self-serving statistics than a tangible surplus.

PATTERNS OF WORLD TRADE AND ECONOMIC RELATIONS

Trade traditionally has been measured by the exchange of tangible goods, both raw materials and finished products. The prominence of oil as a trading Trade traditionally has been measured by the exchange of tangible goods, both commodity, and the economic power exerted in the 1970s by the Organization of Petroleum Exporting Countries

(OPEC), resulted in a considerable shift of wealth caused by remarkable changes in the price of a single commodity. The power of OPEC diminished in the 1980s and 1990s due to an oversupply of oil and conflict both within the oil industry and within OPEC. Since the millennium, OPEC power and oil prices have been on a rise, not surprising to any American who owns a gas powered vehicle. Petroleum remains the ultimately important commodity, and it played a critical role in the decision of the United States to commence the Gulf and Iraq Wars. Extractable raw materials remain the principal source of wealth for many nations. Nations which produce many natural and agricultural resources, from tin to bananas, attempt to create cartels which will give them control of their economic destiny.

Services Trade

In recent years attention on items of trade and therefore value has shifted from an exclusive focus on tangibles and technology, to an area of trade and economic relations far more difficult to define. That area is trade in services such as advertising, banking, insurance, accounting, consulting, entertainment, tourism and the vast area of computer services. U.S. trade in these "invisibles" is measured in billions annually. Trade in tangibles is marred by an increasing deficit, but U.S. trade in services is marked by an increasing surplus.

Many other nations are eager to develop their own services, and to protect them from encroachment by the developed nations. The negotiations in the GATT Uruguay Round on trade in services were an especially difficult part of the overall trade talks. The industrialized nations, led by the United States, for the most part successfully negotiated lowering trade barriers to services, over the objections of such important developing nations as India and Brazil. These nations fear dominance in ownership of services by the industrialized nations. The final agreement reflects many restrictions and reservations by developing nations determined to establish their own service sectors. The ability of the WTO to regulate trade in services will be critical to keeping such service-oriented nations as the United States a part of this important multilateral trade regulating organization.

The Rise of Asia

Viewing the constantly changing world trade patterns as they have developed to this moment, the dominance of the United States which was prevalent decades ago has diminished substantially and is unlikely to reoccur. This trend is attributable to the prominence Japan developed in the 1970s and 1980s in manufacturing and designing products that met consumer demands, to the entry of China and re-entry of India in the world trade arena in the first decade of this century, to the expansion and cooperation of the European nations within the European Union, and to the movement through successive stages of development of many developing nations, especially the "Four Dragons" or "Four Tigers" of Asia—Hong Kong, Korea, Singapore and Taiwan. Increased "world market share" is the goal of every nation, and nations joust over international trade issues. They more closely regulate foreign investment coming into the country, and create new trade incentives to stimulate greater exports to (and foreign investment within) other countries.

The spectacular success of Japan and China as exporters combined with a creativity to block imports has led to a sequence of protests and threats of sanctions by the United States and the European Union. However Japan or China may be accused of being unfair traders and of using a host of nontariff trade barriers (NTBs) to keep foreign goods and investment out, the United States often fails to consider that trade imbalances may be as much caused by domestic failures as by foreign intransigence.

Nontariff Trade Barriers

Japan and China are not alone in using nontariff barriers. They have arisen to protect domestic industry as the earlier protection by high tariffs has diminished. Every nation has developed its own methods of keeping imports at bay. The United States notably employs agricultural quotas and environmental/conservation regulations in this manner. The French provoked a stream of protest by requiring that documentation for imported goods be written in French. France established a "consultative commission for international trade" charged to watch for "abnormal" and excessive imports and unfair export practices of other countries. Meaning, of course, an agency for domestic business to complain to when affected by imports, regardless of the efficiency in production of the domestic business. In the United States, similar complaints are filed with the Office of the U.S. Trade Representative.

Other nations have responded in various ways to the impact of imports. Restricted by their agreements to specific tariff levels as members of the WTO, they have carried nontariff barriers to a new height of originality. These barriers may assume the form of health or safety standards, packing or labeling requirements, and many other rules which may in theory seem justified, but in practice are structured or interpreted so as to eliminate or reduce imports and benefit domestic industries. Lawyers who must be retained to deal with these nontariff barriers, as well as subsidies, dumping or rules of origin, have become the major beneficiaries of these complex trade laws. They alone know how to work through the maze of details in lengthy definitions included in trade laws and multilateral agreements. For example, foreign targets of a U.S. dumping charge must expend enormous resources on responding to such charges, thus making these actions themselves another form of nontariff barrier.

Trade Incentives

Goods which are sold in one nation are not necessarily either goods produced domestically by locally owned manufacturers, or goods produced abroad by foreign owned manufacturers. They may be goods produced *domestically* by *foreign* owned manufacturers. Or they may be goods produced *abroad* by domestic manufacturers. Investing abroad is an alternative to exporting the goods abroad. Foreign investment shares some benefits of trade. The foreign manufacturer receives the profit from the manufacture abroad, but the host nation of the foreign investment creates jobs. Raw materials or parts may be sent by the foreign manufacturer, to create what is little more than an assembly plant in the host nation, or raw materials and parts may be purchased in the host nation, adding to the benefits of permitting investment owned by foreign entities.

While trying to hold imports to reasonable levels, every nation wants to be a major exporter. It is, after all, exports that provide the means to pay for imports. The urge to export leads to another scheme of laws. They are usually laws of encouragement in contrast to the laws of discouragement which typify the import rules. They may be fashioned in the way of granting tax benefits, offering export financing or insurance, overlooking trade restraint elements of permitted export cartels, or tying permitted imports to the level of exports. The United States, for example, in enacting the 1982 Export Trading Company (ETC) Act followed the practice of such nations as Japan in assisting exporters. The ETC Act was designed to permit small and medium U.S. firms to gain information about foreign trade opportunities and techniques and to have easier access to financing for export activity.

The Legal Framework of Trade

Every nation which engages in international economic relations develops a legal framework defining its role. That framework will consist of its own domestic trade laws, including its acceptance of international laws regulating international transactions, and its participation in international organizations which also establish rules. The United States has developed by legislative and executive action an extensive set of domestic rules governing international trade. It has also been a major participant in many organizations which influence or govern trade. The World Trade Organization, successor to the GATT, is by far the most important such organization. The United Nations has played a disappointingly minor role in trade, although more recently UNCITRAL, the United Nations Commission on International Trade Law, has become an important forum for the harmonization of rules affecting trade, such as the Convention on Contracts for the International Sale of Goods (CISG).

Regional economic relations have also increased trade among groups of nations. The European Union and the NAFTA are the two most important areas which have reduced barriers to internal trade, although sometimes at the expense of increasing barriers to external trade. Free trade and customs union agreements have been proliferating in the developing world. But however important participation in bilateral or multilateral trade agreements or organizations may be, the will of a single participant to abide by freer trade rules will be expressed in its domestic trade laws and policies. It is under such laws that multinational enterprises operate.

THE MULTINATIONAL ENTERPRISE (MNE)

One important and controversial business form for engaging in international trade is the multinational enterprise (MNE). Indeed, "intracorporate" trade within a family of MNE companies comprises a very significant share of "international" trade. The most visible MNEs are the largest multinational corporations engaged in business over decades in every sector of the globe. The MNE may also be one of several less structured business forms, such as partnerships and joint ventures, used in business of short duration in only a few places in the world. A transaction may be an international business transaction whether the principal players come from private enterprise, from national or local government, or from a combination of both private enterprise and government.

The MNE has aroused concern and prompted new regulatory attempts by governments, acting singly and in concert. Although history may not yet identify the MNE as having been a primary catalyst in pressing diverse and proud countries into a measure of sustained global order, the utility and proper role of the MNE have engendered vigorous debate involving much unclear data.

The industrialized member countries within the expanding Organization for Economic Cooperation and Development (OECD) have published Guidelines for Multinational Enterprises, adopted by more than 40 nations, which set forth voluntary guidelines for appropriate enterprise behavior. Additionally well received has been the OECD Principles of Corporate Governance. The OECD has focused on corporate governance of state-owned enterprises as well as those privately owned. Representatives from the member countries of the International Institute for the Unification of Private Law (UNIDROIT) worked on an international trade law code regarding the formation and interpretation of contracts, especially leasing agreements. The European Union favors regulating MNE activity on a sector basis, such as in areas of company law, taxation, and employment policy.

International regulation of MNEs shows every prospect of increasing, in part due to the role illicit MNE payments play in generating public demand for closer MNE regulation. Often such payments are a fact of international commercial life, whether they are characterized as "advertising expenses", "commissions", or more simply as "grease" or "bribes". Business enterprises from the United States have often felt seriously constrained by the 1977 Foreign Corrupt Practices Act. Amendments to the Act in 1988 removed the controversial basis for liability when the MNE had "reason to know" that some of their payments through intermediaries might end up in the hands of foreign officials. Further amendments in 1998 to bring U.S. law in compliance with the OECD Convention on Combating Bribery of Foreign Public Officials in International Business Transactions, and the adoption of the Convention in nearly 30 other nations, have somewhat leveled the "foreign payments" playing field.

MNE FINANCIAL PRACTICES: TRANSFER PRICING

Affiliated parts of a multinational enterprise often lend to each other across national borders. Since the enterprise as a whole has goals which each part seeks to assist in achieving, dealing with certain parts of the whole may be structured to advance corporate goals while achieving favorable tax or dividend consequences. The MNE effectively reallocates costs and revenues within its worldwide structure so that profits are increased where tax and exchange controls are considered favorable, and decreased where those controls are considered most severe. This is transfer pricing.

Host nations sometimes impose limits on profits that may be remitted abroad by a foreign investor's local operations. The MNE may seek to offset the effect of these limits on profit remittances. The foreign parent may attempt to charge more for technology transferred to the affiliate, or for raw materials or components sold to the foreign affiliate. The host nation may respond by limiting amounts which may be paid for technology, and by demanding that the raw materials or components be obtained locally. Developing nations have strongly objected to MNEs' transfer pricing practices when the result appears to be very low or no profits in the developing nation because the parent has charged the local subsidiary very high prices for technology, raw materials and components transferred to the subsidiary, but the MNE parent appears to be profitable. Why has the MNE done this? Because the developing nation has high taxes on profits. Or because there are limits on profit remittances due to exchange controls, which are more lenient or do not exist for technology transfers, or for permitted imports of raw materials or components. What may anger the developing nation even more, and also local shareholders when the MNE has agreed to a joint venture with local equity, is when the same transfer pricing practices lead to few profits to distribute as dividends to the local shareholders.

It is not only developing nations which object to artificial transfer pricing practices. Australia, Canada, Japan and the United States formed the Pacific Association of Tax Administrators to combat transfer pricing's possible interrelationship with tax evasion. Developing country monitoring of transfer pricing has not been very effective, partly because of a reluctance of the developed nations to participate in joint efforts which might transfer tax revenue away from the United States, and partly because much intracorporate transfer information is regarded as confidential.

The Organization for Economic Cooperation and Development (OECD) has been working on transfer pricing guidelines for multinational companies for decades. Transfer pricing has also been addressed by individual countries. Within the United States, the IRS has issued regulations under Section 482 of the Internal Revenue Code. These regulations impose penalties for intercompany pricing not conducted under the regulation's arm's-length standards, which adopt a "best method" rule. IRS practices have been criticized as arbitrary and unreasonable. But the IRS claims companies do not properly calculate transfer pricing. The Tax Court has had to resolve these conflicts, and is likely to be a frequent player as the IRS steps up its attack on improper transfer pricing.

Mexico has transfer pricing rules affecting the border industries or maquiladoras. The government has not strictly enforced provisions of the Mexican Tax Code which would require that the maquiladora recognize some level of profit for its services. The reason has been to protect jobs and the entire program itself, but the government could demand taxes on an arm's length basis for the services performed by the maquiladoras. Many foreign companies have used fees for services and transfer pricing resulting in almost no Mexican profits. More recently, Mexico has established minimum maquiladora profit levels as "safe harbors" under is Tax Code. Most firms have moved to take advantage of them, thereby reducing tax risk exposure in Mexico. The experience of the United States and Mexico illustrate how different nations may pursue problems of transfer pricing, from a vigorous attack on the practice to minimal payments to promote social goals, such as job creation.

THE ROLE OF CORPORATE COUNSEL TO A MNE

The role of corporate counsel (house counsel) to a MNE is not different professionally from that of any other brand of lawyer in relation to a client. Unlike many other lawyers, however, counsel is also in a team member relationship with MNE management personnel. Counsel has an employment obligation to support the MNE management structure. Counsel's corporate legal function may be viewed as one vehicle through which headquarters control is exercised over affiliated, sub-parts of the MNE. The access to information and exclusive knowledge of information possessed by counsel are visible and substantial parts of the power dimension of MNE global management. For example, counsel's working relationship with foreign assisting counsel in each country where a sub-part of the MNE operates, and that assisting counsel's working relationship with the principal, MNE sub-part (line) management person within each country, play a substantial role in MNE headquarters control and financial success.

If the principal line management person within each country is willing to explore legal aspects of new business ideas with the assisting counsel in that country, and if assisting counsel has a close reporting and consultative relationship with MNE headquarters counsel, chances increase for the "preventive" side of legal practice to help in shaping management decisions and to reduce large, unanticipated (surgical) legal costs at a later time. The success of counsel's communication with management may generate an ad hoc assignment to a line management function in connection with particular MNE business transactions.

Such closeness can also raise ethical considerations which intersect with counsel's professional responsibilities as a lawyer. For example, currency control measures prevent MNE revenues from being remitted. Moreover, the rate of monetary inflation may be such that revenues left there are subject to substantial devaluation. There is an acute ethical problem for counsel, as a lawyer, who considers the idea that funds might be carried secretly at night into neighboring countries and then exchanged for hard currency and remitted for deposit in a jurisdiction where inflation is not severe.

Corporate line managers are charged with providing needed revenues. Corporate counsel are engaged principally in minimizing legal "overhead" costs of the corporation. Did they teach you how to be an effective cost manager in law school? In addition, requests by line management to put recurring types of company agreements into "standard form" contracts must be squared with the reality of enforcing those contracts in several different national legal systems, with divergent views about the sanctity of contracts made by a corporate body. Counsel may assist in securing approvals from governmental regulatory bodies or persons charged with overseeing

MNE activity, and often must testify on the MNE's behalf before people who need not listen at all or who may only care to listen in an abbreviated way. Many current presidents of corporations in the United States are lawyers and have served as corporate counsel before being appointed president. You might consider how the following hypothetical day for corporate counsel helps prepare lawyers to become MNE presidents.

A HYPOTHETICAL DAY FOR MNE CORPORATE COUNSEL

By way of hypothetical illustration, a typical office day for corporate counsel to a MNE might include work on problems such as: Senegal has served notice that a MNE's revenues worldwide will be taxed unitarily irrespective of the MNE's tax posture in other countries; the MNE's use of its trade name in Mexico is impeded by a "prior use" problem; a Uruguayan appeals court has held that the MNE's trademark is generic and thus not subject to legal protection; a line management employee of the MNE's Austrian subsidiary company needs an "L" visa to spend some time at the MNE's headquarters offices in the United States; new advertising from the MNE's marketing department has possible legal implications if placed in newspapers throughout Europe; reports of resale price maintenance agreements being made by certain companies in Transylvania and Neverland need to be checked in light of antitrust implications under U.S. and EU law.

Moreover, the MNE's products stolen in Hamburg must be traced through INTERPOL; ways must be explored to get blocked currencies from New Country to the MNE's headquarters in the United States; testimony needs to be prepared for presentation to an environmental control authority in Germany; a presentation must be made to the transportation commissioner of the Province of Ontario to secure permits to increase haulage capacity of the MNE's subsidiary company in Canada; charges of employee discrimination in the Far Islands need to be answered; sale-leaseback agreements need to be negotiated in Sydney; a company needs to be formed for tax protection in the Unusual Islands; an expropriation in Bolivia requires attention; the Philippine and Saudi Arabian governments want to increase their equity participation in all existing MNE's joint ventures; certain inquiries by the U.S. Federal Trade Commission need to be answered; someone from the American Bar Association wants counsel to serve on an international trade committee; all standard form contracts used by the MNE and its subsidiary companies are due for another review; line management people are interested in hearing ideas about ways to avoid legal problems, especially transfer pricing issues, in connection with their proposals for new trade activity.

CHAPTER TWO

THE WORLD TRADE ORGANIZATION (WTO) AND INTERNATIONAL MONETARY FUND (IMF)

The need to balance the protection of local industries from harm by foreign competitors and the encouragement of trade across national borders is a recurrent theme in the law of international economic relations. There has been a shift in recent years toward freer international trade because of diminished restrictions on imported goods. However, trade problems associated with the movement of goods across national borders still arise because of restrictive trade devices which impede or distort trade.

Common devices include tariff barriers (e.g., import duties and export duties) as well as certain nontariff trade barriers (NTBs) such as import quotas, import licensing procedures, safety, environmental and other minimum manufacturing standards, import testing requirements, complex customs procedures (including valuation), government procurement policies, and government subsidies or countervailing measures. For example, France once required that all video recorders entering the country had to do so through a small customs post at Poitiers and carry documentation written in French. Product distribution practices have been an effective NTB in Japan. For example, the Japanese have banned from importation food preservatives essential to preserve the edibility of certain agricultural products from abroad.

Efforts by countries to limit disruptive trade practices are commonly found in bilateral treaties of friendship, commerce and navigation (FCN), which open the territory of each signatory nation to imports arriving from the other signatory nation. Such bilateral FCN treaty clauses are usually linked to other preferential trade agreements. In a bilateral arrangement, such linkage will most often be through a reciprocal "most favored nation" (MFN) clause. In a MFN clause, both parties agree not to extend to any other nation trade arrangements which are more favorable than available under the bilateral treaty, unless the more favorable trade arrangements are immediately *also* available to the signatory of the bilateral treaty. In various parts of the world, two or more countries have joined in customs unions or free trade agreements in order to expand commerce between those countries and to acquire increased bargaining power in international trade negotiations. The European Union is a prime example. See Chapter 6.

The General Agreement on Tariffs and Trade (GATT), now replaced by the World Trade Organization (WTO), was an international arrangement dating from 1947 with numerous countries as Contracting States which regularly held multilateral trade negotiations (MTN) seeking ways of making international trade more open. These periodic GATT "Rounds" (Kennedy Round, Tokyo Round, etc.) cumulatively reduced average tariff barriers to 80 percent below those existing in the post WWII era. After the most recent multilateral negotiations, the Uruguay Round finalized in 1994, average tariff rates of developed countries on dutiable manufactured imports were cut from 6.3 percent to 3.9 percent. Tariff reductions are one of the success stories of GATT. But not all nations participated in the GATT or are members of its replacement, the WTO. For example, Russia and Iran are still seeking membership in the WTO. China did not join until 2001, Vietnam in 2007.

THE GATT (1947): HISTORY AND PROVISIONS

Participants in the Bretton Woods meetings in 1944 recognized a post-War need to reduce obstacles to freer trade. They envisioned the creation of an International Trade Organization (ITO) to achieve the desired result. Fifty-three countries met in Havana in 1948 to complete drafting the Charter of an ITO that would be the international organizational umbrella underneath which negotiations could occur periodically to deal with tariff reductions. A framework for such negotiations had already been staked out in Geneva in 1947, in a document entitled the General Agreement on Tariffs and Trade

(GATT). Twenty-three nations participated in that first GATT session, India, Chile, Cuba and Brazil representing the developing world. China participated; Japan and West Germany did not. Stringent trading rules were adopted only where there were no special interests of major participants to alter them. The developing nations objected to many of the strict rules, arguing for special treatment justified on development needs, but they achieved few successes in drafting GATT.

The ITO Charter was never ratified. The United States Congress in the late 1940s was unwilling to join more new international organizations, thus U.S. ratification of the ITO Charter could not be secured. By default, and moving by way of the President's power to make executive agreements, the United States joined 21 other countries in signing a Protocol of Provisional Application of the General Agreement on Tariffs and Trade (popularly called the "GATT Agreement"). One notable feature of this protocol was the exemption of existing trade restraints of the Contracting States. The GATT 1947 Agreement evolved from its "provisional" status into the premier international trade body, GATT the organization based in Geneva. It was through this organization that tariffs were steadily reduced over decades by means of increased membership and GATT negotiating Rounds. Today, the GATT 1947 Agreement has been superceded by the substantially similar GATT 1994 Agreement, part of the World Trade Organization "package" of trade agreements that took effect in 1995.

Trade in Goods: Core GATT Principles

One of the core provisions of GATT 1947 and 1994 is Article I, which makes a general commitment to the long standing practice of "most favored nation treatment" (MFN) by requiring each Contracting Party to accord unconditional MFN status to all other Contracting Parties. Thus, any privilege granted by any Contracting Party to any product imported from any other country (WTO member or not) must also be "immediately and unconditionally" granted to any "like product" imported from any Contracting Parties.

GATT Article III incorporates the practice of according "national treatment" to imported goods by providing, with enumerated exceptions, that the products of one Contracting State, shall be treated in the same manner regarding taxation and regulation as domestic goods. This Article, for example, requires that the products of the exporting GATT Contracting State be treated no less favorably than domestic products of the importing Contracting State under its laws and regulations concerning sale, internal resale, purchase, transportation and use.

In addition to requiring MFN and national treatment, GATT prohibits use of certain kinds of quantitative restrictions. Article XI broadly but not completely prohibits the use of other "prohibitions or restrictions" on imports from Contracting Parties. It specifically prohibits the use of "quotas, import or export licenses or other measures" to restrict imports from a Contracting Party. When such measures are authorized, Article XIII requires nondiscrimination in quantitative trade restrictions, by barring an importing Contracting State from applying any prohibition or restriction to the products of another Contracting State, "unless the importation of the like product of *all* third countries ... is similarly prohibited or restricted." (emphasis added).

The WTO has significantly reduced the number of trade quotas. The Agreement on Textiles eliminated quotas long maintained under the Multi–Fibre Arrangement. Voluntary export restraints (quotas) are severely limited by the Safeguards Agreement. In addition, the WTO removes trade quotas by pressuring for "tariffication," or replacing them with tariffs—sometimes even at extraordinarily high tariff rates. Tariffication is the approach adopted in the WTO Agricultural Agreement. It is expected that high tariff rates will be reduced in subsequent negotiating Rounds. Import licensing schemes are also being phased out under WTO agreements.

GATT Procedures

While GATT does permit nondiscriminatory "duties, taxes and other charges," the powers of a Contracting Party are limited even as to these devices. First, GATT Article X requires that notice be given of any new or changed national regulations which affect international trade, by requiring the prompt publication by any Contracting Party of those "laws, regulations, judicial decisions and administrative rulings of general application." Second, the Contracting Parties commit themselves, under GATT Article XXVIII to a continuing series of multilateral trade negotiations MTN ("from time to time") to seek further reductions in tariff levels and other barriers to international trade. Such negotiations are to be "on a reciprocal and mutually advantageous basis." GATT negotiated tariff rates (called "concessions" or "bindings"), which are listed in the "tariff Schedules", are deposited with GATT by each participating country. These concessions must be granted to imports from any Contracting Party, both because of the GATT required MFN treatment, and also because Article II specifically requires use of the negotiated rates.

Framers of GATT were well aware that a commitment to freer trade could cause serious, adverse economic consequences from time to time within part or all of a country's domestic economy, particularly its labor sector. The GATT contains at least seven safety valves (in nine clauses of the Agreement) to permit a country, in appropriate circumstances, to respond to domestic pressures while remaining a participant in GATT. Two prominent safety valves contained in Article VI deal with antidumping and countervailing duties. In a nutshell, these special tariffs are authorized against what the GATT deems unfair international trade practices. They are detailed in Chapter 3.

THE GATT MULTINATIONAL TRADE NEGOTIATIONS (ROUNDS)

Under the auspices of GATT Article XXVIII, the Contracting Parties committed themselves to hold periodic multinational trade negotiations (MTN or "Rounds"). They have completed eight such Rounds to date. The latest Round failed to start as scheduled late in 1999. An array of "anti-globalization" interests and street protests in Seattle led by labor and environmental groups caused the delay. Regrouping in remote Qatar, the Doha Round was launched in 2001, scheduled for completion in 2005, but barely remains ongoing. Agriculture, services, intellectual property, antidumping duties, tariffs, export subsidies, market access, implementation, electronic commerce, dispute settlement, trade and the environment, trade, debt and finance, and special and differential treatment and assistance for developing countries are on the agenda. Developed WTO countries are particularly pushing the so-called "Singapore" issues of investment, competition policy, transparency in procurement and trade facilitation. At Cancun in 2003, the WTO developing nations rejected these issues while focusing on agricultural trade protectionism by industrial nations. Marathon talks in July of 2008 failed to resolve agricultural trade issues, suggesting that the Doha Round is dead.

While the first five Rounds concentrated on item by item tariff reductions, the "Kennedy Round" (1964–1967) was noted for its achievement of across-the-board tariff reductions. In 1961, GATT began to consider how to approach the increasing trade disparity with the developing world. In 1964, GATT adopted Part IV, which introduced a principle of "diminished expectations of reciprocity". Reciprocity remained a goal, but developed nations would not expect concessions from developing nations which were inconsistent with developmental needs. For the developing nations, nonreciprocity meant freedom to protect domestic markets from import competition. Import substitution was a major focus of developmental theory in the 1960s, and developing nations saw keeping their markets closed as a way to save these domestic industries. Although they also sought preferential treatment of their exports, that was a demand which would remain unsatisfied for another decade.

The "Tokyo Round" (1973–1979) engendered agreements about several areas of nontariff barrier (NTB) trade restraints. Nearly a dozen major agreements on nontariff barrier issues were produced in the Tokyo Round. In the early 1970s, national and regional generalized preference schemes (GSP) developed to favor the exports of developing nations. The foreign debt payment problems of the developing nations suggested that they need to generate revenue to pay these debts, and that developmental theory must shift from import substitution to export promotion.

In 1986, the "Uruguay Round" of multilateral trade negotiations began at a Special Session of the GATT Contracting States. This Uruguay Round included separate negotiations on trade in goods and on trade in services, with separate groups of negotiators dealing with each topic. Subtopics for negotiation by subgroups included nontariff barriers, agriculture, subsidies and countervailing duties, intellectual property rights and counterfeit goods, safeguards, tropical products, textiles, investment policies, and dispute resolution. The negotiating sessions were extraordinarily complex, but were able to achieve a successful conclusion, giving birth to the World Trade Organization in 1995.

THE USTR, FAST TRACK AND BILATERAL TRADE AGREEMENTS

Removing trade barriers is usually done on a reciprocal basis, and requires lengthy bargaining and negotiations between sovereign states. Congress is not adapted to carry on such negotiations, so it routinely delegates limited authority to the President to negotiate agreements reducing import restrictions when the President finds that such restrictions, either of the United States or of a foreign country, are unduly burdensome. Some recent efforts to reduce trade restrictions have been multilateral efforts (e.g., the WTO and the North American Free Trade Agreement). Others have been bilateral, such as the U.S. free trade agreements. In these situations, Congress intermittently since 1974 has given quite broad authority to the President, or his representative, to reduce or eliminate United States tariffs on a reciprocal "fast track" basis. Fast track originated as a compromise after Congress refused to ratify two major components of the Kennedy Round of GATT negotiations.

Since the 1980s, a United States Trade Representative (USTR) is appointed by the President, with the advice and consent of the Senate. The Office of the USTR has been the principal vehicle through which trade negotiations have been conducted in recent years on behalf of the United States. For example, the international setting in which the USTR frequently functions is that provided by the WTO and NAFTA, and to a lesser extent by the International Monetary Fund (IMF). The USTR is the contact point for persons who desire an investigation of instances of noncompliance with any trade agreement.

The Trade Act of 2002 (P.L. 107–210) authorized President Bush to negotiate international trade agreements on a fast track basis, a procedure that requires Congress to vote within 90 legislative days up or down, without amendments, on U.S. trade agreements. In return, Congress receives substantial notice and opportunity to influence U.S. trade negotiations conducted by the USTR. See 19 U.S.C. § 3801 et seq. The President and the USTR quickly completed and Congress approved free trade agreements with Chile and Singapore, and thereafter with Morocco, Australia, Central America/Dominican Republic, Peru, Jordan, Oman, and Bahrain. The President's fast track authority expired in July of 2007 with agreements for Colombia, Panama and Korea not yet approved by Congress. For U.S. free trade partners, fast track suggests that once they reach a deal Congress cannot alter it, though in recent years Congress has effectively tacked on additional requirements, notably regarding labor and the environment.

Hundreds of bilateral free trade agreements lattice the world, including for example the European Union and South Africa, Canada and Costa Rica, China and Chile, Japan and Singapore. Mexico has dozens of bilateral free trade agreements. At this point the only nation without a bilateral free trade deal is Mongolia. A variety of factors help explain why bilaterals have become the leading edge of international trade law and policy, presenting a systemic risk to the WTO. Difficulties encountered in the Uruguay, "Seattle" and Doha Rounds of multilateral trade negotiations are certainly crucial. GATT/WTO regulatory failures regarding bilaterals have also fueled this reality. Yet these "negatives" do not fully explain the feeding frenzy of bilaterals. A range of attractions are also at work. For example, bilaterals often extend to subject matters beyond WTO competence. Foreign investment law is a prime example, and many bilaterals serve as investment magnets. Government procurement, optional at the WTO level, is often included in bilaterals. Competition policy and labor and environmental matters absent from the WTO are sometimes covered in bilaterals. In addition, bilaterals can reach beyond the scope of existing WTO agreements. Services is one "WTO-plus" area where this is clearly true. Intellectual property rights are also being "WTO-plussed" in bilateral free trade agreements.

Whether this amounts to competitive trade liberalization or competitive trade imperialism is a provocative question.

THE WORLD TRADE ORGANIZATION (WTO) AND GATT 1994

The WTO is the product of the Uruguay Round of GATT negotiations, which was successfully completed in 1994. The Uruguay Round produced a package of agreements. These are the Agreement Establishing the World Trade Organization and its Annexes, which include the General Agreement on Tariffs and Trade 1994 (GATT 1994) and a series of Multilateral Trade Agreements (the Covered Agreements), and a series of Plurilateral Trade Agreements.

GATT 1947 and GATT 1994 are two distinct agreements. GATT 1994 incorporates the provisions of GATT 1947, except for the Protocol of Provisional Application, which is expressly excluded. Thus, problems created by exempting existing national laws at the time of the adoption of the Protocol are avoided by this exclusion in the Covered Agreements. Otherwise, in cases involving a conflict between GATT 1947 and GATT 1994, GATT 1947 controls. The WTO will be guided by the decisions, procedures and customary practices developed under GATT.

Annexed to the WTO Agreement are several Multilateral Trade Agreements. As to trade in goods, they include Agreements on Agriculture, Textiles, Antidumping, Subsidies and Countervailing Measures, Safeguards, Technical Barriers to Trade, Sanitary and Phytosanitary Measures, Pre-shipment Inspection, Rules of Origin, and Import License Procedures. In addition to trade in goods, they include a General Agreement on Trade in Services and Agreements on Trade–Related Aspects of Intellectual Property Rights and Trade–Related Investment Measures. Affecting all of these agreements is the Understanding on Rules and Procedures Governing the Settlement of Disputes. Most importantly, *all* of the Multilateral Trade Agreements are binding on *all* Members of the World Trade Organization, now about 150 nations.

In addition to the Multilateral Trade Agreements, there are also Plurilateral Trade Agreements which are also annexed to the WTO Agreement. These agreements, however, are not binding on all WTO Members, and Members can choose to adhere to them or not. They include Agreements on Government Procurement, Trade in Civil Aircraft, International Dairy and an Arrangement Regarding Bovine Meat. States which do not join the plurilateral trade agreements do not receive reciprocal benefits under them.

The duties of the World Trade Organization are to facilitate the implementation, administer the operations and further the objectives of all these agreements. Its duties also include the resolution of disputes under the agreements, reviews of trade policy and cooperation with the International Monetary Fund (IMF) and the World Bank. To achieve these goals, the WTO Agreement provides a charter for the new organization, creating a minimalist institution with limited capabilities, and no substantive or executive competence. The WTO as an institution, for example, has no power to bring actions on its own initiative. Thus, there is a unified administration of pre-existing and new obligations under all agreements concerning trade in goods. In addition, the administration of the new obligations on trade in services, investment and intellectual property are brought under the same roof. Under the provisions of the WTO Agreement, only the Members of WTO can initiate actions via the Dispute Settlement Understanding. Enforcement of WTO obligations is primarily through permitting Members to retaliate or cross retaliate against other members, rather than by execution of WTO institutional orders.

WTO AGREEMENTS AND U.S. LAW

The WTO Covered Agreements concern not only trade in goods, but also trade in services (GATS), and trade-related aspects of intellectual property (TRIPS). The basic concepts that GATT applied to trade in goods (described above) are now applied to these areas through GATS and TRIPS. In the WTO Covered Agreements, the basic concepts of GATT 1947 and its associated agreements are elaborated and clarified. In addition, there is an attempt to transform all protectionist measures relating to agriculture (such as import bans and quotas, etc.) into only tariff barriers, which can then be lowered in subsequent MTN Rounds (a process known as "tariffication"). WTO also contains some superficial provisions on trade-related investment measures (TRIMS). Some of the WTO provisions, particularly those concerning trade in goods, will be discussed in more detail below, in relation to United States trade law.

The United States enacted legislation to implement WTO and the Covered Agreements on December 3, 1994, but did not ratify them as a treaty. The Uruguay Round Implementation Act legislation was submitted to Congress under "fast track" procedures, which required that the agreement and its implementing legislation be considered as a whole, and prohibited Congressional amendments to the implementing legislation. The Congressional authority for "fast track" procedures also required that the President give ninety days notice of his intention to enter into such an agreement.

Neither GATT 1947 nor the WTO Agreement, GATT 1994 and the other Covered Agreements have been ratified as treaties, and therefore comprise international obligations of the United States only to the extent that they are incorporated in United States' implementing legislation. GATT 1947 was not considered controlling by the courts of the United States, and these courts have always held themselves bound to the U.S. legislation actually enacted. The WTO Covered Agreements will be considered to have a non-self-executed status, and therefore are likely to be regarded in the same manner as GATT 1947.

GATT/WTO NONTARIFF TRADE BARRIER CODES

There are numerous nontariff trade barriers applicable to imports. Many of these barriers arise out of safety and health regulations. Others concern the environment, consumer protection, product standards and government procurement. Many of the relevant rules were created for legitimate consumer and public protection reasons. They were often created without extensive consideration of their international impact as potential nontariff trade barriers. Nevertheless, the practical impact of legislation of this type is to ban the importation of nonconforming products. Thus, unlike tariffs which can always be paid, and unlike quotas which permit a certain amount of goods to enter the market, nontariff trade barriers have the potential to totally exclude foreign exports.

Multilateral GATT negotiations since the end of World War II have led to a significant decline in world tariff levels, particularly on trade with developed nations. As steadily as tariff barriers have disappeared, nontariff trade barriers (NTBs) have emerged. Health and safety regulations, environmental laws, rules regulating products standards, procurement legislation and customs procedures are often said to present NTB problems. Negotiations over nontariff trade barriers dominated the Tokyo Round of the GATT negotiations during the late 1970s. A number of NTB "codes" (sometimes called "side agreements") emerged from the Tokyo Round. These concerned subsidies, dumping, government procurement, technical barriers (products standards), customs valuation and import licensing. In addition, specific agreements regarding trade in bovine meats, dairy products and civil aircraft were also reached. The United States accepted all of these NTB codes and agreements except the one on dairy products. Most of the necessary implementation of these agreements was accomplished in the Trade Agreements Act of 1979.

Additional GATT codes were agreed upon under the Uruguay Round ending in late 1993. They revisit all of the NTB areas covered by the Tokyo Round Codes and create new codes for sanitary and phytosanitary measures (SPS), trade-related investment measures (TRIMs), preshipment inspection, rules of origin, escape clause safeguards and trade-related intellectual property rights (TRIPs). The United States Congress approved and implemented these Codes in December of 1994 under the Uruguay Round Agreements Act.

One problem with nontariff trade barriers is that they are so numerous. Intergovernmental negotiation intended to reduce their trade restricting impact is both tedious and difficult. There are continuing attempts through the World Trade Organization to come to grips with additional specific NTB problems. Furthermore, various trade agreements of the United States have been undertaken in this field. For example, the Canada–United States Free Trade Area Agreement and the NAFTA built upon the

The *Beef Hormones* case illustrates NTB issues and a rare outcome in WTO dispute settlement. The EU banned imports of growth enhancing hormone-treated beef from the U.S. and Canada as a health hazard. The WTO Appellate Body ruled that, since the ban was more strict than international standards, the EU needed scientific evidence to back it up. However, the EU had failed to undertake a scientific risk assessment, and its scientific reports did not provide any rational basis to uphold the ban. In fact, the primary study had found no evidence of harm to humans from the growth-enhancing-hormones. The Appellate Body ruled that the ban violated the WTO Sanitary and Phytosanitary Standards (SPS) Code and required the EU to produce scientific evidence to justify the ban within a reasonable time, or to revoke the ban. Arbitrators determined that 15 months was a reasonable time, but the EU failed to produce such evidence and the U.S. retaliated with over $200 million in tariffs on EU exports.

The United States maintains that the European Union must eliminate their ban on hormone-treated beef in order to conform to the ruling. Naturally, the Europeans see things a bit differently. If they can come up with solid scientific evidence that the administration of hormones to beef in the U.S. and Canada poses risks to human health, they can escape retaliation. The EU claimed on the basis of post-dispute studies that one beef hormone was proven harmful to human health, and five others ought to be banned as a precautionary principle. The EU petitioned the WTO to seek removal of the U.S. sanctions. This petition was rejected in 2008 by the Appellate Body, again for want of scientific justification.

THE WTO AGREEMENT ON AGRICULTURE

Agricultural issues played a central role in the Uruguay Round GATT negotiations. More than any other issue, they delayed completion of that Round from 1990 to 1993 and threaten the current Doha Round. The agreement finally reached was a trade liberalizing, market-oriented effort. Each country promised a number of commitments on market access, reduced domestic agricultural support levels and export subsidies. The United States Congress approved of these commitments by adopting the Uruguay Round Agreements Act.

Broadly speaking nontariff trade barriers to international agricultural trade are replaced by tariffs that provide substantially the same level of protection. This is known as "tariffication." It applies to virtually all NTBs, including variable levies, import bans, voluntary export restraints and import quotas. Tariffication applies specifically to U.S. agricultural quotas adopted under Section 22 of the Agricultural Adjustment Act. All agricultural tariffs, including those converted from NTBs, are reduced by 36 and 24 percent by developed and developing countries, respectively, over 6 and 10 year periods. Certain minimum access tariff quotas apply when imports amount to less than 3 to 5 percent of domestic consumption. An escape clause exists for tariffed imports at low prices or upon a surge of importation depending upon the existing degree of import penetration. The efficacy of these "liberalizations" has been severely challenged by developing nations led by Brazil and India in the Doha Round. They claim that agricultural trade restraints combined with huge export subsidies from surplus producers like the U.S. and the EU undermine their agricultural production and exports.

Regarding domestic support for agriculture, some programs with minimal impact on trade are exempt from change under the WTO Agreement. These programs are known as "green box policies." They include governmental support for agricultural research, disease control, infrastructure and food security. Green box policies were also exempt from GATT/WTO challenge or countervailing duties until 2004. Direct payments to producers that are not linked to production are also generally exempt. This will include income support, adjustment assistance, and environmental and regional assistance payments. Furthermore, direct payments to support crop reductions and *de minimis* payments are exempted in most cases.

After removing all of the exempted domestic agricultural support programs, the agreement on agriculture arrives at a calculation known as the Total Aggregate Measurement of Support (Total AMS).

This measure is the basis for agricultural support reductions under the agreement. Developed nations promised to reduce their Total AMS by 20 percent over 6 years, developing nations by 13.3 percent over 10 years. Agricultural export subsidies of developed nations had to be reduced by 36 percent below 1986–1990 levels over six years and the quantity of subsidized agricultural exports by 21 percent. Developing nations must meet corresponding 24 and 14 percent reductions over 10 years.

All conforming tariffications, reductions in domestic support for agriculture and export subsidy alterations were essentially exempt from challenge until 2004 within the GATT/WTO on grounds such as serious prejudice in export markets or nullification and impairment of agreement benefits. However, countervailing duties could be levied against all unlawfully subsidized exports of agricultural goods except for subsidies derived from so-called national "green box policies" (discussed above).

THE GENERAL AGREEMENT ON TRADE IN SERVICES (GATS)

Market access for services is a major focus of the WTO General Agreement on Trade in Services (GATS). Since the United States is the world's largest exporter of services, including for example engineering, computer and professional services, it has a special interest in GATS. The U.S. Congress approved and implemented the GATS agreement in 1994 under the Uruguay Round Agreements Act.

Subsequently, early in 1995, the United States refused to extend most-favored-nation treatment to financial services. The European Union, Japan and other GATS nations then entered into an interim two-year agreement which operated on MFN principles. Financial services was revisited in 1996–97 with further negotiations aimed at bringing the United States into the fold. These negotiations bore fruit late in 1997 with 70 nations (including the United States) joining in an agreement that covers 95 percent of trade in banking, insurance, securities and financial information. This agreement took effect March 1, 1999.

A general right of most-favored-nation treatment in the services sector has been established. National laws that restrict the number of firms in a market, that are dependent upon local "needs tests" or that mandate local incorporation are regulated by the GATS. Various "transparency" rules require disclosure of all relevant laws and regulations, and these must be administered reasonably, objectively and impartially. Specific market access and national treatment commitments are made by various governments in schedules attached to the agreement. The European Union, for example, has refused to make commitments in the audio-visual sector. These commitments may be modified or withdrawn after three years, subject to a right of compensation that can be arbitrated. Certain mutual recognition of education and training for service-sector licensing will occur. State monopolies or exclusive service providers may continue, but must not abuse their positions. Detailed rules are created in annexes to the GATS on telecommunications and air transport services.

WTO DECISION–MAKING

The World Trade Organization is structured in three tiers. One tier is the Ministerial Conference, which meets biennially and is composed of representatives of all WTO Members. Each Member has an equal voting weight, which is unlike the representation in the IMF and World Bank where there is weighted voting, and financially powerful states have more power over the decision-making process. The Ministerial Conference is responsible for all WTO functions, and is able to make any decisions necessary. It has the power to authorize new multilateral negotiations and to adopt the results of such negotiations. The Ministerial Conference, by a three-fourths vote, is authorized to grant waivers of obligations to Members in exceptional circumstances. It also has the power to adopt interpretations of Covered Agreements. When the Ministerial Conference is in recess, its functions are performed by the General Council.

The second tier is the General Council which has executive authority over the day to day operations and functions of the WTO. It is composed of representatives of all WTO Members, and each member has an equal voting weight. It meets whenever it is appropriate. The General Council also has the power to adopt interpretations of Covered Agreements.

The third tier comprises the councils, bodies and committees which are accountable to the Ministerial Conference or General Council. Ministerial Conference committees include Committees on Trade and Development, Balance of Payment Restrictions, Budget, Finance and Administration. General Council bodies include the Dispute Settlement Body, the Trade Policy Review Body, and Councils for Trade in Goods, Trade in Services and Trade–Related Intellectual Property Rights. The Councils are all created by the WTO Agreement and are open to representatives of all Member States. The Councils also have the authority to create subordinate organizations. Other committees, such as the Committee on Subsidies and Countervailing Measures are created by specific individual agreements.

Of the General Council bodies, the two most important are the Dispute Settlement Body (DSB) and the Trade Policy Review Body (TPRB). The DSB is a special meeting of the General Council, and therefore includes all WTO Members. It has responsibility for resolution of disputes under all the Covered Agreements, and will be discussed in more detail below, under Dispute Resolution.

The purpose of the Trade Policy Review–Mechanism (TPRM) is to improve adherence to the WTO agreements and obligations, and to obtain greater transparency. Individual Members of WTO each prepare a "Country Report" on their trade policies and perceived adherence to the WTO Covered Agreements. The WTO Secretariat also prepares a report on each Member, but from the perspective of the Secretariat. The Trade Policy Review Body (TPRB) then reviews the trade policies of each Member based on these two reports. At the end of the review, the TPRB issues its own report concerning the adherence of the Member's trade policy to the WTO Covered Agreements. The TPRB has no enforcement capability, but the report is sent to the next meeting of the WTO Ministerial Conference. It is then up to the Ministerial Conference to evaluate the trade practices and policies of the Member.

Consensus Rules

The process of decision-making in the WTO Ministerial Conference and General Council relies upon "consensus" as the norm, just as it did for decision-making under GATT 1947. "Consensus", in this context means that no Member formally objects to a proposed decision. Thus, consensus is not obtained if any one Member formally objects, and has often been very difficult to obtain, which proved to be a weakness in the operation of GATT. However, there are many exceptions to the consensus formula under WTO, and some new concepts (such as "inverted consensus", discussed below) which are designed to ease the process of decision-making under WTO.

Article IX(1) of the WTO Agreement first provides that "the practice of decision-making by consensus" followed under GATT shall be continued. The next sentence of that provision, however, states that "where a decision cannot be arrived at by consensus, the matter at issue shall be decided by voting", except where otherwise provided. The ultimate resolution of the conflict between these two sentences is not completely clear.

There are a number of exceptions to the requirement for consensus that are expressly created under the WTO Agreement. One such exception is decisions by the Dispute Settlement Body, which has its own rules (see below). Another set of exceptions concerns decisions on waivers, interpretations and amendments of the Covered Agreements. Waivers of obligations may be granted and amendments adopted to Covered Agreements only by the Ministerial Conference. Amendments of Multilateral Trade Agreements usually require a consensus, but where a decision on a proposed amendment cannot obtain consensus, the decision on that amendment is to be made in certain circumstances by a two-thirds majority vote. In "exceptional circumstances", the Ministerial Conference is authorized to grant waivers of obligations under a Covered Agreement by a three-fourths vote. Another exception to the consensus requirement allows procedural rules in both the Ministerial Conference and the General Council to be decided by a majority vote of the Members, unless otherwise provided.

Admission to the WTO

Admission to the World Trade Organization is by "consensus." In theory, this gives each member a veto over applicant countries. In reality, no nation wishing to join has ever formally been vetoed, though many have been long delayed. It took, for example, well over a decade to negotiate acceptable terms of entry for the People's Republic of China. Such negotiations are handled individually by member states, not by the WTO as an organization. United States negotiations with China were particularly lengthy and difficult, one principal issue being whether China should be admitted as a developing or developed nation. (The issue was fudged, with China treated differently within the WTO package of agreements.)

Essentially, applicant counties make an offer of trade liberalization commitments to join the WTO. This offer is renegotiated with interested member nations, some 40 nations regarding China including the European Union which negotiates as a unit (NAFTA does not). Regarding China, the last member to reach agreement on WTO admission was Mexico, which extracted stiff promises against the dumping of Chinese goods. The various commitments made by the applicant in these negotiations are consolidated into a final accession protocol which is then approved by "consensus." Russia is currently well into this negotiation process. Iran's desire to join has basically been frustrated by U.S. refusal to negotiate on WTO entry.

DISPUTE SETTLEMENT UNDER WTO

WTO provides a unified system for settling international trade disputes through the Dispute Settlement Understanding (DSU) and using the Dispute Settlement Body (DSB). The DSB is a special assembly of the WTO General Council, and includes all WTO Members. There are five stages in the resolution of disputes under WTO: 1) Consultation; 2) Panel establishment, investigation and report; 3) Appellate review of the panel report; 4) Adoption of the panel and appellate decision; and 5) Implementation of the decision adopted. There is also a parallel process for binding arbitration, if both parties agree to submit this dispute to arbitration, rather than to a DSB panel. In addition, during the implementation phase (5), the party subject to an adverse decision may seek arbitration as a matter of right.

Although the DSU offers a unified dispute resolution system that is applicable across all sectors and all WTO Covered Agreements, there are many specialized rules for disputes which arise under them. Such specialized rules appear in the Agreements on Textiles, Antidumping, Subsidies and Countervailing Measures, Technical Barriers to Trade, Sanitary and Phytosanitary Measures, Customs Valuation, General Agreement on Trade in Services, Financial Services and Air Transport Services. The special provisions in these individual Covered Agreements govern, where applicable, and prevail in any conflict with the general provisions of the DSU.

Under WTO, unlike under GATT 1947, the DSU practically assures that panels will be established upon request by a Member. Further, under WTO, unlike under GATT 1947, the DSU virtually ensures the adoption of unmodified panel and Appellate Body decisions. It accomplishes this by requiring the DSB to adopt these decisions automatically and without amendment unless they are rejected by a consensus of all Members. This "inverted consensus" requires that all Members of the DSB, including the Member who prevailed in the dispute, decide to reject the dispute resolution decision; and that no Member formally favor that decision. Such an outcome seems unlikely. This inverted consensus requirement is imposed on both the adoption of panel reports or Appellate Body decisions and also on the decision to establish a panel.

The potential resolutions of a dispute under DSU range from a "mutually satisfactory solution" agreed to by the parties under the first, or consultation phase, to authorized retaliation under the last, or implementation, phase. The preferred solution is always any resolution that is mutually satisfactory to the parties. After a final decision, there are three types of remedies available to the prevailing party, if a mutually satisfactory solution cannot be obtained. One is for the respondent to bring the measure found to violate a Covered Agreement into conformity with the Agreement. A second is for the prevailing Member to receive compensation from the respondent which both parties agree is sufficient to compensate for any injury caused by the measure found to violate a Covered Agreement. Finally, if no such agreement can be reached, a prevailing party can be authorized to suspend some of its concessions under the Covered Agreements to the respondent. These suspended concessions, called "retaliation," can be authorized within the same trade sector and agreement; or, if that will not create sufficient compensation, can be authorized across trade sectors and agreements.

Phase 1: Consultation

Any WTO Member who believes that the Measures of another Member are not in conformity with the Covered Agreements may call for consultations on those measures. The respondent has ten days to reply to the call for consultations and must agree to enter into consultation within 30 days. If the respondent does not enter into consultations within the 30 day period, the party seeking consultations can immediately request the establishment of a panel under DSU, which puts the dispute into Phase 2.

Once consultations begin, the parties have 60 days to achieve a settlement. The goal is to seek a positive solution to the dispute, and the preferred resolution is to reach whatever solution is mutually satisfactory to the parties. If such a settlement cannot be obtained after 60 days of consultations, the party seeking consultations may request the establishment of a panel under DSU, which moves the dispute into Phase 2.

Third parties with an interest in the subject-matter of the consultations may seek to be included in them. If such inclusion is rejected, they may seek their own consultations with the other Member. Alternatives to consultations may be provided through the use of conciliation, mediation or good offices, where all parties agree to use the alternative process. Any party can terminate the use of conciliation, mediation or good offices and then seek the establishment of a panel under DSU, which will move the dispute into Phase 2.

Phase 2: Panel establishment, investigation and report

If consultations between the parties fail, the party or parties seeking the consultations (the complainant) may request the DSB to establish a panel to investigate, report and resolve the dispute. It is not uncommon to have several member states, sometimes a dozen or more, join together as complainants. This often creates high profile WTO disputes. The DSB must establish such a panel upon request, unless the DSB expressly decides by consensus not to establish the panel. Since an "inverted consensus" is required to reject the establishment of the panel and the complainant Member must be part of that consensus, it is very likely that a panel will be established. Hundreds of panels have been established since 1995.

The WTO Secretariat maintains a list of well-qualified persons who are available to serve as panelists. The panels are usually composed of three individuals from that list who are not citizens of either party. If the parties agree, a panel can be composed of five such individuals. The parties can also agree to appoint citizens of a party to a panel. Panelists may be either nongovernmental individuals or governmental officials, but they are to be selected so as to ensure their independence. Thus, there is a bias towards independent individuals who are not citizens of any party. If a citizen of a party is appointed, his government may not instruct that citizen how to vote, for the panelist must be independent. By the same reasoning, a governmental official of a non-party Member who is subject to instructions from his government would not seem to fit the profile of an independent panelist.

The WTO Secretariat proposes nominations of the panelists. Parties may not normally oppose the nominations, except for "compelling reasons." The parties are given twenty days to agree on the panelists and the composition of the panel. If such agreement is not forthcoming, the WTO Director–General is authorized to appoint the panelists, in consultation with other persons in the Secretariat.

The "cases" brought to DSB panels can involve either violations of Covered Agreements or nonviolation nullification and impairment of benefits under the Covered Agreements. A prima facie case of nullification impairment arises when one Member infringes upon the "obligations assumed under a Covered Agreement." Such infringement creates a presumption against the infringing Member, but the presumption can be rebutted by a showing that the complaining Member has suffered no adverse effect from the infringement.

The panels receive pleadings and rebuttals and hear oral arguments. Panels can also engage in fact development from sources outside those presented by the parties. Thus, the procedure has aspects familiar to civil law courts. A panel can, on its own initiative, request information from any body, including experts selected by the panel. It can also obtain confidential information in some circumstances from an administrative body which is part of the government of a Member, without any prior consent from that Member. Finally, a panel can establish its own group of experts to provide reports to it on factual or scientific issues.

A panel is obligated to produce two written reports—an interim and a final report. A panel is supposed to submit a final written report to the DSB within six months of its establishment. The report will contain its findings of fact, findings of law, decision and the rationale for its decision. Before the final report is issued, the panel provides an interim report to the parties. The purpose of this interim report is to apprise the parties of the panel's current analysis of the issues and to permit the parties to comment on that analysis. The final report of the panel need not change any of the findings or conclusions in its interim report unless it is persuaded to do so by a party's comments. However, if it is not so persuaded, it is obligated to explain in its final report why it is not so persuaded.

The decisions in panel reports are final as to issues of fact. The decisions in panel reports are not necessarily final as to issues of law. Panel decisions on issues of law are subject to review by the Appellate Body, which is Phase 3, and explained below. Any party can appeal a panel report, and as is explained below it is expected that appeals will usually be taken.

Phase 3: Appellate review of the panel report

Appellate review of panel reports is available at the request of any party, unless the DSB rejects that request by an "inverted consensus." There is no threshold requirement for an appellant to present a substantial substantive legal issue. Thus, most panel decisions are appealed as a matter of course. However, the Appellate Body can only review the panel reports on questions of law or legal interpretation.

The Appellate Body is a new institution. GATT 1947 had nothing comparable to it. The Appellate Body is composed of seven members (or judges) who are appointed by the DSB to four year terms. Each judge may be reappointed, but only once, to a second four year term. Each judge is to be a recognized authority on international trade law and the Covered Agreements. Appointments to the Appellate Body have included a number of distinguished judges, law professors, government trade officials and trade lawyers from a range of developed and developing countries. The review of any panel decision is performed by three judges out of the seven. The parties do not, however, have any influence on which judges are selected to review a particular panel report. There is a schedule, created by the Appellate Body itself, for the rotation for sitting of each of the judges. Thus, a party might try to appear before a favored judge by timing the start of the dispute settlement process to arrive at the Appellate Body at the right moment on the rotation schedule, but even this limited approach has difficulties.

The Appellate Body receives written submissions from the parties and has 60, or in some cases 90, days in which to render its decision. The Appellate Body review is limited to issues of law and legal interpretation. The panel decision may be upheld, modified, or reversed by the Appellate Body decision. Appellate Body decisions are anonymous, and ex parte communications are not permitted, which makes judge-shopping by parties more than usually difficult.

Phase 4: Adoption of the panel or Appellate Body decision

Appellate Body determinations are submitted to the DSB. Panel decisions which are not appealed are also submitted to the DSB. Once either type of decision is submitted to the DSB, the DSB must automatically adopt them without modification or amendment at its next meeting unless the decision is rejected by all Members of the DSB through the form of "inverted consensus" discussed previously.

An alternative to Phases 2 through 4 is arbitration, if both parties agree. The arbitration must be binding on the parties, and there is no appeal from the arbitral tribunal's decision to the DSB Appellate Body.

Phase 5: Implementation of the decision adopted

Once a panel or Appellate Body decision is adopted by the DSB, implementation is a three-step process. In the first step, the Member found to have a measure which violates its WTO obligations has "a reasonable time" (usually 15 months) to bring those measures into conformity with the WTO obligations. That remedy is the preferred one, and this form of implementation is the principal goal of the WTO dispute settlement system. To date, most disputes have resulted in compliance in this manner.

Phase 6: Compensation Option

If the violating measures are not brought into conformity within a reasonable time, the parties proceed to the second step. The parties negotiate to reach an agreement upon a form of "compensation" which will be granted by the party in violation to the injured party. Such "compensation" will usually comprise trade concessions, which are over and above those already available under the WTO and Covered Agreements. The nature, scope, amount and duration of these additional concessions is at the negotiating parties' discretion, but each side must agree that the final compensation package is fair and is properly related to the injury caused by the violating measures. No such compensation agreements have ever been achieved.

Phase 7: Authorized Retaliation

If the parties cannot agree on an appropriate amount of compensation within twenty days, the complainant may proceed to the third step. In the third step, the party or parties injured by the violating measures seek authority from the DSB to retaliate against the party whose measures violated its WTO obligations (the respondent). Thus, complainant seeks authority to suspend some of its WTO obligations benefitting the respondent. The retaliation proposed must ordinarily be within the same sector and agreement as the violating measure. "Sector" is sometimes broadly defined, as all trade in goods, and sometimes narrowly defined, as in individual services in the Services Sectoral Classification List. "Agreement" is also broadly defined. All the agreements listed in Annex IA to the WTO Agreement are considered to be a single "agreement." If retaliation within the sector and agreement of the violating measure is considered insufficient compensation, the complainant may seek suspension of its obligations across sectors and agreements.

Within 30 days of the complainant's presentation of the request to retaliate, the DSB must grant the request, unless the request is rejected by all the members through an "inverted consensus." However, the respondent may object to the level or scope of the retaliation. Upon such an objection, the issues raised by the objection will be examined by either the Appellate Body or by an arbitrator. The respondent has a right, even if arbitration was not used in Phases 2 through 4, to have an arbitrator review in Phase 5 the appropriateness of the complainant's proposed level and scope of retaliation. The arbitrator will also examine whether the proper procedures and criteria to establish retaliation have been followed. The Phase 5 arbitration is final and binding and the arbitrator's decision is probably not subject to DSB review.

In addition to objecting to the level of authorized retaliation, the responding WTO member may simultaneously challenge the assertion of noncompliance. This challenge will ordinarily be heard by the original panel and must be resolved within 90 days. Thus the request for authorized retaliation and objections thereto could conceivably be accomplished before noncompliance is formally determined. In practice, WTO dispute settlement has melded these conflicting procedures such that compliance and retaliation issues are decided together, typically by the original panel.

Retaliation in Action

Retaliation has rarely been authorized, and even less rarely imposed. The amount of a U.S. retaliation permitted after the WTO *Bananas* and *Beef Hormones* decisions were not implemented by the EU was contested. The arbitration tribunals for this issue were the original WTO panels, which did not allow the entire amount of the almost $700 million in retaliatory tariffs proposed by the United States. The U.S. was authorized and levied retaliatory tariffs amounting to about $100 million (*Bananas*) and $200 million (*Beef Hormones*) against European goods because of the EU failure to implement those WTO decisions. Since 2000, Congress has authorized rotating these tariffs in "carousel" fashion upon different European goods. The threat of carousel retaliation contributed to an April 2001 settlement of the *Bananas* dispute.

In a landmark ruling, a WTO panel acting as an arbitrator authorized Ecuador to remove protection of intellectual property rights regarding geographical indicators, copyrights and industrial designs on European Union goods for sale in Ecuador. This authorization was part of Ecuador's $200 million compensation in the *Bananas* dispute. The WTO panel acknowledged that Ecuador imports mostly capital goods and raw materials from the European Union and that imposing retaliatory tariffs on them would adversely harm its manufacturing industries. This risk supported "cross-retaliation" outside the sector of the EU trade violation and likewise contributed to settlement of the *Bananas* dispute. Cross-sector retaliation has also been authorized against the U.S. after losing a GATS dispute to Antigua on Internet gambling restraints.

The amount of EU retaliation permissible after the U.S. lost (for the second time) under WTO subsidy rules concerning Internal Revenue Code extraterritorial export tax preferences (FISCs) was disputed. A WTO panel, serving as an arbitrator, authorized approximately $4 *billion* in EU retaliation against U.S. exports. This retaliation commenced in March of 2004 and escalated monthly until the U.S. capitulated by amending the I.R.C. late in 2004.

Both "compensation" in the second step and "retaliation" in the third step of implementation provide only for indirect enforcement of DSB decisions. There is no mechanism for direct enforcement by the WTO of its decisions through WTO orders to suspend trade obligations. Some commentators believe that retaliation will be an effective implementation device; others believe that it will prove ineffective. The division represented by these conflicting views represents two different approaches to the nature of both international law and international trade law.

One approach seeks a rule-oriented use of the "rule of law"; the other seeks a power-oriented use of diplomacy. The United States and less developed countries have traditionally sought to develop a rule-oriented approach to international trade disputes. The European Union and Japan have traditionally sought to use the GATT/WTO primarily as a forum for diplomatic negotiations, although the EU now ranks second in number of WTO proceedings. These different views created part of the conflict at the December 1999 Seattle WTO meeting (which failed to launch the Millennium Round). If the DSB is a court, its proceedings should be open and "transparent." However, if it is just another form of government-to-government diplomacy, that has always been held in secret.

U.S. INVOLVEMENT IN WTO DISPUTE RESOLUTION

The WTO dispute resolution process has been invoked more frequently than many expected. The

United States has been a complainant or a respondent in about 200 disputes. It lost a dispute initiated by Venezuela and Brazil concerning U.S. standards for reformulated and conventional gasoline. The offending U.S. law was amended to conform to the WTO ruling. It won on a complaint initiated jointly with Canada and the European Union regarding Japanese taxes on alcoholic beverages. Japan subsequently changed its law. When Costa Rica complained about U.S. restraints on imports of underwear, the U.S. let the restraints expire prior to any formal DSB ruling at the WTO. Similar results were reached when India complained of U.S. restraints on wool shirts and blouses. The United States won a major dispute with Canada concerning trade and subsidies for periodicals. This celebrated *Sports Illustrated* dispute proved that WTO remedies can be used to avoid Canada's cultural industries exclusion under NAFTA.

In the longstanding *Bananas* dispute noted above, the United States joined Ecuador, Guatemala, Honduras and Mexico in successfully challenging EU import restraints against so-called "dollar bananas." The EU failed to comply with the Appellate Body's ruling, and retaliatory measures were authorized and imposed. A patent law complaint by the U.S. against India prevailed in the DSB and ultimately brought changes in Indian law regarding pharmaceuticals and agricultural chemicals. In *Beef Hormones,* also noted above, the European Union lost twice before the Appellate Body for want of a "scientific basis" to ban hormone beef imports. It refused to alter its import restraints and presently faces about $200 million retaliatory tariffs on selected exports to Canada and the United States.

The United States prevailed against Argentina regarding tariffs and taxes on footwear, textiles and apparel. It lost a challenge (strongly supported by Kodak) to Japan's distribution rules regarding photo film and paper. In this dispute the U.S. elected *not* to appeal the adverse WTO panel ruling to the Appellate Body. In contrast, the European Union took an appeal which reversed an adverse panel ruling on its customs classification of computer equipment. The U.S. had commenced this proceeding. Opponents in many disputes, Japan, the United States and the European Union united to complain that Indonesia's National Car Programme was discriminatory and in breach of several WTO agreements. They prevailed and Indonesia altered its program.

India, Malaysia, Pakistan and Thailand teamed up to challenge U.S. shrimp import restraints enacted to protect endangered sea turtles. The WTO Appellate Body generally upheld their complaint and the U.S. has moved to comply. The adequacy of U.S. compliance was unsuccessfully challenged by Malaysia. The European Union and the United States jointly opposed Korea's discriminatory taxes on alcoholic beverages. This challenge was successful and Korea now imposes flat non-discriminatory taxes. The United States also complained of Japan's quarantine, testing and other agricultural import rules. The U.S. won at the WTO and Japan has changed its procedures.

In a semiconductor dumping dispute, Korea successfully argued that the U.S. was not in compliance with the WTO Antidumping Agreement. The United States amended its law, but Korea has instituted further proceedings alleging that these amendments are inadequate. The United States did likewise after Australia lost a subsidies dispute relating to auto leather exports. The reconvened WTO panel ruled that Australia had indeed failed to conform to the original adverse DSB decision. A U.S. challenge concerning India's quotas on imports of agricultural, textile and industrial products was upheld. India and the United States subsequently reached agreement on a timeline for removal of these restraints.

Closer to home, New Zealand and the United States complained of Canada's import/export rules regarding milk. Losing at the WTO, Canada agreed to a phased removal of the offending measures. The United States also won against Mexico in an antidumping dispute involving corn syrup, but lost a "big one" when the DSB determined that export tax preferences granted to "Foreign Sales Corporations" of U.S. companies were illegal. The United States expanded the FSC regime by removing the requirement that eligible goods be manufactured in the U.S. It claimed that this change made the FSC program not contingent upon exports, and thus WTO-legal. The European Union challenged this assertion of compliance before the WTO and won. Retaliation finally brought U.S. compliance.

Another "big one" went in favor of the United States. The European Union challenged the validity under the DSU of unilateral retaliation under Section 301 of the Trade Act of 1974. Section 301 has been something of a bete noire in U.S. trade law, but the WTO panel affirmed its legality in light of Presidential undertakings to administer it in accordance with U.S. obligations to adhere to multilateral WTO dispute settlement. The WTO Appellate Body ruled against the United States regarding the legality of the Antidumping Act of 1916 and the royalty free provisions of the 1998 Fairness in Music Licensing act. The Appellate Body also ruled against Section 211 of the Omnibus Appropriations Act of 1998 denying trademark protection in connection with confiscated assets (the "HAVANA CLUB" dispute). U.S. compliance with these rulings has been slow in forthcoming, although the Antidumping Act of 1916 has been repealed.

A WTO Panel ruled in 2002 that the Byrd Amendment violates the WTO antidumping and subsidy codes. The Byrd Amendment (Continued Dumping and Subsidy Act of 2000) authorizes the Customs Service to forward AD and CVD duties to affected domestic producers for qualified expenses. Eleven WTO members including the EU, Canada and Mexico challenged the Amendment. This ruling was affirmed by the WTO Appellate Body and retaliation was authorized. Late in 2005, the U.S. repealed the Byrd Amendment, subject to a contested two-year phase-out.

U.S. involvement in WTO dispute settlement continues to be extensive. The Appellate Body ruled that U.S. countervailing duties against British steel based upon pre-privitization subsidies were unlawful. U.S. complaints against Korean beef import restraints and procurement practices were upheld. Canada's patent protection term was also invalidated by the WTO under a U.S. complaint (WT/DS 170/1). European Union complaints concerning U.S. wheat gluten quotas have been sustained. The *Wheat Gluten* dispute questions the legality of U.S. "causation" rules in escape clause proceedings under Section 201 of the Trade Act of 1974. The United States and other complainants prevailed in a 2002 WTO proceeding against Indian local content and trade balancing requirements for foreign auto manufacturers. These requirements violated the TRIMs agreement. In a David and Goliath dispute, Antigua–Barbuda won a 2004 WTO panel ruling under the GATS against U.S. Internet gambling restraints, the Appellate Body affirming in part. The U.S. won a panel decision against Mexico's exorbitant telecom interconnection rates, but lost a cotton subsidy challenge by Brazil. (retaliation authorized by the Appellate Body in 2008).

Major U.S. safeguard tariffs against steel were invalidated in 2003 by the Appellate Body. The U.S. won an SPS dispute against Japanese quarantine of U.S. apples, while losing an important softwood lumber "zeroing" methodology complaint brought by Canada. In 2006, the Mexico–United States "sugar war" came to a head before the Appellate

Body. Mexico's 20% soft drink tax on beverages not using cane sugar, its 20% distribution tax on those beverages, and related bookkeeping requirements were found to violate GATT Article III and not exempt under Article XX(d). Subsequently, the two countries settled their dispute by agreeing, effective in 2008, to free trade in sugar and high fructose corn syrup. The U.S. failed to persuade the Appellate Body to require the European Union under GATT Article X (3) to undertake a major overhaul of its customs law system targeting inconsistencies therein among the 27 member states. Lastly, the United States lost another "zeroing" dispute under its antidumping law.

The United States has also settled a number of disputes prior to WTO panel decisions, and remains in consultation on other disputes that may be decided by a WTO panel. For the latest summary of all WTO disputes, including many not involving the United States, see www.wto.org.

THE INTERNATIONAL MONETARY FUND (IMF)

Most nations have a national currency and pursue an internal monetary policy to meet their own political and economic goals. Fifteen EU nations have joined in a common currency, the Euro, managed by the European Central Bank. No central authority controls a world monetary system; monetary policy is decentralized. Since 1944, nations have coordinated national monetary policies principally through the International Monetary Fund (IMF).

Both the IMF and the International Bank for Reconstruction and Development (the "World Bank") arose out of the Bretton Woods Conference in 1944. The World Bank was to facilitate loans by capital surplus countries (e.g., then the United States) to countries needing foreign investment for economic redevelopment after World War II. The IMF was to stabilize currency exchange rates, assist countries in their balance of payments, and repair other war damage to the international monetary system. Twenty-nine countries including the United States became party to the IMF Articles of Agreement in 1945. Today, over 150 countries are members of the IMF.

IMF Operations

The IMF goals are to facilitate the expansion and balanced growth of international trade, to assist in the elimination of foreign exchange restrictions which hamper the growth of international trade, and to shorten the duration and lessen the disequilibrium in the international balances of payments of members. The mitigation of wide currency fluctuations is achieved through a complex lending system which permits a country to borrow money from other Fund members or from the Fund (by way of "Special Drawing Rights" or "SDRs") for the purpose of stabilizing the relationship of its currency to other world currencies. These monetary drawing arrangements permit a member country to support its national currency's relative value when compared with national currencies of other countries, especially the "hard" ("reserve") currencies such as the Swiss franc, the Euro, Japanese yen, and United States dollar.

In recent years, IMF loans have normally been "conditioned" upon adoption of specific economic reforms by debtor states, especially in Asia and Latin America. This has led to the perception that the IMF is the world's "sheriff", setting the terms for refinancing national debts and protecting the interests of commercial bank creditors. The IMF has functioned as the first line of negotiation in an international "debt crisis," and commercial and national banks often conform their loans to IMF conditions. These IMF conditions can have dramatic political and social repercussions in debtor nations.

From 2006 onwards, nations have been paying their IMF debt in record numbers. Argentina did so with an assist from Venezuela. Brazil, Russia, Bolivia, Uruguay, Indonesia, the Philippines and others have joined in the flight from IMF loan conditions. The IMF's loan portfolio stood at $100 billion in 2003. By 2009, that portfolio was approaching zero, the IMF was running a budget deficit, and proposing sales of gold to make up the difference. Many commentators wonder aloud what is the role of the IMF without loans?

The IMF, like any bureaucracy in search of a mission, has begun drafting a Code of Best Practices for "Sovereign Wealth Funds" (SWFs). Such

Funds are said to hold over $3 trillion, and are expanding rapidly. Abu Dhabi, Saudi Arabia, Kuwait, Singapore, Russia, China and Norway (for example) all have large SWFs, many of which played an important role in bailing out U.S. banks and securities firms during the 2007–08 sub-prime lending crisis. The primary concern is that SWFs might use their power for political purposes. Their emergence further diminishes the need for IMF loans. As yet the SWFs have not "conditioned" their lending or investment decisions.

Special Drawing Rights (SDRs)

The International Monetary Fund has established a form of international money which is not a national currency and is called a Special Drawing Right (SDR). Certificates of deposit are denominated in SDRs; short-term SDR loans may be obtained commercially; and some OPEC nations have begun to value their national currencies in SDRs. Mechanically, an SDR is an international medium of exchange having a 1991 composite value based 39 percent on the U.S. dollar, 32 percent on the Euro, 18 percent on the Japanese yen, and 11 percent on the British pound. Each exchange rate fluctuation in any one of these "basket currencies" produces commensurately only a smaller, fractional fluctuation in the value of an SDR.

Although the SDR has been talked about as if it is a supranational currency, the SD "Right" is more technically a "unit of account" created by an IMF process. When an IMF member country, having a negative balance of payments position, runs short of its currency "reserves" (which may be its stocks of "hard" "reserve" currencies or gold), the member country may exercise its "Right" to make a "Special Drawing" from the IMF Special Drawing Account (e.g., the country may exercise its Special Drawing Right to ask the IMF to arrange for that country to receive $40 million (U.S.) worth of currency other than gold). Upon receipt of the Drawing "request", the IMF approaches another member country having a fuller stock of "reserves" (which "back up" its national currency), and requests that country to provide currency to the requesting country (e.g. to provide $40 million worth of currency other than gold). In return for having supplied the currency, the supplying country acquires additional Special Drawing Rights (e.g. worth $40 million) which it may revoke if ever its currency "reserves" get too low. Each IMF Member Country participating in the SDR scheme has a finite allocation of SDRs available for its possible use. A net result of the SDR scheme is that countries "swap" currencies to help other countries from time to time in maintaining existing, relative values between their national currency and other currencies of the world.

The EURO Zone

There have also been regional efforts to use the "unit of account" to stabilize relationships among currencies within a region and thereby to promote regularity of currency settlements. Of these regional efforts the "Ecu" of the European Monetary

System (EMS) was the most successful. The Ecu was used by EU countries to establish relative values of Member Country currencies. The Ecu has been succeeded by the Euro, which is a "regional," rather than a national, currency. The Euro is issued and controlled by the European Central Bank.

On January 1, 1999 the Euro became the currency of the 11 Member States of the EMS, replacing the German mark, the French franc and the national currencies of Austria, Belgium, Finland, Ireland, Italy, Luxembourg, the Netherlands, Portugal and Spain. Greece subsequently joined the Euro zone, while Denmark and Sweden rejected participation in national referendums. Ten new EU member states, acceding in 2004, are eligible to participate in the Euro zone if they qualify under relatively stringent economic and financial criteria. Slovenia, Malta and Cyprus have been admitted to the Euro zone. Euro banknotes and coins were issued on January 1, 2002 and are now widely circulated. After an initially steep fall against the U.S. dollar, the Euro has bounced back to well above its opening exchange rate of $1.18 per Euro.

An American trader who incurs expenses and pays bills in U.S. dollars wishes to be paid in U.S. dollars—even for goods or services which are sold outside of the United States. Similarly, a French business person wishes to have Euros. Both have a need for, and must rely upon, the convertibility of currencies (e.g., dollars for Euros and vice versa) so that payments can be made abroad or foreign income can be used to pay bills at home. Convertibility in the international setting has been achieved at different times by using, as a common reference point or standard, different forms of "international money". Gold has been an international money for centuries. The U.S. dollar is both a national currency and a primary form of international money. The Europeans hope to challenge the dollar's supremacy with the Euro.

CHAPTER THREE
RESTRICTIONS ON IMPORTS

Virtually all governments regulate the entry of goods into their jurisdiction. Customs tariffs may be collected, and conformity of the imported goods to local product standards will be reviewed. Much of the law related to restrictions on imports is derived from agreements governing international economic relations, notably those of the World Trade Organization. In this chapter, we will focus on United States law, which is broadly representative of the regulation of imports.

UNITED STATES TRADE LAWS

Rules and sources of law for United States international trade are mostly found in a sequence of specific trade acts which make up the basic framework for import and export trade. To these, however, must be added numerous provisions of other laws which are directed to specific trade issues. For example, the Export Administration Act of 1979 details U.S. export controls, the subject of Chapter 4. United States trade case law tends to be limited. Trade rules have evolved in legislative chambers and multilateral organizations rather than in the courts. There is really no common law of trade; the decisions which do exist are almost exclusively interpretations of the statutory rules.

For U.S. international trade law, there is no easy single statutory source of law. New trade statutes do two things. They create some new trade rules and thus have some permanency standing alone. But they also modify earlier trade statutes. Thus a search often requires checking several U.S. trade laws, although certain subjects tend to be identified with a single trade Act. For example, the Tariff Act of 1930 is where the tariff schedules are located; the Trade Act of 1974 is where rules governing trade with less favored nations, those not benefitting from "normal" MFN status, are found. It is also the source of the trade rules for more than most favored nations, those benefitting for example from the generalized system of preferences (GSP) program. The Trade Agreements Act of 1979 and the Uruguay Round Implementation Act of 1994 cover a number of GATT/WTO trade rules. Trade is thus governed principally by a matrix of separate U.S. trade laws ranging from the Tariff Act of 1930 to the Trade Act of 2002.

These are not the only laws which govern United States trade. There are many other acts which regulate trade, some of which appear as amendments to other laws. For example, the Foreign Corrupt Practices Act, intended to reduce the making of improper payments to government officials abroad, is a relatively brief act which modifies the securities laws. The Caribbean Basin Economic Recovery Act, the ANDEAN Trade Preference Act and the Africa Growth and Opportunity Act extend special duty free import rights to goods from those developing areas. The Buy American Act of 1933 grants government procurement preferences to U.S. manufacturers and service providers to the exclusion of many foreign suppliers.

All of these laws provide the basic domestic law framework governing United States trade. When combined with United States obligations in international and regional organizations and agreements such as the WTO and NAFTA, one begins to understand the complexity and diversity of United States international trade and economic relations law.

U.S. IMPORT LAWS

The first of the principal laws regulating imports to the United States is the Tariff Act of 1930. This is the famous Smoot–Hawley Tariff Act, which raised tariff walls to substantial heights and worsened the world depression of the early 1930s. The severe tariffs of Smoot–Hawley have since been largely diminished for those nations which benefit from most favored nation (MFN) status, but remain for those less favored. One reason the 1930 Act remains in force is that it is the location of the hundreds of pages of tariffs—the tariff schedules. In addition to tariffs, the 1930 Act includes the organization and functions of the International Trade Commission. It controls some of the actions which the Commission may take, including of considerable importance, what are commonly referred to as Section 337 actions challenging unfair practices in import trade. There are extensive provisions for the promotion of foreign trade, and also the major provision protecting American trademarked goods from the entry of counterfeit products, Section 526. And finally, the Tariff Act of 1930 includes the United States rules governing countervailing and antidumping duties.

Although other trade acts were enacted subsequent to the 1930 Act, the next which includes major provisions important to U.S. international trade is the Trade Act of 1974. This Act includes executive negotiating authority for trade agreements with other countries, the creation of the office of the United States Trade Representative and provisions governing the interrelationship of Congress and the President with regard to trade relations. Furthermore, it includes important provisions regulating relief from injury caused by import competition, particularly Section 201 actions, known as "escape clause" or "safeguards" actions. Part of the relief from injury includes adjustment assistance for workers. Another title of the 1974 act addresses the enforcement of United States rights under trade agreements, which are reflected in Section 301 actions.

A separate title governs trade relations with countries not currently receiving nondiscriminatory treatment, meaning essentially nonmarket economies. These provisions are becoming less useful as many nonmarket economies have attempted to shed such status for participation in the world market. They include the little used but potentially important Section 406, allowing "market disruption" actions. Finally, the 1974 Trade Act includes the generalized system of preferences (GSP) scheme, which gives to certain developing nations tariff status even better than most favored nations receive.

The Trade Agreements Act of 1979 is the third important trade act. This Act was passed principally to implement several of the codes negotiated in the Tokyo Round of the GATT, concluded after negotiations in the mid–1970s. Thus, it has sections dealing with government procurement and technical barriers to trade (standards). Changes to the rules governing countervailing and antidumping duties, and to customs valuation, both part of then newly adopted GATT codes, were implemented by this Act, but as amendments to the Tariff Act of 1930 rather than enduring provisions identified with this 1979 Act.

The fourth important act is the Trade and Tariff Act of 1984. In addition to making amendments to the earlier acts, this Act extended "fast track" negotiating authority (discussed in Chapter 2) to the President, which provided for the development of a free trade agreement with Israel. The fifth act is the Omnibus Trade and Competitiveness Act of 1988. This Act authorized the President to enter into the Uruguay Round of GATT negotiations. It also implemented the Harmonized Tariff Schedule of the United States. Special attention was devoted in the 1988 Act to amending Section 301 of the 1974 Trade Act. It is the source of the notorious "Super 301" and "Special 301" procedures whereby the United States targets nations with which it has major trade or intellectual property disputes.

When the United States became a signatory to the North American Free Trade Agreement in 1993, Congress soon thereafter enacted the North American Free Trade Implementation Act, which made NAFTA part of U.S. trade law. Similarly, when the United States became a signatory to the Agreement Establishing the World Trade Organization in 1994, and its associated agreements and understandings, Congress enacted the Uruguay Round Agreements Act, which made the WTO a part of U.S. trade law.

The Trade Act of 2002 renewed, after a notable lapse during the Clinton administration, "fast track" international trade negotiating authority for the President. It is under this authority that President George W. Bush concluded free trade agreements with Chile, Singapore, five Central American nations and the Dominican Republic (CAFTA/DR), Oman, Bahrain, Peru, Colombia, Panama, Morocco, South Korea and Australia. He also pursued agreement on other bilateral free trade deals, a Free Trade Area of the Americas, and the Doha Round of World Trade Organization negotiations, none of which were completed prior to the expiration of fast track in July 2007.

THE ORIGINS OF UNITED STATES TARIFFS

Article I, Section 8, of the United States Constitution authorizes Congress to levy uniform tariffs on imports. Tariff legislation must originate in the House of Representatives. Although tariffs were primarily viewed as revenue-raising measures at the founding of the nation, it was not long before tariffs became used for openly protectionist purposes. The Tariff Act of 1816 initiated this change in outlook. During much of the 19th Century, the United States legislated heavy protective tariffs. These were justified as necessary to protect the country's infant industries and to force the South to engage in more trade with the North (not with Europe). Exceptions were made to the high level of tariffs for selected United States imports. These typically flowed from conditional most-favored-nation reciprocity treaties. The first of these treaties involved Canada (1854) and Hawaii (1875).

As the United States moved into the 20th Century, additional tariffs in excess of the already high level of protection were authorized. "Countervailing duty" tariffs were created in 1890 to combat export subsidies of European nations, particularly Germany. After 1916, additional duties could also be assessed if "dumping practices" were involved. Early American dumping legislation was largely a reaction to marketplace competition from foreign cartels. Throughout all of these years the constitutionality of protective tariffs was never clearly resolved. In 1928, however, the United States Supreme Court firmly ruled that the enactment of protective tariffs was constitutional. This decision, followed by the crash of the stock market in 1929, led to the enactment of the Smoot–Hawley Tariff Act of 1930. This Act set some of the highest rates of tariff duties in the history of the United States. It represents the last piece of tariff legislation that Congress passed without international negotiations. These tariffs remain part of the United States law and are generally referred to as "Column 2 tariffs" under the Harmonized Tariff Schedule (HTS).

Since 1930, changes in the levels of tariffs applicable to goods entering the United States have chiefly been achieved through international trade agreements negotiated by the President and affirmed by Congress. During the 1930s and 40s, the Smoot–Hawley tariffs generally applied unless altered through bilateral trade agreements. The Reciprocal Trade Agreements Act of 1934 gives the President the authority to enter into such agreements, and under various extensions this authority remains in effect today. An early agreement of this type was the Canadian Reciprocal Trade Agreement of 1935.

UNITED STATES TARIFF RATES

United States tariffs generally take one of three forms. The most common is an ad valorem rate. Such tariffs are assessed in proportion to the value of the article. Tariffs may also be assessed at specific rates or compound rates. Specific rates may be measured by the pound or other weight. A compound rate is a mixture of an ad valorem and specific rate tariff. Tariff rate quotas involve limitations on imports at a specific tariff up to a certain amount. Imports in excess of that amount are not prohibited, but are subject to a higher rate of tariff. Thus tariff rate quotas tend to restrict imports that are in excess of the specified quota for the lower tariff level.

These are three sets of United States tariff rates: Column 1 General, Column 1 Special and Column 2. Column 1 General tariff rates, known as most favored-nation (MFN) or "normal" tariffs, are the lower and most likely to be applicable. Column 2 tariff rates, originating in the Smoot–Hawley Tariff Act of 1930, are the higher and least likely to be applicable. In addition, there are a variety of selective Column 1 Special provisions, usually duty free entry programs to which the U.S. subscribes. These include the Generalized System of Tariff Preferences of the United States (GSP), the Caribbean Basin Initiative, the Andean Trade Preference Act, the Africa Growth and Opportunity Act of 2000 and Section 9802.00.80 of the HTS. The North American Free Trade Agreement (NAFTA), and a growing number of bilateral U.S. free trade agreements, generally provide for duty free access.

COLUMN 1 TARIFFS AND THE GATT

The Trade Agreements Extension Act of 1945 authorized the President to conduct multilateral negotiations in the trade field. It was out of this authority that the General Agreement on Tariffs and Trade (GATT) was negotiated. The GATT became effective on January 1, 1948 and was implemented in the United States by executive order. Indeed, despite its wide-ranging impact on United States tariff levels since 1948, the GATT has never been ratified by the United States Congress. Nevertheless, it is the source of the principal tariffs assessed today on imports into the United States. These duties, known as most-favored-nation (MFN) tariffs or "Column 1 tariffs," have been dramatically reduced over the years through successive rounds of GATT/WTO trade negotiations. They are unconditional MFN tariffs, meaning that reciprocity is not required in order for them to apply to WTO member nations.

Column 1 (MFN) tariff status for exports to the United States can also be obtained under U.S. bilateral trade agreements. Chinese goods enjoyed such status long before WTO membership, but were subject to the "Jackson–Vanik Amendment." This provision of the 1974 Trade Act requires tolerably liberal emigration policies of nonmarket economy nations for U.S. Column 1 tariff status to apply. Vietnamese goods qualified under Jackson–Vanik for MFN treatment prior to WTO membership for

Vietnam in 2007. Each year the President issued a "waiver" to facilitate these outcomes.

The term "most-favored-nation" is misleading in its suggestion of special tariff arrangements. It is more appropriate and officially correct to think of MFN tariffs as the "normal" level of U.S. tariffs, to which there are exceptions resulting in the application of higher or lower tariffs. At this point, the average MFN tariff applied to manufactured imports into the United States is approximately 3.5 percent.

FOREIGN TRADE ZONES

"Free trade zones" are located throughout the U.S., many of them near ports and airports. While imported goods remain in the zones, they are not subject to U.S. tariffs. The imported goods are subject to U.S. tariffs when they leave the zones, but only if they are then brought into the United States. If they are exported from the free trade zone to another country, they will never be subjected to U.S. tariffs. Thus, such zones serve as distribution centers, encourage assembly of certain manufactured items for export, provide local employment, and may lessen overall tariffs which must be paid before an assembled item crosses the zone for routine importation into the country. In the U.S., zones are supervised by the Foreign Trade Zones Board (located within the Commerce Department) and by the Customs Service.

CUSTOMS CLASSIFICATION

An importable item must "pass customs". Usually, the passage through customs and physical entry into a country occur simultaneously. When goods arrive at the United States border, the consignee (or an agent, such as a customs broker) files both "entry" and "entry summary" forms which are used to determine the classification, valuation, origin and conformity to product standards of the imported goods. At the same time, a deposit of the amount of estimated customs duties is made with customs officials. A procedure for immediate release of imported goods is available, as is the use of consolidated periodic statements for all entries made during a billing period.

The classification problem may be illustrated as follows: Are parts of a wooden picture frame, imported piece by piece in separate packages for later assembly within a country, to be assessed duties prescribed for wood picture frames or for strips of wood molding? Is "wood picture frame" even an appropriate nomenclature, or should what is commonly known to be a wood picture frame have a tariff nomenclature of "art object" or "forest product" or simply "personal belonging"?

For decades, most of the countries in the world, except the United States and Canada, classified imports according to the Brussels Tariff Nomenclature (BTN), which identifies items along a progression from raw materials to finished products. The

United States had its own system of classification set out in the Tariff Schedule of the United States (TSUS). However, beginning in 1982, the United States initiated steps to convert the TSUS into a Harmonized Commodity Description and Coding System (HS) of classification, in common with the classification system used by most other countries and developed by the Customs Cooperation Council in Brussels. The United States adopted the Harmonized System as the Harmonized Tariff Schedule (HTSUS) for classification of all imports by enactment of the Omnibus Trade and Competitiveness Act of 1988, with an effective date of Jan. 1, 1989. Most nations have adopted HS and use it to classify U.S. exports.

If the importer and the United States customs officials disagree about the proper classification of an imported item, the United States Court of International Trade (CIT) has exclusive jurisdiction to resolve their dispute. In cases decided under TSUS, the CIT has followed its own logic, without reference to decisions of other courts, because the approach of the U.S. statute (TSUS) was so unique. In the cases decided so far under HTSUS, the CIT has continued this tradition in its decisions under the new classification system, rather than viewing the decisions of foreign courts or the Rules accompanying the HS as persuasive.

The U.S. Supreme Court held in *United States v. Mead Corp.*, 533 U.S. 218 (2001) that Customs Service classification rulings are not entitled to full administrative deference. Rather, such rulings are entitled to limited deference depending on their "thoroughness, logic and expertness, fit with prior interpretations, and any other sources of weight."

CUSTOMS VALUATION

Even though an imported item may be classified and have a known rate of duty, expressed as a percentage of the item's value, difficulty may still arise in getting the importer and customs authorities to agree upon the item's value. For decades, United States customs valuation of an imported item was gauged by the American Selling Price (ASP) of the item—i.e., the usual wholesale price at which the same item manufactured in the United States was offered for sale.

However, Article VII of GATT 1947 requires that "value for customs purposes ... should not be based on the value of merchandise of national origin or on arbitrary or fictitious values." The 1979 Tokyo Round produced a Customs Valuation Code, which established the details of an approach which was quite different from ASP. This approach was incorporated into the U.S. Trade Agreements Act of 1979. United States customs valuation is now calculated by the "transaction value" of the imported item and, if that cannot be determined, by certain fall-back methods which are, in descending order of eligibility for use: the transaction value of identical merchandise, the transaction value of similar merchandise, the resale price of the merchandise with allowances for certain factors, or the cost of producing the imported item. "Transaction value" is "the price actually paid or payable for the merchandise when sold for exportation to the United States" plus "certain amounts reflecting packing costs, commissions paid by buyer, any assist, royalty or license fee paid by buyer, and any resale, disposal, or use proceeds that accrue to seller." This approach to valuation forms the core of the new Agreement on Implementation of Article VII of GATT 1994.

RULES OF ORIGIN

Tariff schedules often provide that duties on an imported item vary depending upon the country from which the item comes. Hence, where goods are from, legally speaking, matters. To resolve this issue, "rules of origin" come into play. Two common situations raising questions of origin involve products shipped to the United States from Country "X" that have been manufactured in Country "Y," and products shipped to the United States from Country "X", in which the product was made, but certain component parts of the product have originated in Country "Y".

The core U.S. "rule of origin" provides that an article is a product of a country only if it is wholly the growth, product, or manufacture of that country or in the case of an article which consists in whole or in part of materials from another country, it has been substantially transformed into a new and different article of commerce with a name, character, or use distinct from that of the article or articles from which it was so transformed. For example, this "substantial transformation" test is relevant in determining the rate at which U.S. customs duty is charged (MFN or not). It is also relevant to waivers of the application of United States "Buy American" procurement laws.

Under the proposed WTO Agreement on Rules of Origin, there will be an effort to harmonize the rules of origin on a world-wide basis. A committee of experts is charged with creating rules which are "objective, understandable, and predictable." They are likely to differ from the core U.S. rule. Special rules of origin apply to the various U.S. duty free entry programs, most notably NAFTA which relies principally on changes in tariff classifications and regional value content to determine which goods may freely be traded. See Chapter 7. It is expected that any WTO agreement on rules of origin will adopt similar approaches.

GENERALIZED TARIFF PREFERENCES FOR DEVELOPING NATIONS

The Generalized System of Preferences (GSP) recognizes that economic development of the third world requires the assistance of industrialized nations, and grants preferences to products of developing countries without demanding reciprocity. In addition to obtaining MFN tariff rates, developing countries can ship goods duty free into U.S. and other major industrial markets under GSP. These special arrangements for developing countries are permitted by the provisions of GATT/WTO. They have been implemented by the U.S., the EU, Japan and other major industrialized nations, although each GSP program differs in structure and approach.

Under the United States GSP, goods are admitted duty free if both the product *and* its country of origin meet the statutory requirements. The designation of developing countries as eligible for the GSP benefits has always been to some extent politicized—e.g., by declaring all communist states to be ineligible, and by declaring all but three OPEC member states to be ineligible. In addition, under 1984 amendments, the President must evaluate whether a country recognizes "internationally recognized worker's rights" and adequately protects intellectual property rights before that country can be designated as a GSP beneficiary. Also, the GSP beneficiary designation should not be given to nations which give more preferential treatment to imports from other developed nations than to U.S. products, assist terrorists, expropriate U.S. owned investments, or refuse to cooperate in drug enforcement or recognize international arbitration awards.

The GSP rule of origin requires that the product be shipped directly from the beneficiary developing country to the United States. Where the goods are locally produced from local resources, there is no further problem. However, where the goods exported by the beneficiary country are produced from materials imported into the developing country, further analysis is necessary. In such cases, the present GSP rule of origin requires that at least 35 percent of the value of an item be added within a developing country for the item to be considered as "originating" in that developing country. Thus, Toyotas manufactured in Japan, but shipped to the U.S. through a GSP beneficiary country, would not qualify for GSP duty free treatment. But Toyotas manufactured in the GSP beneficiary country from parts manufactured in Japan could so qualify, if the value of the parts aggregated only 60 percent of the value of the final product. In addition, the Federal Circuit Court of Appeals has ruled that the processing of goods in the GSP country must create two substantial transformations in the identity of the goods for GSP treatment to be available.

Products of particular GSP beneficiary countries can be added or removed to the list of GSP qualified goods by petition of interested persons. The petitions, and the resultant certification or de-certification, are determined by the U.S. Trade Representative, with the advice of the U.S. International Trade Commission (ITC). The criterion used is "import sensitivity," which means that American industry or labor must actively seek protection from this foreign competition. The tendency of the decisions has been not to displace American interests, and to regard the GSP benefits as a "gift" to developing countries.

A separate principle is known as "graduation" from the GSP list. While the principle can be applied to an entire country, it is also used to "graduate" specific products from specific countries from the GSP list to the MFN list. The 1984 amendments required the President to complete a general review of all GSP products to determine whether they were "sufficiently competitive" to graduate. Graduation has had its greatest impact on so-called "newly industrialized countries." In 1989, South Korea, Taiwan, Hong Kong and Singapore were graduated entirely from the GSP list. At the same time, Bahrain, Brunei, Nauru and Bermuda were dropped from the list because their per capita GNP exceeded the statutory limit. In 1995, the Bahamas and Israel were similarly dropped, and in 1997 Malaysia was entirely graduated. U.S. free trade partners, for example Mexico, have been removed from the GSP list of eligible countries.

CARIBBEAN BASIN, ANDEAN AND AFRICAN TRADE PREFERENCES

The European Union has had for many years a policy which grants substantial duty free entry into its market for goods originating in Mediterranean Basin countries. The United States has duplicated this approach for the Caribbean Basin. This is accomplished through the Caribbean Basin Economic Recovery Act of 1983. For these purposes, the Caribbean Basin is broadly defined to include nearly all of the islands in that Sea, and a significant number of Central and South American nations bordering the Caribbean. So defined, there are about 30 nations which could qualify for purposes of the United

States Caribbean Basin Initiative. As with the GSP program, the Caribbean Basin Initiative (CBI) involves presidential determinations to confer beneficiary status upon any of these eligible countries. However, unlike the GSP, there are no presidential determinations as to which specific products of these countries shall be allowed into the United States on a duty free basis. All Caribbean products except those excluded by statute are eligible. Moreover, there are no "competitive need" or annual per capita income limits under the CBI. Lastly, unlike the GSP program which must be renewed periodically, the Caribbean Basin Initiative is a permanent part of the U.S. tariff system. For U.S. free trade partners in the region, CAFTA/DR for example, the CBI is no longer applicable.

The Andean Trade Preference Act (ATPA) of 1991, renewed in the Trade Act of 2002, authorizes the President to grant duty free treatment to imports of eligible articles from Columbia, Peru, Bolivia and Ecuador. Venezuela is not included as a beneficiary under this Act. The Andean Trade Preference Act is patterned after the Caribbean Basin Economic Recovery Act of 1983. Goods that ordinarily enter duty free into the United States from Caribbean Basin nations will also enter duty free from these four Andean countries. The same exceptions and exclusions discussed above in connection with the Caribbean Basin Initiative generally apply.

While the CBI is a permanent part of United States Customs law, the ATPA was only authorized initially for a period of ten years. Furthermore, the guaranteed access levels for Caribbean Basin textile products, separate cumulation for antidumping and countervailing duty investigations, and the waiver of the Buy American Act for procurement purposes are not authorized by the ATPA. Broadly speaking, the passage of the ATPA represents assistance to these nations economically, in return for their help in containing narcotics. U.S. free trade agreements with Peru and Colombia supercede the ATPA, whose continued application to Ecuador and Bolivia is in doubt.

The Africa Growth and Opportunity Act of 2000 granted duty-free and quota-free access to the U.S. market for apparel made from U.S. fabric and yarn. Apparel made from African fabric is capped for duty free entry. The least developed sub-Saharan countries enjoy duty-free and quota-free apparel access regardless of the origin of the fabric. The Act also altered U.S. GSP rules to admit certain previously excluded African products on a duty-free basis, including petroleum, watches and flat goods. Sub–Saharan countries can export almost all products duty-free to the United States. These countries are encouraged to create a free trade area with U.S. support. African exports are subject to import surge (escape clause) protection and stringent rules against transshipments between countries for purposes of taking advantage of U.S. trade benefits.

GOODS INCORPORATING UNITED STATES COMPONENTS

Section 9802.00.80 of the Harmonized Tariff Schedule of the United States (formerly Section 807.00 of the Tariff Schedule of the United States) is an unusual "duty free" provision. This section allows for the duty free importation of United States fabricated components that were exported ready for assembly abroad. If qualified, goods assembled abroad containing U.S. components are subject only to a duty upon the value added through foreign assembly operations. In order for this to be the case, Section 9802.00.80 requires that the components be fabricated and a product of the United States, that they be exported in a condition ready for assembly without further fabrication, that they not lose their physical identity by change in form, shape or otherwise, and that they not be advanced in value or improved in condition abroad except by being assembled and except by operations incidental to the assembly process such as cleaning, lubricating and painting.

If all of the Section 9802.00.80 criteria are met, the tariff that will be assessed upon the imported assembled product will be limited to a duty upon the full value of that product less the cost or value of U.S. made components that have been incorporated into it. Those who seek to take advantage of Section 9802.00.80 must provide the United States Customs Service with a Foreign Assembler's Declaration and Certification. The assembly plant operator certifies that the requirements of Section 9802.00.80 are met, and the importer declares that this certification is correct. Billions of dollars of ordinarily tariffed value have been excluded as a result of this Customs law provision. Motor vehicles, semiconductors, office machines, textiles and apparel, and furniture are good examples of the kinds of products assembled abroad with fabricated U.S. components so as to meet the requirements of Section 9802.00.80. Historically, many of these products were assembled in Japan, Germany or Canada. In recent times, the assembly operations (maquiladoras) to which Section 9802.00.80 frequently applies have more commonly been found in the developing world.

DUTY FREE ACCESS TO THE UNITED STATES

The end-game so far as exporters and importers to the United States are concerned is unlimited duty free access. Except for raw materials and goods from U.S. free trade partners, few exports will ordinarily qualify for such treatment. However, products of developing Andean, Caribbean or African nations may achieve this goal. This is possible because of United States adherence to the duty-free entry programs discussed above.

There are, of course, exceptions and controls (quotas, NTBs) that may apply under these duty free programs. Nevertheless, the United States market is so lucrative that careful study of these external trade rules is warranted. Such studies can realize unusually advantageous trade situations. For example, many developing nations have duty free rights of entry into the European Union under the Lomé/Cotonou Conventions, the Union's Mediterranean Basin Policy or the EU version of the GSP program. The goods of some of these nations may also qualify for duty free access to the United States market. A producer strategically located in such a nation (e.g., Jamaica) can have the best of both worlds, duty free access to the European Union and the United States. Mexico, which in addition to NAFTA has free trade agreements with the European Union, Japan and dozens of other countries, is another premier duty-free export location.

U.S. IMPORT QUOTAS

The United States has employed import quotas for many years. Tariff-rate quotas have been applied to dairy products, olives, tuna fish, anchovies, brooms, and sugar, syrups and molasses. Quite a few absolute quotas originate under Section 22 of the Agricultural Adjustment Act. These quotas are undertaken when necessary to United States farm price supports or similar agricultural programs. They have been used on animal feeds, dairy products, chocolate, cotton, peanuts, and selected syrups and sugars. Some U.S. agricultural quotas are being converted into tariffs under the WTO Agreement on Agriculture. Some quotas imposed by the U.S. are sanctions for unfair trade practices, as against tungsten from China. Other quotas originate in international commodity agreements, and important restraints on textile imports were achieved as a result of the international Multi–Fiber Arrangement, which expired in 2005 under the WTO Textiles Agreement.

The Agricultural Act of 1949 requires the President to impose global import quotas on Upland Cotton. Whenever the Secretary of Agriculture determines that its average price exceeds certain statutory limits, unlike the ordinary restrictive import quota, the importation of Upland Cotton is duty free. Like the U.S. Meat Import Act, this provision tends to be countercyclical to market forces for cotton in the United States. A U.S. cotton subsidy system has been ruled invalid by the WTO Appellate Body in a dispute brought by Brazil.

Lastly, the United States sometimes imposes import restraints for national security or foreign policy reasons. Many of these restraints originate from Section 232 of the Trade Expansion Act of 1962. This provision authorizes the President to "adjust imports" whenever necessary to the national security of the country. Trade embargoes (zero quotas) are sometimes imposed on all the goods from politically incorrect nations (e.g., Cuba). Product-specific import bans also exist for selected goods, e.g., narcotic drugs and books urging insurrection against the United States. The importation of "immoral" goods is generally prohibited, even for private use, and the obscenity of such items is decided by reviewing the community standards at the port of entry. Generally, as well, goods produced with forced, convict or the worst forms of child labor are excluded from the United States. This ban has been applied to certain goods from the People's Republic of China.

If a quota system is created, a fundamental subsidiary issue is: How will the quotas be allocated? The U.S. Customs Service generally administers quotas on a first-come, first-served basis. This approach creates a race to enter goods into the United States. The President is authorized to sell import licenses at public auctions. One advantage of an auction system is its revenue raising potential. Instead of an auction system, the U.S. has ordinarily used a Presidentially managed system of import allocations, especially in regard to agricultural import quotas.

The U.S. Tariff Act of 1930 provides that to the extent practicable and consistent with efficient and fair administration, the President is to insure against inequitable sharing of imports by a relatively small number of the larger importers. In fact, allocating quotas among U.S. importers rarely happens. In the past, quotas were often part of a "voluntary export restraint" (VER) or orderly market agreement (OMA) between the U.S. and one or more foreign governments, and represented adherence by those governments to U.S. initiatives. The negotiations typically concentrated on obtaining foreign government agreement to limitations on exportation of their products into the U.S. market, and did not pursue rules on who might use the resulting allocations. A classic example for many years was Japanese "voluntary" restraints on exporting autos to the United States. The WTO Agreement on Safeguards severely limits the use of VERs and OMAs.

U.S. PUBLIC PROCUREMENT

In federal nations like the United States, procurement can extend to state and local purchasing requirements. The principal United States statute affecting imports in connection with government procurement is the Buy American Act of 1933. This Act requires the government to buy American unless the acquisition is for use outside the U.S., there are insufficient quantities of satisfactory quality available in the U.S., or domestic purchases would be inconsistent with the public interest or result in unreasonable costs.

Buy American

As currently applied, the United States Buy American Act requires federal agencies to treat a domestic bid as unreasonable or inconsistent with the public interest only if it exceeds a foreign bid by more than six percent (customs duties included) or ten percent (customs duties and specific costs excluded). Exceptions to this general approach exist for reasons of national interest, certain designated small business purchases, domestic suppliers operating in areas of substantial unemployment and demonstrated national security needs. Bids by small businesses and companies located in labor surplus areas are generally protected by a 12 percent margin of preference. Bids from U.S. companies are considered foreign rather than domestic when the materials used in the products concerned are below 50 percent American in origin. These rules apply to civil purchasing by the United States government, but are suspended for purchasing subject to the WTO Procurement Code.

The Department of Defense has its own Buy American rules. Generally speaking, a 50 percent price preference (customs duties excluded) or a 6 or 12 percent preference (customs duties included) whichever is more protective to domestic suppliers is applied. However, intergovernmental "Memoranda of Understanding" (MOU) on defense procurement provide important exceptions to the standard Department of Defense procurement rules. Additional procurement preferences are established by the Small Business Act of 1953. Under this Act, federal agencies may set aside certain procurement exclusively for small U.S. businesses. In practice, the federal government normally sets aside about 30 percent of its procurement needs in this fashion. Special set-aside rules apply to benefit socially and economically disadvantaged minority-owned businesses. These preferences are excepted from U.S. adherence to the WTO Procurement Code.

A number of federal statutes also contain specific Buy American requirements. These include various GSA, NASA and TVA appropriations bills, the AMTRAK Improvement Act of 1978, the Public Works Employment Act of 1977, various highway and transport acts, the Clean Water Act of 1977, and the Rural Electrification Acts of 1936 and 1938. Many of these statutes involve federal funding of state and local procurement. All are generally excepted from the WTO Procurement Code as applied by the United States.

In addition to the Buy American Act, state and local purchasing requirements may inhibit import competition in the procurement field. For example, California once had a law which made it mandatory to purchase American products. This law was declared unconstitutional as an encroachment upon the federal power to conduct foreign affairs. A Massachusetts ban on contracting with companies with investments in Myanmar (Burma) was likewise struck down. State statutes which have copied the federal Buy American Act, on the other hand, and incorporated public interest and unreasonable cost exceptions to procurement preferences, have generally withstood constitutional challenge. For example, a lawful Pennsylvania statute requires state and local agencies to ensure that contractors do not provide products containing foreign steel.

A practice known as "unbalanced bidding" has arisen in connection with the Buy American Act. Unbalanced bidding involves the use of United States labor and parts by foreigners in sufficient degree so as to overcome the bidding preferences established by law for U.S. suppliers. This occurs because the United States value added is *not* included in the calculations of the margin of preference for the U.S. firms. Thus foreign bids minus the value of work done in the U.S. are multiplied by the 6, 12 or 50 percent Buy American Act preference. If the U.S. bids are above the foreign bids but within the margin of preference, the U.S. company gets the contract. If the U.S. bids are higher than the foreign bids plus the margin of preference, the foreigners get the contract.

GATT Code and U.S. Response

The Buy American Act was conformed to the GATT Procurement Code negotiated during the Tokyo Round. However, Congress expressed its displeasure with the degree to which that Code opened up sales opportunities for United States firms abroad. It therefore amended the Buy American Act in 1988 to deny the benefits of the GATT Procurement Code when foreign governments are not in good standing under it. United States government procurement contracts are also denied to suppliers from countries whose governments "maintain ... a significant and persistent pattern of practice or discrimination against U.S. products or services which results in identifiable harm to U.S. businesses." Presidential waivers of these statutory denials may occur in the public interest, to avoid single supply situations or to assure sufficient bidders to provide supplies of requisite quality and competitive prices.

The European Union was one of the first to be identified as a persistent procurement discriminator by the USTR. This identification concerned long-standing heavy electrical and telecommunications disputes that were partly settled by negotiation with the EU. The remaining disputes led to U.S. trade sanctions and Union retaliation. This did not occur with Greece, Spain and Portugal (where the EU procurement rules did not apply), and with Germany which broke ranks and negotiated a pathbreaking bilateral U.S. settlement. Japan has also been identified as a persistent procurement discriminator in the construction, architectural and engineering areas.

Where public procurement is involved, and the taxpayer's money is at issue, virtually every nation has some form of legislation or tradition that favors buying from domestic suppliers. The Tokyo Round GATT Procurement Code was not particularly successful at opening up government purchasing. Only Austria, Canada, the twelve European Union states, Finland, Hong Kong, Israel, Japan, Norway, Singapore, Sweden, Switzerland and the United States adhered to that Procurement Code. This was also partly the result of the 1979 Code's many exceptions. For example, the Code did not apply to contracts below its threshold amount of $150,000 SDR (about $171,000 since 1988), service contracts, and procurement by entities on each country's reserve list (including most national defense items). Because procurement in the European Union and Japan is often decentralized, many contracts fell below the SDR threshold and were therefore GATT exempt. By dividing up procurement into smaller contracts national preferences were retained. United States government procurement tends to be more centralized and thus more likely to be covered by the GATT Code. This pattern may help explain why Congress restrictively amended the Buy American Act in 1988.

WTO Procurement Code

The WTO Procurement Code took effect in 1996 and replaced the 1979 Tokyo Round Code. It remains optional for WTO members. The WTO Code expanded the coverage of the prior Code to include procurement of services, construction, government-owned utilities, and some state and local (subcentral) contracts. The U.S. and the European Union applied the new Code's provisions on government-owned utilities and subcentral contracts as early as 1994.

Various improvements to the procedural rules surrounding procurement practices and dispute settlement under the WTO Code attempt to reduce tensions in this difficult area. For example, an elaborate system for bid protests is established. Bidders who believe the Code's procedural rules have been abused will be able to lodge, litigate and appeal their protests. The Procurement Code became part of U.S. law in 1994 under the Uruguay Round Agreements Act. The United States has made, with few exceptions, all procurement by executive agencies subject to the Federal Acquisition Regulations under the Code's coverage (i.e., to suspend application of the normal Buy American preferences to such procurement).

U.S. PRODUCT STANDARDS

There are numerous nontariff trade barriers applicable to United States imports. Many of these barriers arise out of federal or state safety and health regulations. Others concern the environment, consumer protection, product standards and government procurement. Many of the relevant rules were created for legitimate consumer and public protection reasons. They were often created without extensive consideration of their international impact as potential nontariff barriers. Nevertheless, the practical impact of legislation of this type is to ban the importation of nonconforming products from the United States market. Thus, unlike tariffs which can always be paid and unlike quotas which permit a certain amount of goods to enter the United States market, nontariff barriers have the potential to totally exclude foreign exports.

The diversity of U.S. regulatory approaches to products and the environment makes it extremely difficult to generalize about nontariff trade barriers. In 2008, all imports of plants and wood products (even toothpicks) were subjected to new disclosure duties that may inhibit trade. All foods imported into the United States are subject to inspection for their wholesomeness, freedom from contamination, and compliance with labeling requirements (including the 1993 nutritional labeling rules). This examination is conducted by the Food and Drug Administration using samples submitted to it by the United States Customs Service. If these tests result in a finding that the food products cannot be imported into the United States, they must be exported or destroyed.

The Consumer Products Safety Act bars the importation of consumer products which do not comply with the standards of the Consumer Products Safety Commission. Exporters of consumer products must certify that their goods conform to applicable United States safety and labeling standards. Any product that has a defect which is determined to constitute a "substantial product hazard" or is imminently hazardous may be banned from the United States market. The Customs Service may seize any such nonconforming goods. These goods may be modified in order to conform them to U.S. Consumer Products Safety Commission requirements. Otherwise, such goods must be exported or destroyed, an end result notably applied in 2007 to childrens' toys from China.

Generally speaking, the United States maintains an open market for competitive trade in services. One major exception is maritime transport. In this area, the U.S. protects its domestic industry from import competition under the Merchant Marine Act of 1920 ("Jones Act") and other statutes. For example, the shipment of Alaskan oil is reserved for U.S.-flag vessels as is the supply of offshore drill rigs. The Jones Act most notably prohibits foreign vessels from transporting goods or passengers between U.S. ports and on U.S. rivers, lakes and canals. The reservation of goods for U.S.-flag ships (such trade is known as cabotage) is very significant economically, amounting to some $6.4 billion annually with a heavy concentration in petroleum products.

United States environmental or conservation laws notably affecting international trade include:

- The Endangered Species Act of 1973 prohibiting import/export of endangered species.
- The "Pelley Amendment" authorizing import restraints against fish products of nations undermining international fisheries or wildlife conservation agreements.
- The High Seas Driftnet Fisheries Enforcement Act of 1992 banning imports of fish, fish products and sport fishing gear from countries violating the United Nations driftnet moratorium.
- The Sea Turtle Conservation Act prohibiting shrimp imports harvested with adverse effects on sea turtles first used in 1993 against shrimp from several Caribbean nations and now applicable globally to Thailand, India, China and Bangladesh among others.
- The Wild Bird Conservation Act banning imports of tropical wild birds.
- The Antarctic Marine Living Resources Convention Act prohibiting import/export of living resources.
- The African Elephant Conservation Act restricting ivory imports.

WTO Product Standards Law

Under United States law, state and federal agencies may create standards which specify the characteristics of a product, such as levels of quality, safety, performance or dimensions, or its packaging and labeling. However, in accordance with the WTO Technical Barriers to Trade Agreement (Standards Code), these "standards-related activities" must not create "unnecessary obstacles to U.S. foreign trade," and must be demonstrably related to "a legitimate domestic objective" such as protection of health and safety, security, environmental or consumer interests. Sometimes there is a conflict between federal and state standards. For example, federal law licensing endangered species' articles preempted California's absolute ban on trade in such goods. The Office of the USTR is charged with responsibility for implementation of the WTO Standards Code within the United States.

United States standards have been attacked as nontariff trade barriers violating international obligations. Sometimes the standards have been upheld, sometimes not. For example, a binational arbitration panel established under Chapter 18 of the Canada–U.S. FTA issued a decision upholding a United States law setting a minimum size on lobsters sold in interstate commerce. The panel found that, since the law applied to both domestic and foreign lobsters, it was not a disguised trade restriction.

Tuna, Shrimp and Beef Disputes

On the other hand, a GATT panel once found that United States import restrictions designed to protect dolphin from tuna fishers violated GATT 1947. The panel ruled that GATT did not permit any import restrictions based on extraterritorial environmental concerns, whether they were considered disguised trade restrictions or not. This decision suggested difficulty with a number of United States laws which concern health, safety and environmental conditions in exporting nations. A 1994 decision by a second GATT 1947 panel recognized the legitimacy of environmental regulations, but ruled against the tuna boycott by the U.S. because of its focus on production methods and the unilateral imposition of standards by the U.S. In 1997, Congress enacted legislation that replaced the domestic controls on imported tuna with international restrictions stated in the Declaration of Panama. This Declaration, with internationally accepted standards, finally placed U.S. tuna legislation in conformity with its GATT/WTO obligations.

In 1998 the WTO Appellate Body ruled against a U.S. ban on shrimp imports from nations that fail to use turtle exclusion devices comparable to those required under U.S. law. The Appellate Body found the U.S. ban undermined the multilateral GATT 1994 trading system because the security and predictability of the system would be compromised if other Members adopted similar measures. The unilateral use of extraterritorial measures to protect exhaustible natural resources was not "justifiable." The Appellate Body believed international agreement on the subject should be sought.

The standards of other nations have also been challenged as violations of WTO obligations. For example, the United States has challenged European Union bans of imports of meat from the United States, first for containing certain hormones, later for unsanitary conditions in U.S. meatpacking facilities. In the former controversy, the United States retaliated. In 1997 and again in 2008, the WTO Appellate Body ruled against the EU ban on hormone-treated beef, citing the lack of an adequate scientific basis for the ban as required under the WTO Sanitary and Phyto–Sanitary (SPS) Agreement.

RESPONSES OF DOMESTIC PRODUCERS TO IMPORT COMPETITION

The duty payable on an imported item may be increased above that required normally by the posted tariff schedule because of certain "antidumping" measures or "countervailing duties" imposed by the country of importation. Antidumping duties are a trade response to what is considered to be a "dumping" of items into the country of importation at a price which is less than the price or value charged for comparable commodities in the country of origin, usually termed "less than fair value" (LTFV). In other words, antidumping is all about price discrimination. Countervailing duties are a second trade response to unfair "subsidies" given by another country to position its exports more competitively in the international market place. A third alternative for domestic producers responding to import competition is the escape clause (safeguard) or market disruption proceeding which is often added to antidumping and countervailing duty complaints as a shotgun approach to obtain protective relief. All three alternatives are governed by WTO Codes. This creates a reasonably uniform body of trade remedies law in about 150 nations.

Antidumping and countervailing duties are permitted by GATT 1994, and the criteria for them are largely derived from the WTO Covered Agreements. Under the Antidumping and Subsidies Codes, each of these duties may be imposed on products of another Member only if two requirements are met. First, there must be an unfair trade practice, either dumping (sales at less than fair value) or prohibited or actionable subsidies. Second, the practice must cause either "injury" or "adverse trade effects." Under U.S. law, these are proven by showing "material injury" to a domestic industry has actually occurred or is threatened, or the establishment of such an industry must be "materially retarded." Under the WTO Safeguards Code, escape clause proceedings do not require a showing of any unfair trade practice, such as dumping or subsidies, so that the injury standard is higher, and the escape mechanism is available only when increased imports are a "substantial cause of *serious* injury, or the threat thereof" (emphasis added) to an established domestic industry. Causation issues are critical to all three import competition proceedings.

NAFTA uniquely provides for resolution of antidumping and countervailing duty disputes through binational panels. Such panels apply the domestic law of the importing country, and provide a substitute for judicial review of the decisions of administrative agencies of the importing country.

It should be noted that none of these responses available to domestic producers have any relation to restricting goods from a nation because that nation does not allow our goods entry into its markets. Antidumping and countervailing duties deal only with unfair selling prices of the dutiable imported goods themselves, and the escape mechanism deals only with protecting the domestic competitors of the *imported* goods from serious harm.

DUMPING AND ANTIDUMPING DUTIES

The economics of dumping arise from a producer's opportunity to compartmentalize the overall market place for its goods, thus permitting it to offer the product for sale at different prices in different sectors. Only if trade barriers or other factors insulate each market sector from others is there opportunity to vary substantially the product's price. For example, a producer can securely "dump" products in an overseas market at cheap prices and at high volume only if it can be sure that the product market in its home country is immune from penetration by these products. The objective of dumping may be to increase long term marginal revenues or to ruin a competitor's market position.

One of the WTO Covered Agreements is "The Agreement on Implementation of Article VI of GATT 1994," also known as the Antidumping Code. The Antidumping Code provides that a product is to be considered dumped if its export price of the product is less than "normal value," the price which would be charged for the same or a similar product in the ordinary course of trade for domestic consumption in the exporting country. Thus, in evaluating whether an export price constitutes dumping, the best analytic tool is the domestic sales price of comparable goods in the exporting country.

However, such comparable sales may not be available, either because comparable products are not sold domestically, or because the usual retail transaction is not comparable (e.g., leasing rather than a sale). In that situation, the Antidumping Code provides a hierarchy of alternative computation methods to achieve an approximate evaluation. Among these alternatives, the preferred one uses the price for the same or a similar product in the ordinary course of trade for export to a third country. The next preferred alternative is to calculate the cost of production of the exported goods in the country of origin, plus a reasonable amount for profits and for administrative, selling and any general costs, and compare that to the export price of the product when sold for export to the United States.

The WTO Antidumping Code, adopted from the earlier Tokyo Round GATT code, focuses upon dumping determinations (particularly criteria for allocating costs) and material injury determinations (particularly causation). *De minimis* dumping, defined as less than two percent of the product's export price, is not subject to antidumping duties and signatories must terminate such investigations immediately. Cumulation of imports in injury determinations is permitted, as is the filing of petitions by unions and workers. When another signatory challenges the implementation of the Code, World Trade Organization dispute settlement panels have binding authority to resolve the dispute without hearing new evidence and allowing for "competing, reasonable interpretations" of the Antidumping Code under national laws.

U.S. ANTIDUMPING LAW

United States objections to dumping were recorded as the subject of a protest by Secretary of the Treasury Alexander Hamilton in 1791, and have continued to be the subject of investigations. In general, U.S. antidumping statutes compare the price at which articles are imported or sold within the United States with the actual market value or wholesale price of such articles in the principal markets of the country of their production at the time of their export to the U.S. The approach was established by the Antidumping Act of 1916, a rarely used criminal statute, which was considered an unfair competition law, or price discrimination statute, and was functionally similar to the price discrimination statutes applicable to domestic business. The European Union, Japan and others successfully challenged the 1916 Act in WTO dispute resolution proceedings as inconsistent with the Antidumping Code. The United States promised to repeal the Act, and finally did so in 2004.

Other U.S. antidumping provisions found in the Tariff Act of 1930 implement the Antidumping Code. Under these provisions, "dumping" is the sale of imported goods at "less than fair value" (LTFV) or the difference between the product's export price or constructed export price and its "normal value." "Normal value", in turn, is usually determined by the amount charged for the goods in the exporter's *domestic* market (the "home market"). If such sales are both at LTFV and cause or threaten "material injury" to a domestic industry, or retard its development, then an antidumping duty "shall" be imposed. The antidumping duty levied is in addition to the usual customs charged on such products, and is in the amount of the difference between the price at which the goods are sold for export to the United States and the home market price.

Domestic injury determinations are made by the U.S. International Trade Commission (ITC). Since the statute requires a determination of threatened or actual "material injury", or retardation of the establishment of a U.S. industry, much depends upon a workable definition of "material injury." The statutory definition is "harm which is not inconsequential, immaterial, or unimportant." And further provides that, in making a determination of "material injury," the ITC "shall" consider the volume of imports involved, the effect of the imports on U.S. prices for "like products", and the impact of the imports on U.S. producers of "like products", but only in relation to production operations in the United States. The ITC is directed to evaluate both the actual and potential declines not only in production, sales and profits, but also in market share and productivity of the domestic industry. It is also directed to evaluate actual and potential negative effects on employment, growth, ability to raise capital and investment. All effects are to be measured on an industry-wide basis, and not in relation to an individual company; but a threat to a "major portion" of a national industry is sufficient.

Market Economy Dumping Determinations

The procedure for deciding whether to impose antidumping duties involves two governmental agencies: the International Trade Administration (ITA) and the International Trade Commission (ITC). The ITA is part of the Department of Commerce, which in turn is part of the Executive Branch. The ITC, on the other hand, is an independent agency, and was discussed previously in this Chapter. The ITA was originally designed to foster, promote and develop world trade, and to help American companies sell overseas by providing them with information concerning the "what, where, how and when" of imports and exports. It provides business data, educational programs, information sources, foreign license requirements, and procedures for starting a foreign business to individual businesses and trade groups. Since 1980, it has also decided whether import sales were at LTFV or benefitted from improper subsidies. The ITC was established by the Trade Act of 1974, and consists of six persons, appointed by the President with the advice and consent of the Senate, who have "qualifications requisite for developing expert knowledge of international trade problems".

In an antidumping proceeding, the ITA determines whether the imports are being sold at LTFV, and the ITC makes a separate determination concerning injury to a domestic industry. The proceeding may be initiated by either the Commerce Department or by an aggrieved business—or by a group or association of aggrieved businesses. However, the petition must be filed "on behalf of" the entire industry. The ITA then determines whether the petition "alleges the elements necessary for the imposition of a duty", based on the "best information available at the time." The ITC then makes a Preliminary Determination as to injury within 45 days "based on the best information available to it" at that time. If the ITC makes such a finding, the ITA then makes a Preliminary Determination of whether there is "a reasonable basis to believe" that goods are being sold at LTFV. If the ITA makes such a Preliminary Determination, it then proceeds to make a "final determination" concerning sales at LTFV. If sales at LTFV are found by the ITA, the ITC then must make a "final determination" concerning injury.

Any goods imported after an ITA *preliminary* determination of sales at LTFV will be subject to any antidumping duties imposed later, after final determinations are made. Thus this preliminary determination tends to discourage imports, since importers do not know what their liability for duties will be. Foreign exporters are expected to raise their "U.S. prices" to the level of home market prices soon after such a preliminary determination. If they do, the antidumping law will have accomplished its purpose in eliminating dumping.

The ITA final determination of sales at LTFV establishes the amount of any antidumping duties. Since duties are not imposed to support any specific domestic price, they are set not to exceed the "margin of dumping", or the amount the price for domestic consumption in the exporting country exceeds the export price of the product in that country. The antidumping duty is to remain in force only as long as the dumping occurs.

Nonmarket Economy Dumping Determinations

Congress enacted special rules to govern antidumping duty analysis of imports from nonmarket economy countries (NMEs). The rules are based on the assumption that "normal value" cannot be determined by prices in a NME which are bureaucratically determined, and therefore are not sufficiently subject to the forces of competition to form an accurate standard for comparison. (Whether that assumption is accurate for all NMEs is beyond the scope of this Nutshell.) Instead, the ITA will "construct" a "normal value" by determining the factors of production (labor, materials, energy, capital) actually used by the NME to produce the imported goods, then value each of those factors in a market economy country "considered to be appropriate" by the ITA.

If a "normal value" cannot be constructed, an alternative is to use a comparable "surrogate" non-NME country which produces the imported product, and use its domestic price for the imported goods as the "normal value". The alternative construction was the primary method for valuation before 1988, but its results were not very reliable. Although the ITA sought a surrogate of comparable economic development and per capita gross national product, that was not always possible. Although the statutory definition refers to a "nonmarket economy country," which implies use of a single standard for a whole political unit, the ITA has differentiated between imports from China, based on whether particular factors of production are considered to be market driven or not.

U.S. IMPLEMENTATION OF THE WTO ANTIDUMPING CODE

In order to conform U.S. law to the WTO Antidumping Code, the Tariff Act (1930) was amended to provide for a de minimus dumping margin. The ITA in making its preliminary determination, must disregard any weighted average dumping margin that is de minimus, i.e., any average dumping margin that is less than two percent ad valorem or the equivalent specific rate for the subject merchandise. Any weighted average dumping margin that is de minimus must also be disregarded when making final determinations.

Additional Tariff Act amendments have reduced the discretion previously available by imposing strict statutory time limits. In the case of an antidumping petition, the ITA must make an initial determination within twenty days after the date on which a petition is filed. This time limit may be extended to forty days in any case where necessary to poll or otherwise determine support for the petition by the industry and exceptional circumstances exist. Time limits are also imposed on the ITC in their determination of whether there is a reasonable indication of injury.

Further WTO-derived amendments authorize an adjustment to sales-below-cost calculations for start-up costs, thought to be particularly beneficial to high-tech products. There is a new "captive production" section intended to remove such internal sales from ITC injury determinations. The United States, however, failed to fully implement the average-to-average or transaction-to-transaction dumping calculations mandated by the Antidumping Code. Rather, weighted average approaches will only be used in the investigatory phase, not in subsequent administrative reviews where the traditional U.S. calculation of dumping margins by comparing individual U.S. sales to average home or third country sales will continue. Adjustments for profits from further manufacturing, selling and distribution of products in the U.S. are authorized. And the amendments strengthen existing U.S. anticircumvention provisions despite their absence from the WTO Antidumping Code. Also reinforced is U.S. law on exclusion of sales below cost from normal value calculations in the home market.

Still more WTO-driven changes require the ITC to provide all parties to the proceeding with an opportunity to comment, prior to the Commission's vote, on *all* information collected in the investigation. Imports from a country subject to investigation must be deemed negligible if they amount to less than three percent of the volume of all such merchandise imported into the United States in the most recent 12–month period preceding the filing of the petition for which data are available. If imports from a country are deemed negligible, then the investigation regarding those imports must be terminated. The Commission is ordinarily required to consider cumulation of imports from two or more countries when the imports are subject to investigations as a result of petitions filed on the same day. The Commission must make any cumulative analysis on the basis of the same record, even if the simultaneously filed investigations end up with differing final deadlines.

The International Trade Commission must consider the magnitude of the dumping margin (although not the magnitude of the margin of subsidization) in making material injury determinations. Lastly, the Commission must conduct a review no later than five years after an antidumping or countervailing duty order is issued to determine whether revoking the order would likely lead to continuation or recurrence of dumping or subsidies and material injury. Known as the "sunset provision," this new WTO requirement results in review of all existing antidumping and countervailing duty orders.

Interpretation of the WTO Antidumping Code

The WTO Appellate Body has taken a restrictive view of what constitutes permissible antidumping duties. In the *EC–Bed Linen from India* dispute, for example, the Appellate Body ruled against "zeroing," a methodology used in dumping margin calculations by the United States and other countries. Both positive and negative dumping margins should be weighed in calculating weighted average dumping margins. However, the Federal Circuit Court of Appeals has held "zeroing" a reasonable interpretation of the U.S. antidumping statute, calling the Appellate Body opinion not "sufficiently persuasive." In the *Thai-steel from Poland* dispute, the Appellate Body rejected a cursory material injury determination stressing that all relevant economic factors must be considered.

In the *United States–Hot–Rolled Steel from Japan* dispute, the Appellate Body found bias in the determination of normal value when low-priced sales from a respondent to an exporter were automatically excluded. The Body also indicated that injury determinations must include an analysis of captive production markets in addition to merchant markets. Causation in such determinations must be rigorously scrutinized. A WTO panel has ruled that the Commerce Department's refusal to revoke an antidumping order against South Korean DRAMS was inconsistent with Article 11.2 of the Antidumping Code. Hence, U.S. regulations regarding the likelihood of continued dumping after a three-year hiatus are suspect under the Code. The Court of International Trade, on the other hand, found the U.S. regulations in question consistent with the WTO Antidumping Code. The Court took the position that the WTO panel ruling was not binding precedent, merely informative.

The WTO Appellate Body ruled against the "Byrd Amendment" (Continued Dumping and Subsidy Act of 2000) allowing firms to receive U.S. antidumping duties. Millions of dollars have been collected by U.S. steel, bearings, candy, candle, cement, computer chip, lumber and other companies under the Byrd Amendment. Awaiting repeal of the Byrd Amendment, the European Union, Canada, Japan and others imposed WTO-authorized retaliatory trade sanctions on U.S. exports to their markets. Repeal was finally accomplished in a late 2005 budget bill, subject to a contested two-year phase-out.

SUBSIDIES AND COUNTERVAILING DUTIES

Tariffs payable on an imported item may be increased above the usual posted tariff schedule amount because of a "countervailing duty." Such duties are levied as an offset by the country of importation upon an imported item the production or export of which has been helped by an unfair "subsidy" in the country of origin. Subsidies come in many forms (e.g. tax rebates, investment tax credits, other tax holidays, subsidized financing); rapidly developing countries offer routinely to give some form of subsidy for initial foreign investment which may have an intended export aspect. In the United States, the EXIMBANK offers low cost loans to overseas buyers of products exported from the United States; other countries have similar programs.

In theory, the countervailing duty offsets exactly the unfair subsidy. Proponents of countervailing duties argue that they are necessary to keep imports from being unfairly competitive even though "fair" subsidies in other countries may be penalized by the countervailing duty. Opponents of countervailing duties argue that there is no coherent standard of "fairness" vs. "unfairness" rationally to justify such duties. They point out that, absent a predatory motive by a foreign government, there is no more reason to justify government intervention in favor of a producer disadvantaged by foreign competition than disadvantaged by domestic competition. The result in each case is that the domestic resources used by the disadvantaged producer are shifted to their next highest value use and, viewing the world market as a unity, production efficiency worldwide is increased thereby. Opponents of countervailing duties point out also that it is often difficult to identify a subsidy.

WTO SUBSIDIES CODE

International concern with unfair subsidies and countervailing duties is reflected in Articles VI, XVI, and XXIII of the GATT 1947 and in the "Agreement on Subsidies and Countervailing Measures" (the SCM Agreement), which is part of the Covered Agreements under WTO. The United States legislation implementing the SCM Agreement changed many concepts under U.S. law. Under the SCM Agreement, the authorities of the importing signatory have the power to impose a countervailing duty (CVD) in the amount of the subsidy for as long as the subsidy continues. The CVD may only be imposed after an investigation, begun on the request of the affected industry, has "demonstrated" the existence of (1) a subsidy; (2) adverse trade effects, such as injury to a domestic industry; and (3) a causal link between the subsidy and the alleged injury.

Under the SCM Agreement there is an attempt to shift the focus of subsidy rules from a national forum, as it was exclusively under GATT, to the multinational forum provided by the Subsidies Committee under WTO and the SCM Agreement. Subsidies complaints can now be brought either in the national forum or the WTO. Three classes of subsidies were established: (1) prohibited ("red light"); (2) permissible, but actionable if they cause adverse trade effects ("yellow light"); and (3) non-actionable and non-countervailable ("green light")(expired in 2000). There are special rules which require LDCs to phase out their export subsidies and local content rules, but over eight and five years, respectively. Transitional economies are also required to phase out both export subsidies and local content rules, but over a seven year period.

The WTO Subsidies Code creates rules for CVD procedures. The commencement of CVD proceedings, the conduct of CVD investigations, the calculation of the amount of subsidy, and the right of all interested parties to present information are covered. Dispute settlement in the subsidies area will focus upon whether another country's trade interests have been seriously prejudiced. A presumption of such prejudice will exist whenever the total *ad valorem* subsidization of a product exceeds five percent, and when the subsidy is by way of debt forgiveness or to cover operating losses.

The multilateral dispute settlement procedure under WTO first provides for consultations between the complaining Member and the subsidizing Member. If these do not resolve the dispute within 30 days for a "red light" subsidy, or 60 days for a "yellow light" subsidy, either party is entitled to request that the DSB establish a panel to investigate the dispute and make a written report on it. The DSB panel will have 90 days (red light), or 120 days (yellow light), to investigate and prepare its report. The panel report is appealable on issues of law to the Appellate Body. The Appellate Body has

30 days (red light), or 60 days (yellow light), to decide the appeal. Panel and Appellate Body decisions are adopted without modification by the DSB unless rejected by an "inverted consensus." See generally, Chapter 2.

If a prohibited or actionable subsidy is found to exist, the subsidizing Member is obligated under WTO to withdraw the subsidy. If the subsidy is not withdrawn within a six month period, the complaining Member can be authorized to take countermeasures. Such countermeasures may not be countervailing duties, but may instead comprise increased tariffs by the complaining Member on exports from the subsidizing Member to the complaining Member.

U.S. COUNTERVAILING DUTY LAW

The U.S. statutory provisions on countervailing duties on products imported from WTO Members is set forth in the Tariff Act of 1930. Duties may be imposed if it is found that the product is subsidized and that as a result a U.S. industry is materially injured or threatened with such injury or its development is materially retarded.

A "subsidy" is defined as a "financial contribution" by a governmental entity which confers a benefit to the manufacturer of the subsidized product. It includes governmental grants, loans, equity infusions and loan guarantees, as well as tax credits and the failure to collect taxes. It can also include the governmental purchase or providing of goods or services on advantageous terms. Further, direct governmental action is not required; a subsidy can also be created if any of the above are provided through a private body. In addition to a "financial contribution" and a "benefit", a subsidy must be specific to a particular industry or enterprise. Red light subsidies are "deemed" to be specific in WTO proceedings, and this concept is incorporated into the provisions on U.S. domestic proceedings for countervailing duties. However, specificity must be proven for other types of actionable subsidies.

Red, Yellow, Amber and Green Light Subsidies

"Red light" (prohibited) subsidies include financial contributions which are conditioned upon the export performance of the beneficiary, even where that condition is only one of several criteria (export subsidies). It includes both subsidies legally conditioned on export performance and also those which are in fact tied to actual or anticipated exportation or export earnings. It does not include, however, all financial contributions to all enterprises which happen to export. "Red light" subsidies also include financial contributions which are conditioned on the use of local goods (import substitution subsidies).

"Yellow light" (permissible, but actionable) subsidies are permissible under the SCM Agreement, but only so long as they do not cause "adverse trade effects." These subsidies include "financial contributions" which benefit specific enterprises or industries, but are not contingent upon export performance and were not insulated under "green light" criteria (below). Under U.S. law, such subsidies are subject to countervailing duties if they cause or threaten material injury to an industry in the United States, or materially retard the establishment of an industry in the United States. The definition of "material injury," or a threat thereof, or material retardation of establishment, is the same as in antidumping proceedings, discussed above.

However, there are references in that U.S. definition to two provisions in the SCM Agreement—those dealing with "red light" and "dark amber" subsidies—with instructions that the ITC consider the nature of the subsidy in determining whether the subsidy imposes a material threat to an industry. "Dark amber" subsidies are ones which exceed five percent of the cost basis of the product, or provide debt forgiveness, or cover the operating losses of a specific industry or of an enterprise more than once. This "dark amber" type of subsidy (halfway between "red" and "yellow") was a five year experiment under the SCM Agreement to provide "permissible, but actionable" subsidies in which there is a presumption of "adverse trade effects", and the subsidizing Member had to rebut that presumption. The dark amber provisions lapsed in 2000.

A new concept found in WTO, and incorporated in U.S. law, was the "green light" (non-actionable) subsidy. Such subsidies were not subject to countervailing duties if they met the rigorous criteria established in the SCM Agreement. Such subsidies included those for industrial research and development, regional development and adaptation of existing plant to new environmental standards. Green light subsidies were a five year experiment under the SCM Agreement to insulate certain governmental grants from countermeasures by other Members. They were not renewed after that period.

Enforcement Procedures

If a subsidy is either prohibited ("red light") or actionable ("yellow light"), it may be subject to either national or multinational actions. It will be subject to action within the U.S. legal system to impose a countervailing duty on imports of the subsidized product. It will also be subject to multilateral process within the WTO to obtain the withdrawal of the subsidy by the offending Member.

The procedure for deciding whether to impose countervailing duties under domestic U.S. law is the same as that for antidumping duties, described previously, and involving both the ITA and ITC making both preliminary and final determinations. An ITA preliminary determination that a countervailable subsidy exists subjects any goods imported after that date to any countervailing duties imposed later, and therefore usually has the effect of reducing imports of such goods.

The Federal Circuit Court of Appeals in *Georgetown Steel Corp. v. United States*, 801 F.2d 1308 (Fed. Cir. 1986) ruled that economic incentives given to encourage exportation by the government of a nonmarket economy (NME) cannot create a countervailable "subsidy." The court's rationale was that, even though an NME government provides export oriented benefits, the NME can direct sales to be at any set price, so the benefits themselves do not distort competition. The court also suggested that imports from NMEs with unreasonably low prices should be analyzed under antidumping duty provisions. The opinion gives little guidance on the key issue of determining which nations have NME. Late in his administration, President George W. Bush issued regulations allowing CVD against NMEs, first applied to steel pipe from China.

U.S. ESCAPE CLAUSE (SAFEGUARD) PROCEEDINGS

GATT Article XIX permits suspension of tariff concessions and MFN treatment if increased quantities of imports threaten or cause *serious* injury to a domestic industry. In the United States, suspension of tariff concessions is obtained through "escape clause proceedings," also called Section 201 proceedings under the Trade Act of 1974. In the United States, decisions about import adjustments are made by the President upon recommendation of the International Trade Commission (ITC), the successor to the United States Tariff Commission. A petition requesting import relief for the purpose of "facilitating positive adjustment to import competition may be filed with" the ITC by any entity which is "representative of an industry." Such entities may be an industry member firm, a trade association, a labor union or even a "group of workers," so long as they are representative of the industry. The petition must specify the purposes for which import relief is being sought, and ought to present the industry's plan for meeting import competition. The ITC then investigates to determine whether the increase in imports is "a substantial cause of serious injury", or threatens serious injury, to the domestic producers of the imported item.

The statutory criteria for these issues require the ITC to consider:

(A) with respect to serious injury, the significant idling of productive facilities in the domestic industry, the inability of a significant number of firms to carry out domestic production operations at a reasonable level of profit, and significant unemployment or underemployment within the domestic industry;

(B) with respect to threat of serious injury, a decline in sales or market share, a higher and growing inventory ... , and a downward trend in production, profits, wages, or employment (or increasing underemployment) in the domestic industry concerned ... ; and

(C) with respect to substantial cause, an increase in imports (either actual or relative to domestic production) and a decline in the proportion of the domestic market supplied by domestic producers.

In responding to such a petition, the ITC will consider such economic factors as whether, for the entire industry, production and employment is declining or merely static, there is significant idle capacity, and a significant number of the firms operate at a reasonable level of profit. Even if serious injury is found, the imports must also be a "substantial cause" of that injury. This "substantial cause" requirement means a cause which is important and not less than any other cause. Competing causes can include inept management, negative general economic or market trends, and technological innovations.

Protective Relief

The statute requires the ITC to report its findings to the President within four months after the petition is filed. If the ITC finds that imports have increased, and that this increase has been a "substantial cause" of actual or threatened serious injury to the industry, the President "shall" take all appropriate and feasible action to facilitate efforts by the industry to make "a positive adjustment to import competition." Even though the word "shall" is used, there are many open provisions which allow the President to resist taking protective action. Thus, unlike antidumping and countervailing duty proceedings, the President has control over both whether any relief will be given in a Section 201 proceeding, and what form of relief will be granted.

One reason why protective escape clause relief is difficult to obtain is the fact that most trading partners of the United States are entitled to take compensatory action if the President decides to provide such relief. They are authorized to do this by the General Agreement on Tariffs and Trade. This is the case because escape clause proceedings do not concern any unfair trade practice. Rather, they are simply a reaction to the fact of increased import competition. This perspective helps explain why the President frequently decides that it is not in the national economic interest of the United States to impose escape clause relief.

If relief is given, it can be either protective relief or adjustment assistance. The former is directed toward the imported goods and can include increased tariffs, tariff rate quotas (tariffs which increase after reaching a certain quota), trade quotas or "orderly marketing agreements" (OMAs). The likelihood of such action being taken has in the past prompted some countries to agree "voluntarily" to lessen pressure on the country of importation by restraining their exporters or otherwise entering into such "orderly market agreements". Japanese auto export restraints to the United States and Europe were two prime examples.

Adjustment Assistance

Escape clause proceedings often lead to adjustment assistance to workers and firms. This assistance is designed to accommodate the increased imports, not to prevent or reduce the imports. Escape clause relief is always considered temporary, but adversely affected workers may be provided with "adjustment assistance" payments and other displacement benefits. For example, automobile workers have been paid such assistance because foreign automobile manufacturers enjoyed great marketing success in the United States. Trade adjustment assistance decisions are made by the U.S. Department of Labor. Adjustment assistance is also available to workers whose plants relocate to U.S. free trade partners, or GSP, CBI, Andean or African trade preference countries.

Trade adjustment assistance programs of the United States were expanded in 2002, including for the first time worker assistance with health insurance, coverage of "secondary workers," a new pilot program on wage insurance for older workers, benefits for family farmers and ranchers, and expanded training and income support. This expansion came in conjunction with the Trade Promotion Authority ("fast track") granted by Congress to the President for free trade agreements and the Doha Round WTO negotiations.

THE WTO SAFEGUARDS AGREEMENT

A Safeguards Code on escape clause and related "gray area" protective measures was agreed upon during the Uruguay Round. This WTO code was approved and implemented by Congress in December of 1994 under the Uruguay Round Agreements Act. One of its more important prohibitions is against seeking, undertaking or maintaining voluntary export or import restraint agreements (VERs and OMAs). Substantive and procedural escape clause rules are also established, notably on proof of "serious domestic injury," opportunities to present evidence and a maximum four-year period of protection (extendable to eight years). The right to retaliate when another country invokes escape clause relief is suspended for the first three years of such invocation. Special rules limit the use of escape clause measures to exports from developing nations and extend the potential for their use on imports by such nations.

Interpretation

The WTO Appellate Body rulings concerning the Safeguards Agreement stringently limit use of escape clause remedies. In 2001, for example, three rulings went against U.S. safeguard measures. In *U.S.–Wheat Gluten from the EC*, the Appellate Body emphasized the critical issue of causation. The U.S. International Trade Commission's analysis of factors other than imports that may have caused domestic industry injury lacked clarity and was inadequate. In addition, U.S. notice of intent to impose safeguards had to be "immediate," sufficient to allow a "meaningful exchange" of consultations. In *U.S.–Lamb Meat from New Zealand*, the Appellate Body reiterated that all causation factors must be isolated and examined. Further, it rejected the "domestic industry" definition adopted by the ITC because growers were included. Exclusion of free trade partners (Canada, Mexico) from escape clause remedies is not permissible if their imports were included in the injury determination. Both of these decisions emphasize the need for the ITC to find "unforeseen developments" in its injury determinations. No guidance is given by the Appellate Body on this term.

The third 2001 Appellate Body ruling against U.S. safeguards concerned cotton yarn from Pakistan. This decision came under the Agreement on Textiles and Clothing. The Appellate Body rejected exclusion of vertically integrated yarn producers from the definition of "domestic industry." Similarly, exclusion of Mexican yarn from the relief was not permissible. In 2002, the Appellate Body ruled against U.S. safeguards on line pipe from Korea, finding under strict scrutiny a number of substantive and procedural errors.

U.S. Steel Tariffs

In March of 2002, President Bush imposed tariffs of up to 30 percent on imported steel over three years. This escape clause relief was tempered by exclusions for selected steel from selected countries. Most Australian and Japanese steel products, for example, were not subject to these U.S. tariffs. About half of all EU steel imports were exempt. Canada and Mexico were fully exempt. Numerous WTO members commenced dispute proceedings under the WTO Safeguards Agreement. In 2003, the Appellate Body ruled the U.S. tariffs on steel illegal under the WTO Safeguards Agreement. The Appellate Body held that the U.S. erred in utilizing the protective tariffs some four years after the surge of steel imports during the Asian economic meltdown, and that exclusion of NAFTA partners Canada and Mexico was improper. The European Union threatened over $2 billion annually in retaliatory tariffs on U.S. exports of clothing, citrus and boats, products thought to be politically damaging to the Bush Administration. In November 2003, the United States lifted its escape clause steel tariffs.

U.S. COURT OF INTERNATIONAL TRADE

Except for internal NAFTA trade, judicial review of final determinations by the ITA and ITC concerning antidumping or countervailing duties is by the Court of International Trade (CIT). Under NAFTA, these reviews are exclusively undertaken by binational panels. The CIT also hears appeals from ITC determinations in escape clause proceedings, but in these cases review is limited to procedural irregularities or clear statutory misconstructions. The Court of International Trade was established in 1980 as the successor to the Court of Customs. The CIT is an Article III court, possessing all the legal and equity powers of a Federal District Court, including that of jury trial, but with three general limitations. These limitations prohibit its issuance of injunctions or writs of mandamus in challenges to trade adjustment rulings, allow it to issue only declaratory relief in suits for accelerated review, and limit its power to order disclosure of confidential information to a narrowly defined class of cases.

The CIT has "exclusive" subject matter jurisdiction over suits against the United States, its agencies, or its officers arising from any law pertaining to revenue from imports, tariffs, duties or embargoes or enforcement of these and other regulations. The court's exclusive jurisdiction also includes any civil action commenced by the United States that arises out of an import transaction, as well as authority to review final agency decisions concerning antidumping and countervailing duty proceedings and trade adjustment assistance eligibility. The geographical jurisdiction of the CIT is nationwide, and it is even authorized to hold hearings in foreign countries. However, the CIT does not have jurisdiction over disputes involving public safety or health restrictions on imports, because of the need in such cases for uniformity of treatment of both domestically produced goods and imports, which can be insured only by referring such issues to U.S. District Courts.

CIT decisions are appealed first to the Court of Appeals for the Federal Circuit (formerly the Court of Customs and Patent Appeals), and ultimately to the United States Supreme Court.

CHAPTER FOUR
CONTROLS ON EXPORTS

A merchant in the United States wishing to export goods must consider all limitations imposed by the importing nation which affect the proposed transaction. Foreign import controls may or may not be comparable to the U.S. import controls discussed in Chapter 3. For nations which are members of the WTO, the controls are likely to be relatively similar. But the merchant in the United States must also consider that the United States may have *export* controls which affect the goods. Additionally, if there are any third party nation components in the goods to be exported, the export controls of that third nation must also be considered. For example, if a U.S. manufacturer of shirts made of materials from India wishes to export the finished shirts to Pakistan, it must consider whether India prohibits the trade of any of its products to the final destination of Pakistan. Another example is Cuba, which has been acquiring many U.S. products through third nations, even though the United States has a trade embargo against Cuba for most manufactured products.

Control of the re-export (including transshipment or diversion) of goods from a foreign nation is difficult to police and creates ill feeling on the part of the re-exporting nation. Assume that India is engaged in a trade embargo against Canada and attempts to halt the export from the United States to Canada of the shirts mentioned above made in the United States from Indian-sourced material. The U.S. government might ignore the Indian demand, just as Canada and Argentina ignored demands by the United States to halt shipping to Cuba automobiles made in GM and Ford subsidiary plants in Canada and Argentina, respectively.

Why does a nation control exports? Exports earn revenue and create jobs. This suggests that export controls are imposed more for political or foreign policy reasons, than for economic reasons. But sometimes the controls have a mixture of these goals. For example, exports are limited to protect national security (military weapons, controlled by the Arms Export Control Act of 1976), fear of spread of nuclear components (partly controlled by Nuclear Nonproliferation Act), preservation of natural resources (endangered species, subject to an international convention—CITES), reserving resources for domestic use (certain hardwoods for making furniture), or holding resources for sale at expected higher prices in the future (oil).

Export controls, which may assume such various forms as quotas, taxes (fees) or even prohibitions, are almost uniquely domestic rather than international. Export controls are mentioned in the GATT and WTO agreements, but as a practical matter there are no GATT or WTO obligations which affect significantly a country's use of export controls. Introductory GATT language speaks of helping developing nations "share in the growth of international trade," which certainly must include exports. But the WTO package of Covered Agreements is clearly an *import* trade rules regime. It is thus to U.S. law that we turn to discover the framework for the governance of U.S. exports.

U.S. EXPORT POLICY

To understand the U.S. regulation of imports, one must thus turn to a complex matrix of trade acts and agreements. To understand the regulation of exports as opposed to imports, the path is somewhat less cluttered. There is no extensive sequence of laws regulating U.S. exports.

A nation tends to encourage its exports, rather than limit them. Limitations are imposed principally for reasons of national security or shortage of certain raw materials. There is one major U.S. export law which is especially important to those engaging in international trade. It is the Export Administration Act of 1979 (EAA). This Act makes a number of Congressional policy statements indicating an intent to restrict export controls only to the extent necessary. It outlines the licensing procedure for exports, requiring a license only in a limited number of specific export situations. It includes the concept of "foreign availability", that export controls should not be placed on goods which are readily available from other sources. Additionally, it is within the EAA that Congress has placed the foreign antiboycott provisions, which prohibit U.S. persons from taking part in boycotts against countries friendly to the United States. The provisions of this Act, as in the case of several trade laws, are followed up by extensive administrative regulations. Finally, the EAA contains very severe penalties for violating U.S. export controls, including loss of all export rights.

U.S. export policy involves questions of *where* and *what* goods may be shipped abroad. There is usually less immediacy about controlling the nature of the goods as opposed to their destination. Restrictions are often introduced to punish nations for something so distasteful that limits on U.S. exports to that country are thought justified, despite economic losses caused by the diminished exports. The President is in a better position than Congress to respond quickly to foreign acts which may justify immediate export controls and U.S. rules reflect this reality. For example, President Reagan took action after the Soviets imposed martial law in Poland, prohibiting the export of component parts for the Siberian oil pipeline. The President's decision generated substantial adverse reaction from several European nations which were the location of U.S.-owned subsidiaries affected by the order.

Foreign actions which lead to controls may be either related to the exports themselves, such as their diversion from friendly to boycotted nations (e.g., Mexico to Cuba), or actions unrelated to the exports, such as the martial law imposed in Poland. When a foreign nation's allegedly hostile acts persist, the Congress usually joins the President in limiting exports by enacting special legislation, such as the boycotts of Cuba and North Korea. This legislation tends to consist of controls implemented not by the Department of Commerce, but by the Department of the Treasury. Treasury controls currency, and without the ability to move currency across borders, trade is quickly diminished.

THE EXPORT ADMINISTRATION ACT AND REGULATIONS

U.S. exports are principally governed by the Export Administration Act (EAA), and several hundred pages of associated regulations. Congress' power to regulate exports as expressed in these laws originates in the foreign commerce clause. It is the same provision establishing Congressional authority to regulate imports. This power often conflicts with the President's conception of his foreign affairs powers, and can lead to disagreements with the executive branch over the extent to which Congress may restrict Presidential discretion in limiting exports to achieve foreign policy goals.

The Export Administration Act is of limited duration. The last one was enacted in 1979 and amended (extended) in 1985. It expired in 1994. Since that time the executive and legislative branches have not been able to agree on the substance of a new act. President George P. Bush vetoed one attempt in 1990 to adopt a new EAA because he believed that his powers were unduly restricted by Congress. In order to continue controls over exports, every President since 1994 has extended the duration of the EAA by declaring a state of emergency under the International Emergency Economic Powers Act (IEEPA).

The policy of the United States toward export controls is set forth in Section 3 of the Export Administration Act of 1979, which provides that:

It is the policy of the United States to use export controls only after full consideration of the impact on the economy of the United States and only to the extent necessary—

(A) To restrict the export of goods and technology which would make a significant contribution to the military potential of any other country or combination of countries which would prove detrimental to the national security of the United States;

(B) to restrict the export of goods and technology where necessary to further significantly the foreign policy of the United States or to fulfill its declared international obligations; and

(C) to restrict the export of goods where necessary to protect the domestic economy from the excessive drain of scarce materials and to reduce the serious inflationary impact of foreign demand....

* * *

It is the policy of the United States ... to oppose restrictive trade practices or boycotts fostered or imposed by foreign countries against other countries friendly to the United States or against any United States person.

THE PROCESS OF LICENSING EXPORTS

U.S. merchants contemplating exports of their products must understand the licensing regulations. Prior to 1996 essentially *all* commercial exports had to be licensed. But that was deceptive. Most exports required only a *general* license (i.e., one which did not require individual application and approval), which the exporter acquired by use of the Department of Commerce form "Shipper's Export Declaration." The exporter actually issued its own general license. But in some cases the exporter needed to obtain a *validated* license (i.e., one authorizing a specific export, issued after approval of an application). Time and changing attitudes generated many variations of licenses, such as a general license GLV allowing shipments of limited value which otherwise would have required a validated license, or a validated license authorizing multiple exports to approved distributors or users in noncontrolled countries, or sales to foreign subsidiaries, or sales to an entire activity or project, or sales of replacement or spare parts for goods previously sold. The general and validated license framework was replaced in 1996, with an allegedly easier to use process. Some critics suggested it did little but alter the labels, rather than change the substance of the process. That was probably an unfair evaluation, the process has proven to be easier.

Commerce Control List

Whether or not a license is required depends primarily on two issues; the type of goods or technology to be exported, and the destination country. The Bureau of Industry and Security (BIS) of the Department of Commerce implements the Export Administration Regulations (EAR) and thus maintains the Commerce Control List (CCL). This includes all items subject to export controls, except for those under the control of another branch of the government, such as the control of defense articles and services by the Department of State. The transfer by Executive Order of encryption devices from State to Commerce in 1996 was particularly contentious. The CCL is divided into ten general categories (e.g., "Category 3—Electronics"). Within each category are five different groups of products, identified by letters A through E (e.g., "Group C—Material"). Three further numbers identify the reasons for control (national security, possible use by terrorists, etc.). Together this makes a four digit and one letter Export Control Classification Number (ECCN, i.e., 3A001).

The Commerce Control List Supplement No. 1 includes the many variations of ECCNs. For each ECCN, this Supplement includes the License Requirements, the License Exceptions, and the List of Items Controlled. Gradually this list has been relaxed, notably to allow exports of high performance computers in 2002. The 1996 revisions provide a fairly easily understood path through the maze of regulations by means of a 29 step process to determine whether a license is needed, and if needed whether there are applicable exceptions. Use of the process involves reference to the Commerce Country Chart, which helps identify countries subject to controls for such reasons as national security, missile technology, U.N. or U.S. embargo, etc. For example, Country Group A includes several dozen nations with which the U.S. generally has good political and trade relations. Country Group E, contrastingly, includes the few nations currently subject to either a U.N. or U.S. trade embargo, such as Cuba.

Licensed Exports

When a license is required, a critical decision usually made by counsel to the exporter, application is made to the BIS in the Department of Commerce. The application must be approved and the license issued before the goods or technology may be exported. In many cases, a license will only be issued upon certain conditions, such as limiting the capability of the export product, restricting it to civilian use and prohibiting its use for any military or intelligence gathering purposes, or prohibiting resale to another controlled country. There is often a considerable negotiating process between the exporter and the BIS. When a license is issued, the exporter is responsible for the performance of all terms and conditions of the license, both by the foreign licensee and by foreign buyers or subsequent buyers. It is important for the exporter to know what conditions might be imposed on the license at the time the original contract is signed, so that such conditions may also be imposed in the contract on the foreign parties.

Speed may be important in processing an application for a license. But the administration of the EAA often has been characterized by delay, uncertainty and lack of accountability, as conflicts arise between national defense and export promotion policies. Many sensitive items have nevertheless evaded export controls, demonstrated in the 1980s sale to the USSR by Toshiba of Japan and Kongsberg of Norway of propeller milling machines and numerical controllers, respectively, which allowed the manufacture of submarine propellers which would function as quietly as U.S. submarines. The companies were subjected to sanctions prohibiting some trade to the United States.

Licensing Timetable

Although delay is attendant to many export applications, there is a timetable which governs processing license applications. Within 10 days after proper submission, the Secretary of Commerce must acknowledge receipt of the application and advise about any other applicable procedures. Unless referral to another government department is necessary, the license should be granted formally or denied within 90 days. Even if referral is necessary, the statutory timetable requires issuance or denial within 180 days of the application. If the exports are to certain countries designated terrorist supporting nations, Congress may have to be advised and the approval period is further extended.

Before its demise, a multilateral review by COCOM might extend the review period to 240 days. COCOM was the Coordinating Committee of the Consultative Group on Export Controls. It was an informal multilateral organization of the U.S. and its military allies (NATO countries less Iceland, plus Japan) established to regulate certain strategic materials exports to communist countries. The U.S. rules were often more restrictive than were those of COCOM, and COCOM review was sometimes used as leverage to grant rather than to deny an application. COCOM members continually tried to convince the United States to relax some of its export rules. But the United States often acted alone in regulating sensitive exports, as it did in 1990, when President George P. Bush announced the "Enhanced Proliferation Control Initiative," which expanded controls on items used in chemical and biological weapons. Following changes in Eastern Europe and the breakup of the USSR, COCOM was abolished in 1994, with promises by many of its members to create a new organization for multilateral export review. The successor organization, established in 1995 and composed of about 28 nations, is the Wassenaar Arrangement on Export Controls for Conventional Arms and Dual–Use Goods and Technologies. Its purpose is similar to that of COCOM.

The statutory timetable of the EAA is not always met, despite Congressional attempts to mandate administrative conduct. Failures to comply with the timetables often frustrate contemplated export contracts. Courts occasionally permit suits to enjoin the Department of Commerce's noncompliance with the statutory timetable, but in one case 29 months elapsed between the filing of the license application and court injunction mandating compliance. Fortunately, recent experience suggests a more rapid review process by Commerce.

SANCTIONS FOR EAA VIOLATIONS

Civil and criminal sanctions for violation of the EAA are formidable. A business which "willfully" violates any provision of the statute, its regulations or a license, knowing that the exports are destined for a controlled country or for its benefit, can be fined $1 million, or five times the value of the exports, whichever is *greater*. Fines of more than $1 million have been levied. An individual engaged in the same violation is subject to 10 years in prison or a fine of $250,000, or both. Similar sanctions may be applied to a business or an individual with a license who knows of a diversion of exported goods to military use by a controlled country and fails to report the diversion. The most feared sanction, however, is the ability of the Secretary of Commerce to suspend, revoke or deny the authority to export *any* goods which are subject to the EAA. This is considered an "administrative action" and is available whether or not the violation is willful.

BOYCOTT PROVISIONS AND
U.S. EXPORT LAWS

Boycotts affect both exports and imports. The United States uses trade boycotts as a means to achieve political goals, although there is considerable debate regarding their effectiveness. A boycott by many nations, such as that imposed under U.N. auspices against South Africa in the 1970s and 1980s, was only questionably effective, and certainly caused a loss of jobs for those it was intended to benefit. But formal apartheid ended and the boycott deserves partial credit. When a boycott is by only one nation against another, contrastingly, such as the U.S. boycott of trade with Cuba, the likelihood of success in achieving a political goal is considerably diminished. The intention of the Cuban boycott has been to remove Fidel Castro from leadership. Some fifty years later a Castro continues in office, frequently invoking the U.S. boycott as justification for Cuban policies.

U.S. boycotts which prohibit trade, both exports and imports, tend to be the subject of specific legislation directed towards identified countries. Enforcement is shifted from the Department of Commerce to the Department of the Treasury. The Office of Foreign Assets Control (OFAC) within Treasury is the responsible agency for controlling these specific boycotts. The pattern of governance is a broad assets control law with additional laws directed to specific countries, such as the Cuban

Assets Control Regulations. The various country specific regulations prohibit specific transactions and transfers. By controlling the flow of currency, whether to pay for imports or be paid for exports, trade is thereby controlled. Terminating the flow of currency is intended to terminate trade. It works, but not completely, because considerable trade may take place through third nations. Many U.S. goods are sold in Cuba, transferred first to middle-men in such nations as Mexico or Panama. Unilateral boycotts which are unpopular in other nations are difficult to enforce.

U.S. boycott policy, as expressed in such laws as the Cuban Democracy Act of 1992, the Iran and Libya Sanctions Act of 1996, the Cuban Liberty and Democratic Solidarity (Libertad) Act of 1996 ("Helms–Burton"), and the Burmese Freedom and Democracy Act of 2003, may attempt to reach the conduct of third party nations toward the boycotted country. Using such devices as exerting extraterritorial power over owned or controlled entities located in third nations, the United States attempts to draw into the boycott these third nations. It is not surprising that third nations have often responded with extremely strong criticism about interference with their sovereignty by the United States. Curiously, the United States is attempting to mandate conduct by these third party nations which it expressly rejects in the U.S. *anti*boycott provisions, when other nations attempt to have the United States assist in a foreign boycott.

ANTIBOYCOTT PROVISIONS
OF U.S. EXPORT LAWS

While boycotts are governed as outlined above by regulations enforced by the Department of the Treasury, the Export Administration Act addresses a special problem relating to exports, *antiboycotts.* The provisions are a direct consequence of the Arab nations' economic boycott against Israel commenced initially in 1954. When the Arab boycott was extended beyond the primary level (no trading with Israel), to the secondary level (no trading with any nation's enterprise which trades with Israel), and to the tertiary level (no trading with any third party nation's enterprise trading with Israel if it obtained components from a nation trading with Israel), Congress began to debate whether U.S. companies ought to be allowed to assist the boycott of a nation friendly to the United States. After several years of debate and the failure of voluntary controls to have any effect, the EAA was amended to prohibit any U.S. person from complying with, furthering or supporting any boycott by a foreign nation against another foreign nation which is friendly to the United States.

The statute was intended to achieve a political end, that is to assist Israel, although the language of the law never refers to any country by name. The EAA provisions include broad language which directs the President to issue regulations prohibiting any U.S. person from doing business in a boycotted country; refusing to hire or discriminating against any U.S. person; furnishing a broad range of information; or paying, honoring or confirming letters of credit, where such action would comply with, further or support the boycott of a country friendly to the United States. But the provisions also require the regulations to recognize certain exceptions, such as compliance with various requirements of the boycotting country which are essentially nonsupportive of that nation's boycott. A further provision requires any U.S. person who receives requests which might provide information which would help the boycott to not only refuse such requests, but to report those requests to the Secretary of Commerce. The reporting requirements are extensive. A company is even denied the right to point out errors in the boycotting nation's policy, such as to note that the company is on the black list of the boycotting nation, even though it has never traded with the target nation of the boycott. Such a clarification is considered to support the boycott and is thus prohibited.

The regulations which have been issued in accordance with the EAA antiboycott provisions are extensive, providing both rules and (in very small print) numerous examples of acts which would or would not violate the law. The examples, when comprehensible, are not always consistent. But they provide some guidance as to the policy behind the regulations.

Sanctions

Since the 1977 amendments to the EAA which introduced the antiboycott provisions, relatively few cases have reached the courts. There have been many challenges by the Department of Commerce's Office of Antiboycott Compliance, but most have ended in a consent decree. The same severe sanctions as outlined above for violations of the United States export laws apply to violations of the antiboycott provisions, but consent decrees often have resulted in negotiating the minimum fines under the EAA, $10,000 per violation, substantially less than the costs and adverse publicity of litigation. For example, in 1995 U.S. subsidiaries (and a corporation counsel) of the French L'Oreal S.A. agreed to pay fines of $1.4 million for allegedly furnishing or agreeing to furnish information by the subsidiaries to the French parent about business relationships with Israel. The penalties were among the highest negotiated under the laws.

Although the EAA and regulations have provided the teeth to attacking the Arab boycott of Israel, two other laws have also been used. The Internal Revenue Code denies certain tax benefits to a person "participating" in an international boycott, and the Sherman Act (antitrust laws) addresses refusals to deal as anticompetitive activity. But since the adoption of the EAA antiboycott provisions, the tax and antitrust laws have been infrequently applied.

FOREIGN CORRUPT PRACTICES ACT

One final issue of exports involves the practice of U.S. companies in making payments to foreign government officials or agents to encourage purchasing the company's products or services (or accept or extend its direct foreign investment). During the Watergate investigations of payments to U.S. political candidates, it was discovered that many U.S. companies had been making payments to foreign officials. The response was swift. The Foreign Corrupt Practices Act was passed in 1977. The original law included only three substantive sections, one establishing accounting standards which required disclosure of foreign payments, and two governing payments to foreign officials and to "other" persons, where those persons "knew or had reason to know" the payments would be passed on to a foreign official. The law included no definitions and only a brief exclusion for payments which were "ministerial" in nature. These were the familiar, minor "grease" payments so often necessary to pass goods through customs. The law was ambiguous, and from the beginning U.S. businesses requested that the Department of Justice issue guidelines. None were forthcoming. Like the antiboycott laws discussed above, few cases reached the courts, most being settled with consent decrees and nominal fines, thus avoiding the label "corrupt payor."

1988 Amendments

Business interests continued to press for changes, which were finally forthcoming in the 1988 trade law. The most significant change was replacing the "reason to know" language with a requirement that any payment to a third person be made "knowing that" it would be passed on to a foreign official. But new definition provisions state that "knowing" may well include reason to know. Having "a firm belief" or being "aware" is sufficient to constitute "knowing." Another important amendment is the further clarification of permissible "grease" payments. Payments are allowed for a "routine government action," which includes obtaining permits to do business, processing papers, providing certain routine services such as police protection or telephone or power, and "actions of a similar nature." But it specifically does not include any decision by a foreign official regarding new business or retaining old business, decisions which are more than merely routine government actions.

The law further includes an affirmative defense section which stipulates several payments which are not prohibited. They include payments permissible under the *written* laws of the other nation, and reasonable and bona fide expenditures such as travel and lodging if related to the promotion or performance of the contract. Other changes to the FCPA in 1988 include some clarification of the accounting provisions. A final change in 1988 removed what was known as the Eckhardt provision, which prohibited bringing a suit directly against an employee without first having received a judgment finding the employer in violation of the Act. With the removal of the Eckhardt provision, corporate officers may find themselves scapegoats, and required to defend charges while the company remains free of any litigation.

OECD Code

A few individual nations have attempt to prohibit payments by their nations' entities, but some nations encourage such payments by allowing them to constitute deductions against taxes as ordinary business expenses. Attempts within the United Nations to govern payments to foreign officials on the international level failed. The U.S. Trade Representative began an intense effort in 1996 to gain agreement by other nations to prohibit such deductions. The international organization Transparency International urged adoption of laws prohibiting such payments, and has published annual lists of the most corrupt nations. Finally, efforts of the Organization for Economic Cooperation and Development (OECD) led to the 1997 OECD Convention on Combating Bribery of Foreign Officials, which obligates signatories to criminalize bribery of foreign officials. Some 40 industrialized nations participate. The United States signed the Convention and amended the FCPA in 1998. The 1998 amendment slightly broadens the definition of wrongful conduct to include payments which "secure an advantage."

SECTION 301 AND SUPER 301

Section 301 of the Trade Act of 1974 is one of the most politically motivated provisions of U.S. trade laws. Basically, this section applies when U.S. rights or benefits under international trade agreements are at risk or when foreign nations engage in unjustifiable, unreasonable or discriminatory conduct.

Thus Section 301 primarily focuses on the activities of foreign governments. Although it has been used to protect U.S. markets from foreign imports, Section 301 has been most notably applied to open up foreign markets to U.S. exports, investments and intellectual property rights. The focus has been on foreign market access for U.S. goods and services.

Section 301 of the Trade Act of 1974 authorizes and in some cases mandates unilateral U.S. retaliation if another nation is in breach of a trade agreement or engaging in unjustifiable, unreasonable or discriminatory conduct. Amendments contained in the Trade and Tariff Act of 1984 broadened the scope of Section 301 to include retaliatory action against foreign country practices in connection with *services*. Special remedies are allowed, including denial of "service sector access authorizations." Presumably, for example, the U.S. Trade Representative (subject to presidential directives) could deny access to foreign banks by withholding licenses from federal authorities.

Section 301 Procedures

Petitions for action under Section 301 are filed with the U.S. Trade Representative, who undertakes appropriate relief after investigation, consultation with the relevant foreign country and other interested parties, and an affirmative determination of a Section 301 "offense." The USTR may self-initiate Section 301 proceedings, a practice increasingly undertaken since 1988. Remedies are mandatory (subject to various exceptions) when U.S. trade agreement rights are being denied or an unjustifiable foreign country practice is found. Remedies are discretionary when unreasonable or discriminatory practices are involved. The remedies available include suspending trade agreement concessions, various import restraints, and bilateral agreements with the offending country. The USTR chooses the remedy subject to presidential "direction." The remedy chosen need not have any connection with the complaints.

Perhaps the most critical difference between the Section 301 offenses concerns "international legal rights," which is part of the definition of unjustifiable practices. Discriminatory practices are those which deny national or MFN treatment, but there is no reference to doing so inconsistently with U.S. legal rights. Unreasonable practices are expressly not premised on international legal rights, and only need to be "unfair and inequitable." There is a long list of examples of unreasonable practices in Section 301(d)(3)(B).

The statutory definitions of unreasonableness were expanded in 1988. They include inequitable treatment in connection with market opportunities, investment and protection of intellectual property rights. There is no requirement that such behavior violate an international agreement to which the United States is a party. This has the advantage of not linking relief to international dispute settlement procedures. Thus, Section 301 is a statutory provision of remarkable breadth.

Most Section 301 proceedings have been resolved through negotiations leading to alteration of foreign country practices. Ultimately, if the President or the USTR is not satisfied with any negotiated result in connection with a Section 301 complaint, the United States may undertake unilateral retaliatory trade measures. Unlike subsidy, dumping, escape clause and market disruption proceedings, Section 301 of the Trade Act of 1974 has no origins in or other imprimatur of legitimacy from the GATT or World Trade Organization. Indeed, the unilateral nature of Section 301 is thought by many to run counter to the multilateral approach to trade relations embodied in the GATT and WTO. Nevertheless, the WTO Appellate Body has affirmed the legality of Section 301 provided the President does not employ it in a manner inconsistent with the WTO agreements, particularly the Dispute Resolution Understanding. See Chapter 2.

Super 301

Section 301 received hostile responses from U.S. trade partners, especially after the amendments to Section 301 implemented in 1988 through the Omnibus Trade and Competitiveness Act. These amendments include the so-called "Super 301 procedures" which required the USTR to initiate Section 301 proceedings against "priority practices" in "priority countries" identified by the USTR as most significant to U.S. exports. In May of 1989, the USTR initiated Super 301 procedures against the following:

(a) Japanese procurement restraints on purchases of United States supercomputers and space satellites, and Japanese technical barriers to trade in wood products;

(b) Brazilian import bans and licensing controls; and

(c) Indian barriers to foreign investment and foreign insurance.

Super 301 was timed to dovetail with the Uruguay Round of GATT negotiations scheduled to end in late 1990. Some saw it as a clever U.S. bargaining chip. It was anticipated that intergovernmental negotiations concerning alleged unfair trading practices would be undertaken in the 12 to 18 months that followed. This proved to be true for Japan and Brazil, but not India, which refused to even discuss its Super 301 listing. Settlements were negotiated with Japan and Brazil which significantly opened these markets to U.S. exporters.

The Super 301 procedures and designations created in Section 301 of the Trade Act of 1974 were limited in application to 1989 and 1990. Super 301 was perceived to be an acceptable alternative to the "Gephardt Amendment" which would have required 10 percent annual reductions in U.S. trade deficits with countries having excessive and unwarranted trade surpluses. Either way, Japan was clearly the main target of the Gephardt Amendment, Super 301 and continuing efforts to renew Super 301. These efforts, a notable rise in Japan's 1993 trade surplus with the United States and the failure of a trade summit early in 1994, all contributed to the revival of Super 301 in 1994 by President Clinton. This revival was undertaken for two years by executive order and (once again) may have forestalled more severe trade sanctions by Congress. The Uruguay Round Agreements Implementation Act in 1995 codified President Clinton's executive order. Since then, executive orders have occasionally continued to give life to Super 301.

Effect of WTO Dispute Settlement

U.S. adherence to the WTO package of Covered Agreements, including the Dispute Settlement Understanding (DSU), has reduced the frequency with which it unilaterally invokes Section 301. The DSU obligates its signatories to follow streamlined dispute settlement procedures under which unilateral retaliation is restrained until the offending nation has failed to conform to a WTO ruling. See Chapter 2. However, disputes falling outside the scope of the WTO agreements and disputes with nations who are not WTO members, remain vulnerable under Section 301.

CHAPTER FIVE

FREE TRADE AGREEMENTS AND CUSTOMS UNIONS

There is a massive movement towards free trade agreements and customs unions throughout the world, though not often of the consequence of that occurring in Europe and North America. Some of these developments are a competitive by-product of European and North American integration. Others simply reflect the desire (but not always the political will) to capture the economic gains and international negotiating strength that such economic relations can bring. This is particularly true of attempts at free trade and customs unions in the developing world. As discussed in Chapter 2, the explosion of such agreements creates systemic risks for the World Trade Organization. It reports that nearly all of its members are partners in one or more regional or bilateral trade agreements. Here is a sampling of such agreements: Hong Kong–China, Japan–Singapore, Russia–CIS states, New Zealand–China, Mexico–Israel, Canada–Peru, EU–South Africa, Chile–South Korea, the South Asian Free Trade Area (India, Pakistan, Bangladesh, Nepal, Bhutan, Sri Lanka) ... and the list goes on. One reason for this proliferation of free trade and customs union agreements may be doubts about the prospects of success for the Doha Round of WTO negotiations.

There is a continuum of sorts, a range of options to be considered when nations contemplate economic integration. In "free trade areas," tariffs, quotas, and other barriers to trade among participating states are reduced or removed while individual national trade barriers vis-à-vis third party states are retained. "Customs unions" not only remove trade barriers among participating states, but they also create common trade barriers for all participating states as regards third-party states. "Common markets" go further than customs unions by providing for the free movement of factors of production (capital, labor, enterprise, technology) among participating states.

"Economic communities" build on common markets by introducing some harmonization of basic national policies related to the economy of the community, e.g. transport, taxation, corporate behavior and structure, monetary matters and regional growth. Finally, "economic unions" embrace a more or less complete harmonization of national policies related to the economy of the union, e.g. company laws, commercial treaties, social welfare, currencies, and government subsidies. The difference between an economic community and an economic union relates only to the number and importance of harmonized national policies.

All such agreements are inherently discriminatory in their trade impact. As nonuniversalized trade preferences, they tend to simultaneously *create trade* among participating states and *divert trade* between those states and the rest of the world. Thus, while trade creation may represent an improvement in the allocation of scarce world resources, trade diversion may generate an opposite result.

With free trade agreements, diversionary trade effects are usually not distinct because of the absence of a common trade wall against outsiders. Trade diversion nonetheless occurs. "Rules of origin" in free trade area agreements keep third-party imports from seeking the lowest tariff or highest quota state and then exploiting the trade advantages within a free trade area. Under rules of origin, free trade areas are "free" only for goods substantially originating therein. This causes member state goods to be preferred over goods from other states. Rules of origin under a free trade agreement can be as trade diversionary as common external tariffs in customs unions.

GATT ARTICLE 24

Article 24 of the GATT (1947 and 1994) attempts to manage these internal trade-creating and external trade-diverting effects. Free trade area and custom union proposals must run the gauntlet of a formal GATT/WTO review procedure during which "binding" recommendations are possible to bring the proposals into conformity. Such recommendations might deal with Article 24 requirements for the elimination of internal tariffs and other restrictive regulations of commerce on "substantially all" products originating in a customs union or free trade area. Or they might deal with Article 24 requirements that common external tariffs not be "on the whole higher or more restrictive" in effect than the general incidence of prior existing national tariffs. The broad purpose of Article 24, acknowledged therein, is to facilitate trade among the GATT contracting parties and not to raise trade barriers.

It is through this review mechanism that most free trade and customs union agreements have passed *without* substantial modification. The GATT, not economic agreements, most often has given way. For example, during GATT review of the 1957 Treaty of Rome creating what we now call the European Union, many "violations" of the letter and spirit of Article 24 were cited. The derivation of the common external tariff by arithmetically averaging existing national tariffs was challenged as more restrictive of trade than previous arrangements. Such averaging on a given product fails to take account of differing national import volumes. If a product was faced originally with a lower than average national tariff and a larger than average national demand, the new average tariff is clearly more "restrictive" of imports than before. Averaging in high tariffs of countries of low demand quite plausibly created more restrictions on third-party trade. If so, the letter and spirit of Article 24 were breached.

Despite these and other arguments, the Treaty of Rome passed through GATT study and review committees without final resolution of its legal status under Article 24. Postponement of these issues became permanent. GATT attempts—through the lawyer-like conditions of Article 24 to maximize trade creation and minimize trade diversion—must be seen as generally inadequate. Treaty terms became negotiable demands that were not accepted. Decades later, the ineffectiveness of GATT/WTO supervision of free trade and customs union agreements continues. At best Article 24 exerts a marginal influence over their contents. Whether the extraordinary proliferation of preferential agreements undermines or supports WTO trade policies is hotly debated.

GATS INTEGRATED SERVICES' AGREEMENTS

Since 1995 "economic integration agreements" (EIAs) covering services are permitted under Article 5 of the General Agreement on Trade in Services (GATS). Such agreements, which can be staged, must have "substantial sectoral coverage," eliminate "substantially" all discrimination in sectors subject to multilateral commitments, and not raise the "overall" level of barriers to trade in GATS services compared to before the EIA. EIAs involving developing nations are to be accorded "flexibility". Like GATT Article 24 customs unions, there is an Article 5 duty to compensate EIA nonparticipants.

Review of GATS Article 5 notifications is undertaken, when requested by the WTO Council for Trade in Services, by the Committee on Regional Trade Agreements. Thus, whereas CRTA examinations of GATT Article 24 agreements are required, such examinations are optional under GATS. Nevertheless, numerous Article 5 examinations have been conducted, including notably the services components of NAFTA, the EEC Treaty (1957) and EU Enlargement (2004), Japan's FTAs with Singapore, Mexico and Malaysia, China's FTAs with Hong Kong and Macau, and various U.S. bilaterals. None of these examinations have resulted in a final report on consistency with GATS Article 5. This pattern continues the GATT/WTO record of regulatory failure regarding economic integration agreements.

DEVELOPING WORLD INTEGRATION

Developing nations in Africa, the Caribbean, Central America, South America and Southeast Asia (among others) had free trade and customs union agreements in place as early as the 1960s. In 1979, under what is commonly called the Enabling Clause, the GATT parties decided to permit developing nations to enter into differential and more favorable bilateral, regional or global arrangements among themselves to reduce or eliminate tariffs and nontariff barriers applicable to trade in goods. Like Article 24, the Enabling Clause constitutes an exception to MFN trade principles. It has generally been construed to authorize third world free trade area and customs union agreements. Whether the Enabling Clause was intended to take such agreements out of Article 24 and its requirements, or be construed in conjunction therewith, is unclear. However, the creation of alternative notification and review procedures for Enabling Clause arrangements suggests Article 24 is inapplicable.

Notification to GATT of Enabling Clause arrangements is mandatory. Since 1995, the WTO Committee on Trade and Development (CTD) is the forum where such notifications are reviewed, but in practice not examined in depth. Enabling Clause arrangements should be designed to promote the trade of developing countries and not raise external trade barriers or undue trade difficulties. Consultations with individual GATT members experiencing such difficulties must be undertaken, and these consultations may be expanded to all GATT members if requested. Unlike GATT Article 24 and GATS Article 5, neither compensation to nonparticipants nor formal reporting on the consistency with the Enabling Clause of developing nation arrangements is anticipated. The ASEAN–China (2004), India–Sri Lanka (2002), and "revived" Economic Community of West African States (ECOWAS 2005) agreements illustrate notified but unexamined preferential arrangements sheltered by the Enabling Clause.

Africa

Several groups have been formed in Africa. In 1966 the central African countries of Cameroon,

Central African Republic, Chad, Congo (Brazzaville) and Gabon formed the Economic and Customs Union of Central Africa (Union Douaniere et Économique de l'Afrique Centrale: UDEAC) to establish a common customs and tariff approach toward the rest of the world and to formulate a common foreign investment code. Implementation has proceeded very slowly. In 1967 Kenya, Tanzania and Uganda created the East African Community (EAC) in an attempt to harmonize customs and tariff practices among themselves and in relation to other countries. The practical effect of that Community has frequently been negated by political strife. In 1974 six French speaking West African nations formed the West African Economic Community (known by its French initials CEAO). This Community is a sub-group within and pacesetter for ECOWAS, the Economic Community of West African States.

ECOWAS was created in 1975 by Dahomey, Gambia, Ghana, Guinea, Guinea–Bissau, Ivory Coast, Liberia, Mali, Mauritania, Niger, Nigeria, Senegal, Sierra Leone, Togo and Upper Volta to coordinate economic development and cooperation. Some progress on liberalized industrial trade has been made and a Cooperation, Compensation and Development Fund established. During the 1980s the pace of regionalization quickened. ECOWAS countries agreed upon formulative policies for the Community, especially regarding air transport, communications, agriculture, freedom of movement between Member States, currency convertibility, and a common currency. ECOWAS (now the West African Economic and Monetary Union, WAEMU)and CARICOM have agreed upon policies and programs for mutual promotion of inter-Community trade. In June of 1991, the Organization of African Unity (OAU) member states agreed to a Treaty Establishing the African Economic Community. This wide-ranging Treaty embraces 51 African nations, and includes a regional Court of Justice. In September of 1995, 12 southern African countries, with South Africa under Mandela participating for the first time, targeted free trade under the Southern African Development Community. A 20–member Common Market for Eastern and Southern Africa (COMESA) has also been announced.

Islamic World

Bahrain, Kuwait, Oman, Qatar, Saudi Arabia, and United Arab Emirates have formed the Gulf Cooperation Council (GCC) with objectives to establish freedom of movement, a regional armaments industry, common banking and financial systems, a unified currency policy, a customs union, a common foreign aid program, and a joint, international investment company, the Gulf Investment Corporation (capitalized in 1984 at two and one-half billion dollars). The Council has already implemented trade and investment rules concerning tariffs on regional and imported goods, government contracts, communications, transportation, real estate investment, and freedom of movement of professionals. Progress has been made on a Uniform Commercial

Code and a Commission for Commercial Arbitration of the Gulf states. In 1987, the GCC entered into negotiations with the EU which resulted in a major 1990 trade and cooperation agreement. In 2003, the non-Arab states of Iran, Pakistan, Turkey, Afghanistan and five Central Asian nations joined together in an Economic Cooperation Organization Trade Agreement (ECOTA). In 2004, Jordan, Egypt, Tunisia and Morocco concluded their Agadir free trade agreement.

Latin America and Caribbean

Other regional groups have been established in Latin America and the Caribbean. Since 1973, the Caribbean countries of Barbados, Belize, Dominica, Jamaica, Trinidad–Tobago, Grenada, St. Kitts–Nevis–Anguilla, St. Lucia, and St. Vincent have participated in the Caribbean Community (CARICOM), an outgrowth of the earlier Caribbean Free Trade Association. In 1958 Costa Rica, El Salvador, Guatemala, Honduras and Nicaragua formed the Central American Common Market (CACM), another victim of political strife, but still functioning in a limited way. Numerous countries in Latin America were members of the Latin American Free Trade Association (LAFTA) (1961) which had small success in reducing tariffs and developing the region through cooperative industrial sector programs. These programs allocated industrial production among the participating states.

The Grand Anse Declaration commits CARICOM to establishment of its own common market. The

Latin American Integration Association (LAIA) (1981), the eleven member successor to LAFTA, is continuing arrangements for intra-community tariff concessions. They agreed to a 50 percent tariff cut on LAIA goods. Antigua, Dominica, Grenada, Montserrat, St. Kitts–Nevis, St. Lucia, St. Vincent and the Grenadines have formed the Organization of Eastern Caribbean States (OECS) in part "to establish common institutions which could serve to increase their bargaining power as regards third countries or groupings of countries". Some 37 nations signed the Association of Caribbean States agreement in 1994 with long-term economic integration goals.

Latin America became a central focus in the 1990s of economic integration. Mexico not only has a free trade agreement with the United States and Canada, it has also agreed to free trade with Colombia, Venezuela, Chile, Bolivia, Costa Rica, Nicaragua, Guatemala, Honduras, El Salvador, Peru and Uruguay. It has even negotiated free trade agreements with the European Union and EFTA (European Free Trade Assn). Argentina, Brazil, Paraguay and Uruguay signed a treaty establishing the MERCOSUR (Southern Cone) common market in March of 1991 and Chile and Bolivia joined them as Associates in 1996. Venezuela under Chavez is seeking MERCOSUR membership and influence. All of this activity occurs against the background of the Free Trade Area of the Americas (FTAA) initiative of Presidents Clinton and George W. Bush. See Chapter 7.

ANCOM ("The Cartegena Agreement") was founded by Bolivia, Chile, Colombia, Ecuador, and Peru in 1969 primarily to counter the economic power of Argentina, Brazil and Mexico and to reduce dependency upon foreign capital and technology. Its Decision No. 24 regulating foreign investment and technology transfers was widely copied during the 1970s. A major boost came in 1973 with the addition of Venezuela, but some of the fragile dynamics of the regional grouping are illustrated by Chile's withdrawal in 1977, Bolivia's withdrawal in 1981 and resumption of membership barely four months later, and Peru's economic (but not political) withdrawal in 1991 and return in 1996. In 2003 the ANCOM and MERCOSUR groups nominally agreed upon free trade, at least partly to counterbalance United States power in the FTAA negotiations. The United States, pursuing in turn a divide and conquer strategy, has been negotiating bilateral free trade agreements with all ANCOM members save Venezuela.

A CASE STUDY: THE ASSOCIATION OF SOUTHEAST ASIAN NATIONS (ASEAN)

Some interesting moves toward third world free trade and rule-making have been taken by the Association of Southeast Asian Nations (ASEAN). Its problems, failures and successes are representative of third world attempts at legal and economic integration. ASEAN has its genesis in the 1967 Bangkok Declaration, with common trade rules in various states of growth, implementation and retrenchment. ASEAN has internal tariff preferences, industrial development projects, "complementation schemes," and regional joint ventures, all discussed below.

An important juncture in the integration process is the point in time at which member countries of a regional group accept a supranational mechanism for enforcing the regime's law irrespective of national feelings and domestic law within a member country. The 1957 Treaty of Rome provided for a supranational European Court of Justice, which decided quickly upon a mandatory enforcement stance regarding national (Member State) compliance with regional law. ASEAN does not have a comparable enforcement mechanism. A vigorous administrator can also make regional law a reality. In Europe, the Commission frequently issues regulations and decisions which are binding within the territories of Member States. These rules are enforced through fines and penalties, and ultimately by the Court of Justice and European Court of First Instance. Violations are investigated and, if necessary, prosecuted by the Commission. See Chapter 6. In contrast, the ASEAN Secretary–General once remarked that ASEAN's Secretariat was "a postman collecting and distributing letters." The surrender of national sovereignty to ASEAN institutions has been a painfully slow process. That said, NAFTA provides an alternative example of achieving free trade without significantly surrendering national sovereignty to regional institutions. See Chapter 7.

Declarations and Summits

ASEAN was formed in 1967 by Indonesia, Malaysia, the Philippines, Singapore and Thailand. Brunei joined in 1984, Vietnam in 1995. Laos and Myanmar(Burma) joined in 1997, and more recently Kampuchea (Cambodia) became a member. Rarely have such culturally, linguistically and geographically diverse nations attempted integration. The Bangkok Declaration establishing ASEAN as a cooperative association is a broadly worded document. Later proposals were made for a formal ASEAN treaty or convention, but were rejected as unnecessary. The Bangkok Declaration sets forth numerous regional, economic, cultural and social goals, including acceleration of economic growth, trade expansion and industrial collaboration.

The Bangkok Declaration establishes several mechanisms, but little supranational legal machinery, to implement its stated goals. An annual ASEAN Meeting of Foreign Ministers is scheduled on a rotational basis among the Member States. Special meetings are held "as required". The Declaration provides for a Standing Committee composed of the Foreign Minister of the State in which the next annual Ministerial Meeting is to be held, and includes the ambassadors of other ASEAN States accredited to that State. The Declaration also provides for "Ad Hoc Committees and Permanent Committees of specialists and officials on specific subjects". Each Member State is charged to set up a National Secretariat to administer ASEAN affairs within that Member State and to work with the Ministerial Meeting and the Standing Committee.

There have been relatively infrequent meetings of the ASEAN heads of government. This contrasts with the semiannual European "summits" that have kept that group moving forward along the path of integration. The third ASEAN summit was held in Manila in 1987. This summit produced an agreement for the promotion and protection of investments by ASEAN investors (national and most-favored-nation treatment rights are created), made revisions to the basic ASEAN joint venture agreement, and continued the gradual extension of regional tariff and nontariff trade preferences. Goods already covered by the ASEAN tariff scheme were given a 50 percent margin of preference. New items received a 25 percent preferential margin. The nontariff preferences generally co-opt GATT rules, e.g. regarding technical standards and customs valuation.

The fourth ASEAN summit in 1992 committed the parties to the creation of a free trade area within 15 years. Five years were cut from this schedule by agreement in 1994, but operational reality has eluded ASEAN free trade. In 2003, a "watershed" date for complete integration in an ASEAN Economic Community targeted 2020. In 2007, this target date was changed to 2015, a reflection of the fear that ASEAN risks being overwhelmed by the powerhouse economies of China, India and Japan.

ASEAN TRADE RULES AND INDUSTRIAL PROJECTS

Between 1967 and 1976, few steps were taken to further the economic cooperation called for in the Declaration. As with most third world regional groups, ASEAN required a period in which its members got to know and trust each other. The annual Ministerial Meetings did facilitate, however, the formation of committees to study economic development projects and economic cooperation, to establish a working relationship with the EU, and to develop close ties with private sector industries within ASEAN Member States.

Early ASEAN economic cooperation focused upon showcase "industrial projects." A "Basic Agreement" and a set of general "Guidelines" govern their creation and operation. ASEAN industrial projects were modeled on the ANCOM "sectoral programs of industrial development" (SPIDs). They are largely government owned industrial development projects. Several of these projects are now in place with the assistance of Japanese financing, notably the ammonia-urea plants in Indonesia and Malaysia. SPIDs are supported by certain monopoly production rights and tariff preferences. Foreign investors may participate in ASEAN industrial development projects through finance, supply, managerial, technical or limited equity relationships.

Freer Trade

ASEAN cooperation has accelerated. Rather than focusing upon the creation of common, protective external tariffs, ASEAN has fostered freer trade by instituting preferential tariffs for goods originating in other Member States. Tariff reductions have been negotiated pursuant to the Agreement on ASEAN Preferential Trading Arrangements. The "Manila Agreement" is aimed primarily at encouraging the establishment of preferential tariffs with respect to basic commodities, particularly rice and crude oil, products of ASEAN industrial projects, and products expanding intra-ASEAN trade. Some of the tariff preferences are negotiated on a bilateral basis; others are negotiated multilaterally by the ASEAN states.

By late 1982, tariff reductions had been agreed for approximately 9,000 products, and the scope of the preferences extended well beyond foodstuffs and textiles. Since then, the ASEAN preferential tariff arrangements have been extended to approximately 2,000 additional items each year. Across the board tariff cuts on items of lesser import value have also increased intra-ASEAN trade opportunities. Progress notwithstanding, these efforts stop short of the automatic tariff elimination schedules of the European Union and NAFTA. As ASEAN moves toward freer trade within the bloc, overhead costs for investors, practical sources of supply materials, and product marketing opportunities may undergo substantial change.

The "Framework Agreement on Enhancing ASEAN Economic Cooperation" (1993) as accelerated in 1994 envisions an ASEAN free trade area (AFTA) that will cover goods but not services or unprocessed agricultural products. The ASEAN countries also signed an agreement on Common Effective Preferential Tariffs (CEPT). Under this agreement, internal tariffs on manufactured products were reduced to 20 percent by 1998. To qualify, at least 40 percent of the content of the goods must originate within ASEAN, a relatively "liberal" rule of origin. Vegetable oils, cement, chemicals, pharmaceuticals, fertilizer, plastics, rubber and leather products, pulp, textiles, ceramic and glass products, gems and jewelry, cooper cathodes, electronics and wooden furniture are included in this first round of tariff cuts. The goal was to have all tariffs on manufactured goods fall to no less than five percent by 2000. Once again this goal proved elusive. There are ongoing efforts to reduce the number of goods excluded from the CEPT.

Only five percent of ASEAN trade takes advantage of the CEPT. One reason for such a low percentage is unilateral tariff cuts below MFN commitments: Thailand from 41% to 18%, Indonesia from 25% to 8%. Such preference erosion makes it less likely that ASEAN traders will document origin to achieve free trade.

International Impact

ASEAN has entered into negotiations with all of its major world trading partners, dealing with them as ASEAN rather than as individual states. For example, ASEAN negotiated a limited number of preferences for its products entering the EU, and annually negotiates with its biggest trading partners, including the United States. ASEAN has free trade agreements with China, Japan, India, and

Australia–New Zealand. These negotiations exemplify ASEAN seeking bargaining strength through unity. However, unlike the EU, where virtually all major trade relations are determined by the Union, ASEAN states also pursue individual commercial negotiations with trade partners. Singapore and Thailand, for example, have negotiated or are seeking bilateral free trade agreements with the United States, Japan and others. This less than completely united regional approach to trade relations is indicative of the gradual development of ASEAN supranationalism and more in tune with NAFTA than the European Union.

Likewise, there is no ASEAN legislature and no ASEAN court. There is a voluntary ASEAN Law Association and an "emerging law" within ASEAN as evidenced by the various rules, agreements and guidelines supporting economic cooperation in the region. For example, ASEAN has established certain rules covering the "origin" of products subject to its tariff preferences. Under these rules, products not wholly produced or obtained within ASEAN cannot qualify for preferential tariff treatment unless they are processed so that the total value of the materials originating from nonASEAN countries or from an undetermined origin does not exceed 50 percent of the FOB value of the products. However, if the final process of manufacture is performed within ASEAN, the goods will qualify for ASEAN tariff preferences. The value of the nonoriginating materials is determined CIF at importation. In the case of goods entering another ASEAN nation from Indonesia (the least developed ASEAN nation prior to Vietnam), the nonASEAN component cannot exceed 40 percent. Reductions in these local content requirements were adopted in 1987. An investor producing goods in an ASEAN country might need to work with these rules so as to qualify for regional tariff reductions.

ASEAN COMPLEMENTATION SCHEMES AND JOINT VENTURES

Complementation Schemes

ASEAN has encouraged development in the private business sector by urging the formation of numerous regional "Federations" or "Clubs" in various areas of industry and commerce. Sponsored by the ASEAN Chambers of Commerce and Industry, the Clubs are ASEAN-wide and have been formed to assist with "Complementation Schemes." Complementation involves the reduction, as needed, of trade barriers between Member States so that entire manufacturing processes, such as automobile assembly, make maximal use of ASEAN products. Moreover, each participating country produces a component which can be traded within ASEAN as parts for assembly into a more finished manufacture. Each Club, such as the ASEAN Federation of Cement Manufacturers, plays an initiating role in proposing tariff reductions for products which are of concern to that industry. Formation of the Clubs, while not envisioned in principal ASEAN Agreements, has been encouraged at the Ministerial Meetings. Club recommendations are approved tentatively by the Committee on Industry, Minerals and Energy of the ASEAN Governments. Recommendations are forwarded from that Committee to the Economic Ministers and Foreign Ministers for final approval.

General Guidelines and a Basic Agreement for ASEAN industrial complementation schemes were completed in 1980 and 1981. The Guidelines have been approved by the Economic Ministers of ASEAN and include "exclusivity" provisions guaranteeing (with limited exceptions) that no similar public or private projects to manufacture a product covered by a complementation scheme will be approved by any Member State of ASEAN. The Guidelines also provide that complemented products will be given priority in other ASEAN countries having foreign exchange controls. Additional Guidelines deal with the percentage of equity ownership by non-ASEAN nationals, tax incentives, remittances, repatriation of profits and expropriation. In 1983, the ASEAN Foreign Ministers approved an ASEAN auto parts complementation scheme involving local content requirements, exclusivity rights and tariff preferences. Many foreign investors or licensors are potential beneficiaries of this scheme (e.g., a Ford Motor Co. subsidiary has an auto body plant in the Philippines). Despite its origins in the private sector, the success of ASEAN automotive complementation is problematic. The desire to produce "national cars" not "ASEAN cars" is strong and supported by local subsidies. Malaysia, for example, now produces the Proton Saga in cooperation with Mitsubishi Motors.

Joint Ventures

Since 1982, ASEAN has focused on creating rules for ASEAN Industrial Joint Ventures which involve participation by only two ASEAN Member States, permit foreign equity participation up to forty nine percent, contain limited monopoly rights and grant extensive tariff preferences. A set of general Guidelines and a Basic Agreement on ASEAN joint ventures have been promulgated. ASEAN joint ventures may be proposed through the private sector initiative of industry clubs, few of which seem to have taken up the opportunity as yet. A 1987 revision of the Basic Agreement on joint ventures permits exclusivity privileges and protection against unfair trade practices. ASEAN joint ventures are a unique contribution to regional development and represent an investment alternative holding out the possibility of significant economies of scale. Eight joint ventures were approved in 1991, including enamel and heavy equipment production by Indonesia and Malaysia, aluminum hydroxide by Indonesia and Thailand and four food products' joint ventures with the Nestlé Co. In general, the ASEAN trade and investment programs have been hard to implement because of tariff exemptions and nontariff trade barriers. The need to solve such problems is heightened by China's rapidly growing economy and foreign investment magnetism.

ASEAN complementation schemes and joint ventures present potential antitrust law problems for U.S. participants insofar as American foreign commerce is affected. For example, if Ford Motor Co.'s participation in the automotive complementation scheme reduces U.S. export or import opportunities, the scheme could fall within the extraterritorial reach of the Sherman Act. If so, United States prosecutors and plaintiffs will surely claim that ASEAN "clubs" amount to government sponsored cartels. There may also be U.S. customs law problems when and if complemented "ASEAN cars" are exported to the American market. Such cars could, for example, be subject to countervailing tariff duties if it is determined that ASEAN has subsidized their production and the U.S. auto industry is threatened with injury. These potential legal problems may deter involvement in ASEAN joint ventures and complementation schemes by U.S. firms and their business affiliates within the region.

EAST ASIAN INTEGRATION

East Asia, ranging from Japan in the North to Indonesia in the South, enjoyed truly remarkable economic growth during the 1980s and 1990s. When the Asian financial crisis hit in 1997–98, the region took it on the chin economically, but bounced back quickly. United States and other foreign investors participated in this growth largely on a country-by-country basis. All signs are that rapid growth, especially in China, will continue.

East Asia, unlike Europe or NAFTA, has not developed a formal agreement with uniform trade, licensing and investment rules. Only recently has the APEC (Asia–Pacific Economic Cooperation) group even begun to address this idea. The APEC group is comprised of 18 Asia–Pacific nations including the United States. Late in 1994 the APEC nations targeted free trade and investment for industrial countries by 2010 and developing countries by 2020. Nine industries have been selected for initial trade liberalization efforts.

With the European Union and the North American Free Trade Area maturing rapidly, one provocative question is the future of Japan. It is not in the interests of any nation that Japan should feel economically isolated or threatened. Yet it is hard to imagine incorporating Japan into the NAFTA, though some have suggested this. To some degree, what appears to be happening is that regional integration in East Asia is growing along lines that follow Japanese investment and economic aid decisions. Japan now has "economic cooperation" agreements with ASEAN, Thailand, Malaysia, the Philippines, Indonesia and Brunei.

The role of China in all of this is critical. China and Japan are clearly rivals for economic leadership of the region. China is pushing for influence in the East Asian economic sphere. Hong Kong's return in 1997 and Macau in 1999 moved in this direction. China is cultivating trade and investment relations with Singapore, South Korea, Taiwan and, to a lesser extent, Japan. ASEAN and China have a free trade agreement, achieved before that of Japan. Some commentators foresee, as a practical matter, the emergence of a powerful Southern China coastal economic zone embracing Hong Kong, Taiwan, Guangdong and Fujian.

CHAPTER SIX

THE EUROPEAN UNION[1]

The European Union (EU), often called the Common Market, is a supranational legal regime with its own legislative, administrative, treaty-making and judicial procedures. To create this regime, 27 European nations have surrendered substantial sovereignty to the EU. European Union law has replaced national law in many areas and the EU legal system operates as an umbrella over the legal systems of the member states.

The original six member states of Belgium, France, Italy, Luxembourg, the Netherlands, and West Germany, were joined by Denmark, Ireland and the United Kingdom in 1973, Greece in 1981, Portugal and Spain in 1986, and Austria, Finland and Sweden in 1995. Norway failed to join as planned in 1973 and again in 1995 after national referenda. Switzerland is not a member, though closely linked via bilateral agreements with the EU. Greenland (admitted with Denmark) withdrew in 1983. The Norwegians and Greenlanders strongly disliked the Union's Common Fisheries Policy. This Policy regulates the type and number of fish that can be caught in European waters, significantly

1. For much more extensive coverage, see Folsom's *EUROPEAN UNION LAW in a Nutshell*.

subsidizes the fishing industry, and protects it from foreign competition. Its most controversial feature requires common access to all fishing grounds beyond six (sometimes twelve) miles.

Turkey, an Associate for many years, formally applied for membership in 1987. It may be unable to join because of Greek hostility and the requirement of a unanimous Council vote on new members. There are also questions as to Turkey's commitment to democracy and its "European" status. Turkey's candidacy as an EU member state has also been diluted by the rush of Central European applicants after the fall of the Soviet Union. Estonia, Poland, the Czech Republic, Hungary, Slovenia, Malta, Lithuania, Latvia, Slovakia, and Cyprus joined in 2004. Bulgaria and Romania became members in 2007. Thereafter, Croatia, Bosnia, Montenegro, Macedonia and Albania appear next in line, with or without Turkey.

THREE COMMUNITIES

Technically, there were three original European economic communities: the European Coal and Steel Community (ECSC) established in 1952 and now expired, and the European Economic Community (now the European Community) (EC) and the European Atomic Energy Community (EURATOM), both established by Treaties of Rome in 1957. Each community has its own founding treaty and secondary law. The EC must take pride of place in importance and effect on the lives of the citizens of the member states. While each community originally had an organization separate from the other, since a Merger Treaty of 1965, all three communities have had common institutions: The Council of Ministers, the Commission, the European Parliament, and the European Court of Justice (ECJ). A Court of First Instance was created in 1989 to reduce the caseload of the ECJ. In addition, the Maastricht Treaty on European Union of 1993 covers foreign affairs, security, justice and home affairs.

The ECSC was formed in direct response to World War II and waning Allied control of German steel and coal production. Whereas the EC Treaty specifies that it is of unlimited duration, the ECSC Treaty expired in 2002, when it was merged into the EC Treaty. Nevertheless, it was the Coal and Steel Community that gave birth to the major institutions of European economic integration. The ECSC was a curious combination of French regulatory "dirigisme" (price and output controls, tariff protection, investment subsidies) and more market oriented policies (internal free trade, competition rules, adjustment assistance). Many European coal and steel firms are government owned, which generally tended to cause the ECSC to protect these industries from world market forces. The ECSC levied taxes directly upon coal and steel companies, a power not found in the Rome Treaty.

EURATOM was formed to promote the peaceful use of nuclear energy. It has sponsored research and development, joint ventures and free movement of related products and persons. EURATOM is rarely in the news, but played an important role when the EU revised its regulations after Chernobyl.

The European Union has an aggregate population exceeding 500 million and a gross "national" (Union) product exceeding $8000 billion. It is the largest market for exports from the United States. No other regional legal regime rivals Europe in detail of rulemaking and the extent to which its member states have achieved integration. Anyone doing business with Common Market nations will have contact with EU law, which is vast and intricate. There are law school courses devoted entirely to a study of the European Union.

MULTIPLE OFFICIAL LANGUAGES

There are problems of language in interpreting European law. The Coal and Steel Treaty sought to avoid these problems by making French the only official language of that treaty. Presently, there are over twenty working languages within the Common Market. Each working language can be consulted on questions of interpretation. However, with Treaty of Rome terms (such as Article 234) it is important to remember that English was not an official language prior to 1973 when the British joined. Thus, with reference to older legal documents and the Treaty of Rome, the French, German, Dutch or Italian versions are arguably more authoritative. The French version is considered the most authoritative of all because the Treaty of Rome was originally drafted in French. At a minimum, reference to different versions will promote greater understanding of the law. Attorneys practicing European law routinely consult different language versions of regulations, directives, decisions and treaties.

EUROPE WITHOUT INTERNAL FRONTIERS

The Treaty of Rome is intended to achieve the harmonious development of economic activities of member states through: (1) the pursuit of trade and economic growth, a common customs tariff and commercial policy towards third countries, and an elimination of tariffs and quotas within the Community; (2) the abolition of internal obstacles to the free movement of persons, services and capital; (3) the adoption of common agricultural, fishery and transport policies; (4) the fostering of a system of "nondistorted competition"; and (5) the approximation (harmonization) of laws of member states so far as required for the proper functioning of the Common Market. Specific areas of policy include rules on competition, taxation, government contracts, state monopolies, free movement, transportation, the customs union, agriculture, dumping practices, state subsidies, regional development, monetary policy, trade relations, commercial policy, social policy and the European Investment Bank.

Free Movement

Development of the Common Market has not been easy. National interests and laws have often frustrated treaty rules and regional policies. This "hardening of the arteries" of trade and growth caused major revisions to the Treaty of Rome in 1987. These were undertaken through the Single European Act. Their principal focus was on nontariff trade barriers to trade and free movement. Enhanced policies for worker health and safety, foreign policy cooperation, research and development and the environment were also anticipated. The goal was, by the end of 1992, to establish a Europe "without internal frontiers". Hundreds of new legislative acts have been adopted in pursuit of a truly Common Market.

Realization of the goal of a Europe without internal frontiers *for people* has proved harder to achieve. The Benelux states, Germany, Italy, Spain, Greece, Portugal and France agreed to remove their internal frontier controls on people under the 1990 "Schengen Accord." This accord is the product of intergovernmental agreement, not legislation. It is not expected that Ireland and the United Kingdom will participate. The Schengen Accord covers such sensitive issues as visas, asylum, immigration, gun controls, extradition and police rights of "hot pursuit." The main points of contention were cross-border traffic of immigrants and criminals, especially terrorists and drug dealers. These issues were resolved largely by promises of greater intergovernmental cooperation, notably through computer linkages. The Schengen Accord finally became operational in 1995. Its application to the ten 2004 entrants (save Cyprus) took effect in 2008.

EU Citizenship—Rights of Residence

There has been increasing attention on the creation of what it is called a "People's Europe." This focus is multidimensional. It includes traditional Free Movement Rights of Workers (below), the self-employed, and their families, and of professionals and others operating in the services sector. The "People's Europe" has been expanded to include general rights for nonworkers, such as students, the retired, and others to reside anywhere. The Maastricht Treaty on European Union formally introduced the idea of European citizenship and brought with it a selected bundle of civil rights. These include the right to run for office and vote wherever resident in local and European Parliament elections, and the right to be represented abroad diplomatically by other member state consular or embassy services. European Community passports have replaced national passports, and driving licenses have been standardized. In 2004, EU health insurance cards were introduced to facilitate access to "necessary" care when traveling in other member states. The ECJ has repeatedly ruled that citizens exercising their free movement and residence rights cannot suffer discrimination under home country programs, for example pension and unemployment benefits.

A general right of free movement for purposes of residence throughout the Union has been recognized since 1990 and benefits students, retirees and the populace at large. This right should be distinguished from the free movement rights of workers.

The chief concern about a general right of residence is coverage for health and social welfare purposes, and a possible run towards those states with more generous programs. Council Directive 90/364 extends a general right of residence to all member state nationals and their families (including cohabitants) provided they do not become a burden on the public finances of the host country. Spouses and dependent children (even those who are not nationals) are entitled to work in the country where the nonworking member state spouse has taken up residence. These principles also apply to employees and the self-employed who have retired.

Tens of thousands of students are now exchanged under the ERASMUS and SOCRATES programs each year. It has been extended to students from EFTA and many Central European countries. The Rome Treaty was amended by the 1993 Maastricht Accord to authorize cooperative action and "incentive measures" on education, vocational training, youth, cultural and public health affairs. The Bologna Process started in 1998 brought a common bachelor-masters degree system to 46 European nations, including all from the EU.

TREATY ON EUROPEAN UNION (1993)

In 1993, the Treaty of Rome was amended substantially by the Maastricht Treaty on European Union (TEU). The tasks of the Union thereafter included creation of an economic and monetary union with emphasis upon price stability. The listing of activities in pursuit of that goal was expanded to include environmental, social, research and development, trans-European network, health, education, development aid, consumer protection, energy, civil protection, internal market, visas and other policy endeavors. On the other hand, the TEU sought to limit regional activities to those areas where the results are best achieved at the European (versus national) level. This is known as the "subsidiarity principle" and is the subject of intense controversy.

The Treaty on European Union also added what amount to side agreements ("separate pillars" in Eurospeak) on a common foreign and security policy and cooperation regarding justice and home affairs. Like the 1987 Single European Act's provisions on foreign policy, these side agreements did not amend the EC Treaty and stand on their own as separate international agreements. As such, they are not subject to the judicial review of the Court of Justice. The Treaty on European Union of 1993 called for yet another round of intergovernmental negotiations to revise both the TEU and the Treaty of Rome. Late in 1997, these negotiations bore fruit in the Amsterdam Treaty, which then faced national referenda and court challenges during the ratification process.

Amsterdam Treaty (1999)

The Amsterdam Treaty of 1999 was in many respects best known for what it did not accomplish, namely major institutional and agricultural policy reforms in anticipation of European Union membership expansions. The Treaty did significantly extend Parliament's co-decision legislative powers, and institutionalized procedures to deal with "serious and persistent" member state violations of democracy, human rights and the rule of law. It authorized legislative action to secure "freedom, security and justice"(an effective transfer of much of the TEU justice and home affairs power), including asylum, extradition and the essentials of the Schengen Accord, all subject to Court of Justice review but also British, Danish and Irish opt outs.

Additional legislative powers cover employment incentives, public health, fraud prevention, customs cooperation, transparency principles and social policy (formerly the Social Protocol). A complex provision on "flexibility" seeks to allow, subject to detailed controls, some member states to establish "closer cooperation" than others. This provision appears to reflect the realities of less than comprehensive participation in existing policies and programs such as defense, the common currency, the Schengen Accord and the like. Lastly, the Amsterdam Treaty added a special protocol on the principles of subsidiarity and proportionality, and attempts to secure greater support for common foreign and security policies.

TREATY OF NICE (2003)

With the Amsterdam Treaty in place, and new memberships looming, yet another round of intergovernmental negotiations was swiftly commenced. By 2001, the Treaty of Nice was signed and sent on its way for national ratifications. Like the Amsterdam Treaty and its predecessors, Nice amends the Treaty of Rome, notably creating "triple majority" legislative voting in the Council, authorizing the creation of specialized "judicial panels" attached to the Court of First Instance, and increasing the possibility of closer cooperation ("flexibility") by less than the Union's full membership. More significantly, the Enlargement Protocol to the Treaty of Nice establishes the rules of governance once the ten (eventually twelve) new members accede to the European Union. These byzantine institutional changes for the European Council, Commission, Parliament and Courts are covered in the *European Union Law* Nutshell. Lastly, a Charter of Fundamental Rights was "proclaimed" at Nice, but not made binding as a matter of law, and therefore not subject to ratification.

Ratification of the Treaty of Nice and its Enlargement Protocol ran into unexpected opposition in Ireland. Often cited as a model of how the European Union can benefit small countries, Irish law mandates a national referendum on EU ratifications. In the first vote, admittedly a low turnout, the Irish people soundly rejected the Treaty of Nice. Fear of loss of regional benefits to the economically struggling new members may have been critical to this surprising result. A year later, in 2002, after a major persuasion campaign by the Irish government and no provision for "opt-outs," the people voted "yes" on Nice by a wide margin. Shortly thereafter, the accession of the new member states to the European Union was finalized. The Treaty of Nice took effect in 2003.

DEFEAT OF A CONSTITUTION FOR EUROPE (2005)

The growth in membership in the European Union raises fundamental issues of governance. The Nice Enlargement Protocol offers patchwork solutions, but will they measure up to the task? Less than a year after signing on to the Nice Treaty, the heads of state meeting at the Laeken Summit of the European Council established the 105–member Convention on the Future of Europe. Popularly referred to as a "constitutional convention," this body's very existence recognized that the traditional means of governance as revised by the Enlargement Protocol may not be up to the task.

Members of the Convention were drawn from national governments and parliaments, the European Parliament, and Commission. The 12 future member states had nonvoting observer status at the Convention. Chaired by former French President Valery Giscard d'Estaing and driven by an inner 12–member praesidium, the Convention became a focal point for change. Lobbying on all fronts was intense, running from strong federalists to states rights' advocates. In June of 2003, the Convention released its draft Treaty establishing a Constitution for Europe, some 260 pages of complex text merging the Rome, Maastricht TEU and EURATOM treaties. The draft went under review by the EU member states, which unanimously signed off on a final version in June of 2004. The Constitution needed individual ratification in all 25 member states, which it dramatically failed to obtain in French and Dutch referenda. Many variables seem to have been at work: Dislike of national leaders (especially President Chirac of France), visions of Turkish membership in the EU, use of the provocative "C" word (Constitution), job competition from the new member states, and resentment of the Brussels elite. These NO votes were so definitive that virtually all suggestions for "reworking" the Constitution failed to gain traction. With its 50th Anniversary looming, European Union integration was at a standstill.

THE PROPOSED REFORM TREATY

By 2007, with the defeat of the European Constitution fading, EU leaders went back to work on advancement of the Union. Presidents Sarkozy of France and Merkel of Germany, in particular, pushed for a "mini-treaty" during the summer of 2007. Gone was all reference to the "C" word. Promoted as technical amendments to the TEU and Rome Treaty, a proposed "Reform Treaty" (Treaty of Lisbon) emerged late in that year from an Intergovernmental Conference. All references to the European Community would be expunged in favor of European Union, and the Treaty of Rome renamed the "Treaty on the Functioning of the Union." All member states save Ireland were ready to proceed with ratification *without* calling for national referendums. Most did so prior to the dramatic rejection of the Lisbon Treaty by Irish voters in June of 2008. Although its future is in doubt, the target date for implementation of the Reform Treaty is 2009, prior to June elections for the European Parliament.

The Reform Treaty would notably create a two and a half year EU Presidency elected by the Council, establish an EU diplomatic service under a foreign policy chief, eliminate national vetoes on justice and home affairs (migration, criminal justice, judicial and police cooperation) (the UK and Eire can opt out), and render the Charter of Fundamental Rights binding law (subject to a second UK opt out). The Union will also accede to the European Convention on Human Rights. Over Polish objections, legislative voting rules in the Council would be simplified to a double majority representing 55% of the states and 65% of the EU population, phased in between 2014 and 2017. Qualified majority voting will be eliminated. With few exceptions, EU legislation would be co-decided under "normal legislative procedures" by the Council and the Parliament, which also gets to approve the full EU budget.

The European Central Bank would officially be designated an EU institution, despite its fear that this could jeopardize independence. At French insistence, "undistorted competition" as a basic goal would be removed from Treaty-status to a protocol.

Conceivably, such a change could limit EU powers to control government subsidies or mergers and acquisitions. The Commission would be reduced in size to two-thirds the number of member states, a majority of whose national parliaments could force re-examination on subsidiarity grounds of any legislation proposed by the Commission. The President of the Commission will be nominated the Council and elected by the Parliament. For the first time, a right of member state withdrawal from the Union would be established.

GOVERNANCE: THE COUNCIL OF MINISTERS

The Council consists of representatives of the ruling governments of the member states. Specialized Ministers from national governments routinely meet (e.g., Economic and Finance Ministers, Foreign Ministers). Collectively, such Ministers comprise the Council when they act on regional affairs. The principal function of the Council is to coordinate the economic policies of the member states in fulfillment of the objectives of the Treaty of Rome. It exercises important power in approving legislation and international agreements. Since the Council often has the final word on such matters, it possesses considerable power to advance or retard European integration.

Most provisions of the Treaty of Rome state specifically which legislative steps and powers are conferred on the Council. However, there is a general enabling power entitling the Council, acting on a proposal from the Commission and after consulting the Parliament, to take action. This power may be used only where the powers necessary to attain one of the objectives of the Treaty of Rome have not been provided. Environmental regulations and directives, for example, were originally a product of unspecified Treaty law.

The Committee of Permanent Representatives (COREPER) (established by the 1965 Merger Treaty) is a subordinate institution composed of member states' "civil servants", usually at the ambassadorial level. Its main function is to prepare the work of the Council and to maintain close communication with the Commission and with civil servants in member states. In practice, COREPER undertakes to make all noncontentious decisions for the Council, leaving to the Council only the task of formal adoption.

The Principle of Subsidiarity

The Treaty on European Union (Maastricht 1993) and to a lesser extent the Single European Act (1987) formalized "subsidiarity" and "proportionality" principles. The Amsterdam Treaty of 1999 added a Protocol on the application of the principles of subsidiarity and proportionality. These much debated principles hold that the region can act in areas where it does not exclusively have power only if the member states cannot sufficiently achieve the objectives, i.e., "by reason of scale or effects [the] proposed action [can] be better achieved by the Community" (subsidiarity principle). In all cases, European action must not go beyond what is necessary to achieve the objectives of the Treaty of Rome (proportionality principle).

Subsidiarity is a kind of "states' rights" amendment intended to limit the growth of regional government in Europe. An inter-institutional agreement by the Council, Commission and European Parliament on the application of subsidiarity principles by all institutions was quickly negotiated. Subsidiarity guidelines were adopted by the European Council in 1992 and a Protocol implemented in 1999 with the Amsterdam Treaty. Moreover, the Commission regularly reviews proposed and existing legislation in light of the subsidiarity principle. This has caused a number of legislative proposals and acts to be withdrawn or amended. Under the Subsidiarity Protocol, moreover, if a third or more of the national Parliaments give reasoned opinions that a proposal breaches the subsidiarity principle, the Commission must reconsider.

GOVERNANCE: THE COMMISSION AND LAW–MAKING

A principal European institution is the Commission, which is located in Brussels, Belgium. Since 1958, hundreds of Commission decisions and regulations in economic and social areas have moved the Common Market toward closer union. The Commission is independent of the member states. Its 27 Commissioners (one from each member state) are selected by Council appointment. They do not represent member states or take orders from member state governments. The Commission is charged with the duty of acting only in the best interests of the region, and serves as the guardian of the treaties. Each Commissioner supervises specific Directorates (Departments) administering regional policies: Agriculture, External Relations, Competition, etc. And each has an extensive staff of highly paid and tax sheltered Eurocrats. The proposed Reform Treaty would reduce the quantity of Commissioners to two-thirds the number of member states.

Member states with special interests in certain policies usually are able, by common accord in the Council, to have "their" Commissioner supervise the Directorate in which they are most interested. Hence, a French Commissioner is often the head of the Agriculture Directorate, a British Commissioner often heads the Directorate for External Relations, and so on. Commissioners serve four-year terms and are frequently reappointed. However, there have been some failures to reappoint Commissioners who lose the faith of their home governments. Prime Minister Thatcher, in particular, refused to renew a British Commissioner who had "gone native" (became too much of a European Union enthusiast).

Powers of the Commission

One Commission function is to ensure that the provisions of the treaties are carried out. To do so, it has power to render law enforcement decisions and to formulate legislative proposals (regulations, directives) for the Council. It also exercises powers conferred upon it by the Council. Moreover, the Commission has asserted a power to act without express Council authority in situations involving overriding public interest. The EC Treaty enables the Commission to enforce, through the Court of Justice, the observance of Treaty provisions and secondary law by individuals, other regional institutions and by member states. In this capacity, the Commission has been an aggressive prosecutor of European law.

The Commission maintains relations with many international organizations such as the GATT and WTO. With Council mandates, it negotiates most commercial treaties on behalf of the Union. The EU has an extensive network of trade treaties, especially in the Mediterranean basin and in Central and Eastern Europe, and with former colonies of member states.

Legislative Involvement

The Commission has an important function as the only institution which proposes and drafts European legislation. Proposed legislation is submitted to the Council for adoption. The Council is obliged to consult and in some cases cooperate or co-decide with the European Parliament before enacting legislation. Cooperation procedures often resulted in adoption of amendments proposed by Parliament. Co-decision procedures additionally give Parliament a veto over legislative proposals and are dominant today. Such mandatory procedures are the linchpin around which dynamic changes in structure are emerging. Slowly, the European Parliament is becoming a principal legislative body. This institutional power struggle and policy debate has lasted for decades.

The Commission's exclusive power to draft legislation has made it the focal point of lobbying activities in which United States counsel often participate. For example, U.S. lobbying in connection with the European computer software directive is said to have been extremely heavy. More recently, Parliament's ever increasing roles in the legislative process have made it another lobbying center.

GOVERNANCE: THE EUROPEAN PARLIAMENT

The European Parliament is an institution in the course of change. The European Parliament historically played an advisory role. Since 1979 its members have been elected directly by the citizens of the member states (prior to 1979 appointment was by nomination of the national legislatures of member states). The number of MEPs correspond very roughly to the populations of each country. MEPs serve five year terms, and are presently divided into transnational political groups. The European Parliament is a kaleidoscope of European politics.

The Parliament has the power to put questions to the Commission and the Council concerning regional affairs. It also has the power to censure the

Commission, in which event all the Commissioners are required to resign as a body. In 1999, in the midst of controversy over fraud and mismanagement, the threat of such a censure combined with an investigatory report caused the commission to resign en mass. In the event of inaction by another institution, the Parliament can bring an action against that institution in the Court of Justice. For example, the Parliament sued the Council for failing to act on establishing a common regional transport policy, prevailing as a matter of law (but not remedy) before the European Court. The Council failure to act on transport policy was not enforceable since the duty to act was too imprecise.

Diverse Legislative Roles

At a minimum, the Parliament has a right to be consulted and to give an "opinion" as part of the legislative process. That opinion is not binding upon the Commission or Council, but it may prove awkward if that opinion is disregarded. For example, the Court of Justice has held that the Council acts illegally if it legislates without waiting for the Parliament's opinion. Left unanswered is how long Parliament may delay the giving of an opinion.

The Single European Act (1987) granted Parliament a greater "cooperative" voice in developing selected policies (e.g., free movement of workers, the right to establish a business, the freedom to provide services throughout the Common Market). Basically, when the Treaty of Rome required adherence to cooperative procedures, the Parliament often proposed amendments. By an absolute majority, the Commission re-examined the legislative proposal in their light. If the Commission rejected the amendments suggested by the Parliament, they were excluded from the legislative proposal but transmitted to the Council with the Commission's opinion on them. In either case, unanimity within the Council was required to alter the legislative proposal. Again, in either case, a qualified majority vote in the Council in most cases adopted the measure into law.

The "cooperation procedure" applied selectively. Most significantly, it applied to nearly all internal market measures. With the development of the cooperation procedure, and success in persuading the Commission and Council to adopt its amendments, Parliament advanced its legislative agenda.

The European Parliament acquired significant powers under the Maastricht Treaty on European Union (1993), the Amsterdam Treaty (1999) and the Nice Treaty (2003). On legislation, under the "co-decision" procedure, it has what amounts to a legislative veto over selected matters if conciliation through direct negotiations with the Council cannot be achieved. Co-decision applies, for example, to single market, education, culture, health, consumer protection, environmental, transportation and research affairs. The Amsterdam Treaty and Nice Treaty considerably expanded the number areas subject to co-decision. Thus, there are now three distinct European Union legislative processes, each defined in terms of the role Parliament plays: consultative, cooperative and co-decisional. Since the Amsterdam Treaty, co-decision is the most prevalent legislative process.

Budgetary Powers

Significantly, the EC Treaty gives the Parliament power to amend or propose changes in the budget, drafted by the Council, regarding treaty-mandated matters. This has increased Parliamentary influence over "compulsory expenditures" (mostly agricultural subsidies). Since 1975, Parliament has had ultimate control over "non-compulsory" expenditures, about 40 percent of the budget. As a practical matter, this gives the Parliament influence over expenditures in many of the new and important policy areas. However, Parliamentary amendments to the Council's draft budget cannot exceed the maximum rate of increase allowed under the Treaty. This maximum involves a complex calculation by the Commission of regional inflation and gross domestic product (GDP) rates as well as national budget variations. Parliament, at the end of a laborious process with multiple communications to the Council, adopts the final budget.

Parliament and the Council often quarrel over creation of the budget, with Parliament prevailing more and more. Parliament and the Council review how the Commission has implemented the budget. Upon Council recommendation, Parliament gives the Commission a "discharge" of its budgetary duties. The Court of Auditors assists the Parliament and Council in these tasks, which are reasonably routine. Parliament has refused to discharge the Commission, resulting in tighter controls thereafter. Parliament's power over the purse is increasing and its President reportedly remarked: "As long as Parliament does not have more power in other fields, there will be conflicts on the budget." Under the Reform Treaty Parliament obtains considerably more power over the budget.

THE EUROPEAN COURT OF JUSTICE AND COURT OF FIRST INSTANCE

The European Court of Justice is to ensure that in the interpretation and application of the Treaty of Rome "the law" is observed. The Court has construed this assignment to include enforcement of international and customary law as well as regional law. The Court of Justice has also created new law, such as in the area of fundamental human rights, by analyzing the "general principles of law common to member states." This development is consistent with (but not specifically authorized by) the 1977 Joint Declaration on Fundamental Rights of the Council, Commission and Parliament. The Declaration commits Europe to safeguarding representative democracy, the rule of law, social justice and respect for human rights, principles also embodied in the EU Charter of Fundamental Rights and Freedoms (2000).

ECJ Procedures

Twenty-seven Justices (one from each state) comprise the European Court of Justice in Luxembourg.

They are appointed for six year terms by the common accord of the member states and are routinely reappointed to the Court. Most of the Justices and most of the lawyers appearing before the Court (who must be members of the national bars) have been trained in the civil not common law tradition. This imparts a distinctly Continental approach to the Court's procedures and the style of its opinions. For example, the *Court* (not the parties) may call witnesses, hire experts, and order documents produced (limited cross-examination rights are permitted). Thus, appeals to the European Court of Justice can review questions of both law and fact.

The Court has several Advocates–General, a position not found in Britain or the United States. These are civil service lawyers who evaluate cases before the Court and give advice in public opinions. The Court receives written and oral argument by counsel, and then hears the opinion of the Advocate–General, which it may adopt or reject. Lawyers working with European law often refer to such opinions for more extensive legal and policy reasoning than ordinarily appears in the judgments of the European Court. Advocate–General opinions are especially helpful in attempting to project trends or new developments in the law, since they often raise hypotheticals extending beyond the facts of the case.

The brief judgments of the Court of Justice are written in the civil law tradition without dissenting opinions, thus masking divisions within the Court. The Court of Justice has demonstrated a preference for following and citing its own precedents, but has not hesitated to reverse itself as needed. Americans may be comfortable with this approach, but it has caused some consternation in British circles where a strict attitude toward the binding nature of precedent prevails and nothing less than amazement on the Continent.

Linkage with National Courts

The Court is independent of other European institutions and of the member states. It acts in a number of different capacities—civil, administrative, constitutional—and has jurisdiction over European matters throughout the member states. The Court has a powerful voice in the interpretation of regional law. National courts must observe and enforce European law, but the Court of Justice is its final arbiter. Perhaps the most useful channel for assuring this result is the ability of the Court to give "preliminary rulings" on questions referred directly to it by any court of a member state. Lower courts may in their discretion (not the litigants' prerogative) make such references. Courts of last resort in the member states *must* refer regional legal issues to the European Court of Justice. However, courts of last resort sometimes avoid references by invocation of the French administrative law doctrine of "acte clair" or its equivalent. They argue that the law is so clear as to not warrant a referral. This doctrine has now been refined and adopted by the European Court as part of its law.

Power Struggles and Member State Prosecutions

The Court is frequently called upon to review acts or the failure to act of regional institutions. Interested persons, member states and other institutions may raise such challenges before the Court. But the Parliament can as a rule only challenge failures to act, not the myriad of legislative and administrative acts pouring forth from the Council and Commission. Appeals to annul existing acts are limited. For example, the party against whom a Commission law enforcement decision (including decisions to impose fines or penalties) is taken may appeal to the Court. And Europe's institutions can litigate their power struggles before the Court by challenging regulations, directives, decisions and failures to act. These struggles have led to a series of provocative cases entitled Commission v. Council, Parliament v. Council, etc.

National courts and law enforcement institutions are responsible for implementing judgments of the Court of Justice, e.g., collection of fines and penalties levied under competition law against enterprises. When a member state refuses to comply with European law, the Court is often called on to render judgment against that state in actions commenced by the Commission. Its opinions have authority and respect, but prior to 1993 no practical means of enforcement against member states. Noncompliance is a problem, and states have been known to exhaust all their appeal rights and drag their feet before complying. The Maastricht Treaty on European Union authorizes the Court to levy fines and penalties against recalcitrant member states. The first such fine was levied against Greece for failure to implement an insurance directive.

Court of First Instance

The European Court of First Instance (CFI) was authorized by Single European Act amendments to the Treaty of Rome in 1987. The CFI is "attached" to the European Court and its jurisdiction is limited to actions or proceedings by individuals or legal persons. Thus the Court of First Instance cannot hear prosecutions of member states by the Commission, references of European legal issues from national courts, nor challenges of Council or Commission acts or failures to act when these are initiated by member states or other regional institutions. It can hear such challenges and related "pleas of illegality" when they are privately initiated. Additional grants of jurisdiction to the CFI cover the dumping and external subsidies law fields.

The purpose, in general, behind creation of the Court of First Instance (CFI) was to relieve the European Court of some of its caseload. It commenced doing this in November of 1989. However, there is a right of appeal on points of law from the CFI to the European Court. The Council Decision establishing the CFI indicates that such appeals lie on grounds of lack of competence, procedural failures that adversely affect the appellants' interests, and infringement of European law by the CFI. Any failure by the CFI to follow prior ECJ decisions could amount to such an infringement.

Judges of the European Court of Justice and Court of First Instance are of noted caliber and the court is held in high esteem.

THE NATURE OF EUROPEAN LAW

The treaties establishing the European communities and European Union are more than international treaties among contracting sovereign states. They transfer sovereign rights concerning legislative, administrative and judicial powers from member states to regional institutions. For example, the EC Treaty grants the power to enter into international agreements and treaties. In areas where member states have clearly transferred "competence" to the region, international agreements may be made only by the European Union. Since the EC Treaty is broad in scope and more transfers of competence occur each year, this theoretically amounts to a substantial transfer of national sovereignty.

European law includes the EC, EURATOM and TEU treaties and all subordinate legislation made thereunder. Member states have adopted much of this law as national law. For example, upon the entry of the United Kingdom, the UK Parliament enacted the European Communities Act of 1972. Section 2(1) of that Act provides that "all such rights, powers, liabilities, obligations ... created or arising by or under the Treaties ... are without further enactment to be given legal effect ... in the United Kingdom".

Regulations and Directives

Europe's institutions normally legislate through regulations and directives. The EC Treaty empowers both the Council and the Commission, or (less frequently) the Commission acting with Council authority or the Council and the Parliament acting together, to create such law in most areas of regional policy. A regulation has general application, is binding in its entirety, and is applicable directly in all member states. Regulations are self-executing and create rights and obligations for member states, and for their citizens as well. Most regulations concern the common agricultural policy, but they are also important in competition law.

A directive is binding, as to intended result and timing, upon the member state to which it is addressed but leaves to the state the choice of form and method of implementation. Thus, member states must enact or amend their laws or regulations, or do whatever is needed, to carry out directives. Directives have frequently been used to harmonize national policies of concern to the Common Market, e.g., tax systems, company law, customs, investment control, mobility of labor, recognition of professionals, products liability (using a strict liability standard), environmental law, etc.

Doctrine of Direct Effect

European law can affect citizens of member states directly without the intervention of the national legislatures of the member states. This is only true of *directly effective* law. National courts are obliged to enforce directly effective European law, and citizens may invoke such law in national courts. EC regulations are always directly applicable. The Court of Justice ultimately determines which of the many Treaty terms, international treaty obligations and Council directives are directly effective law. It has, for example, decided that equal pay for equal work is a directly effective Treaty provision. This decision allows individuals to challenge pay discrimination in public and private sector jobs. A flight attendant for Sabena Airlines was thus able to allege illegal discrimination on the basis of regional law before a Belgian work tribunal. Indeed, European law in this area enshrines the principle of "comparable worth," a controversial issue in United States employment law.

Directives issued to implement the equal pay for equal work mandate job classifications to measure the comparable worth of one job with another. The Commission successfully enforced one such directive in a prosecution before the European Court of Justice against the United Kingdom. The British Sex Discrimination Act of 1975 did not meet the directive's standards because employers could block the introduction of job classification systems. Danish law's failure to cover non-unionized workers also breached the directive on equal pay for equal work. Dutch law allowing for compulsory retirement of women at age 60 and men at age 65 violated the directive. But implementation of these directives under German law, notably by constitutional provisions, sufficed to meet regional standards. The case law on equal pay and (more broadly) equal treatment is vast.

The Court of Justice has consistently held that when Treaty provisions are clearly defined and intended to impose concrete legal obligations and rights upon individuals, member states and regional institutions, they are directly effective law. Various EC Treaty provisions concerning tariffs, quotas, state monopolies, competition, nondiscrimination on grounds of nationality and others have been held to have this effect. Such provisions can be contrasted with the more numerous "aspirational" Treaty terms which do not establish directly effective legal norms. Similar criteria govern the legal consequences of international treaty obligations and regional directives. The Court has held, for example, that Article XI of GATT (which broadly prohibits quotas in international trade) is binding but not directly effective law. In the Court's view, GATT rules were not intended to create legal rights and obligations for individuals, only governments. Thus a Dutch importer could not challenge regulations applying quotas to apples from outside the Common Market.

National Legal Remedies for Directly Effective Law

Directly effective European law conveys at the national level immediate legal rights and obligations. What remedies can be secured in national courts and tribunals when regional law has these effects? The Treaty of Rome does not provide a ready answer. In general, the Court of Justice has held that directly effective rights must be enforceable in the national courts by means of remedies that are real, effective and nondiscriminatory. Interim or preliminary judicial and administrative remedies may be required to protect directly effective rights when national *or* regional law is challenged.

In a major decision, *Francovich*, the Court of Justice has ruled that member state liability for damages to individuals caused by the state's infringement of European law is inherent in the scheme of the Treaty of Rome. This obligation follows from member state duties under Article 10 to ensure fulfillment of European law. The case involved an Italian failure to implement a directive on employee benefits in the event of insolvency. Whether or not the unimplemented directive is of direct effect does not matter, and faulty implementation or retention of contrary domestic law also gives rise to state liability whenever three conditions are met: (1) the law infringed is intended to confer individual rights; (2) the infringement is sufficiently serious; and (3) there is a direct causal link between the breach and damages sustained. Member state liability generally tracks Community tort liability under Article 288 and also extends to administrative acts and omissions. In a second major decision, *Kobler*, the Court of Justice has held that member states can be liable to individuals for damages when their *national courts* exceptionally breach EU law.

EU LAW ENFORCEMENT

Both the Council and the Commission are empowered to render law enforcement decisions, which are binding upon the persons addressed. The Commission undertakes most prosecutions for violations of European law by member states, institutions, individuals and enterprises. Such decisions, and regulations and directives, must state the reasons upon which they are based. They are subject to judicial review by the European Court of Justice or Court of First Instance.

Grounds for Appeal

In the exercise of its power of review, the Court may declare a Council or Commission act void on four grounds: (1) lack of competence; (2) infringement of an essential procedural requirement; (3) infringement of the Treaty or any rule of law relating to its application; and (4) misuse of powers. These grounds for appeal originate in French administrative law, which should be consulted to amplify their meaning. They also illustrate the significance of different official languages to the law. When first commenced, English was not an official language of the Common Market. Attorneys operating prior to 1973 (the membership date of the UK and Eire) worked in German, Dutch, Italian and French.

It is standard procedure in analyzing European law to compare text in various official languages to uncover nuances and arguments not always apparent in English. This is especially helpful when dealing with pre–1973 law (now officially translated into English), including the Treaties. For example, the appeal ground translated from as "misuse of powers" is much better understood as "détournement de pouvoir", a narrow term of art in French administrative law. Furthermore, "misuse of powers" (a term of art in British administrative law), while broader than "détournement de pouvoir," is not as broad as "abuse of powers or abuse of discretion" in United States law. Hence, American attorneys should avoid projections of their legal concepts into European law.

Supremacy

If a conflict arises between regional law and the domestic law of a member state, the Court of Justice has held that the former prevails. The Treaty binds member states in an identical way, not subject to the particularities of domestic law. There is no supremacy clause, but the Court has ruled that *supremacy of European law* is absolutely necessary to make the Common Market work and is implied by the very existence and structure of the EC Treaty. For the most part, national courts have followed this interpretation, which invalidates conflicting national law. However, several national courts have held that conflicts between European law and national *constitutional* rights should be resolved in favor of the latter. These rulings have not significantly affected the operation of the Common Market, but serve as a reminder that its law on human rights needs development.

It is often said that the doctrines of direct effect and supremacy represent the twin pillars of the European Court's integrationist jurisprudence. Without the cooperation of national courts, especially in using the preliminary ruling reference procedure and in following the rulings of the Court, this jurisprudence would lack widespread, effective implementation.

European law and domestic law co-exist in the sense that they are both enforced through the national courts. It is even possible for regional law and domestic law to apply simultaneously in connection with the same business transaction (possibly causing multiple liabilities), but only to the extent that uniform implementation of European law is not prejudiced. For example, certain rights and powers came into question because of a Council regulation which made it obligatory upon member states to install recording tachygraphs on trucks. The United Kingdom government failed to make such installation mandatory. The Commission issued a decision ordering the installation, but the UK government did not comply. The Commission brought the matter before the Court of Justice. The UK government argued that: (a) to introduce mandatory legislation would cause political difficulties and great economic damage; (b) the costs were prohibitive compared with benefits; and (c) the regulation should not apply to trucks not involved in international trade because no other member states would be prejudiced. The Court rejected all these arguments and considered them directly contrary to the legal force of an EC regulation. That the objectives of the regulation could have been achieved by other means was irrelevant.

FREE MOVEMENT OF GOODS

The Treaty of Rome attempts to achieve free movement of goods by establishment of a customs union to eliminate, between the member states, customs duties and all other charges having "equivalent effect." This elimination applies both to goods having their origin within member states and to those emanating from elsewhere which are in "free circulation." Thus, potatoes from Canada in free circulation in Britain may not be subjected to Irish import licenses. The elimination of internal tariffs was actually completed ahead of schedule, and is being phased in for new members.

A common customs tariff (CCT) with the outside world has also been established. This was originally derived by arithmetically averaging the tariffs of the member states. CCT customs duties are now negotiated by reciprocal agreement with third countries, most often through the GATT by the Commission. The combined effect of the removal of internal tariffs and the creation of the CCT has been to increase trade among member states and reduce trade with non-member states. For example, Britain's trade with Europe increased from 33 to 41 percent of its total trade volume in the first eight years of membership. This increase came largely at the expense of Britain's formerly extensive Commonwealth trade.

Quantitative restrictions on imports between member states and measures having an equivalent effect are also prohibited. A number of Commission directives and Court rulings have stringently enforced this provision against trading rules even remotely capable of hindering regional trade. For example, the Court of Justice ruled that the Belgian Royal Decree mandating cubic package sales of margarine was a measure equivalent to a quantitative restriction upon imports because of its capacity to hinder trade.

Cassis Formula

In a famous case, the Court of Justice held that Belgium could not block the importation via France of Scotch whiskey lacking a British certificate of origin as required by Belgian customs law. The Court of Justice decided that any national rule directly or indirectly, actually or potentially capable of hindering internal trade is generally forbidden as a measure of equivalent effect to a quota. However, *if* European law has not developed appropriate rules in the area concerned (here designations of origin), the member states may enact "reasonable" and "proportional" (no broader than necessary) regulations to ensure that the public is not harmed. Products meeting reasonable national criteria may be freely traded elsewhere in the region. This *Cassis* formula is the origin of the innovative "mutual reciprocity" principle used in significant parts of the single market legislative campaign.

The Court has used a Rule of Reason analysis for national fiscal regulations, public health measures, laws governing the fairness of commercial transactions, and consumer protection. Environmental protection and occupational safety laws of the member states have been similarly treated. Under this approach, for example, a Danish "bottle bill" requiring returnable soft drink and beer containers was generally upheld. The Danes successfully argued that this law was environmentally necessary and reasonable.

The Court of Justice has made it clear that all of the Rule of Reason justifications for national laws are temporary. Adoption of Common Market legislation in any of these areas would eliminate national authority to regulate trading conditions. These judicial mandates, none of which are specified in the Treaty of Rome, vividly illustrate the powers of the Court of Justice to expansively interpret the Treaty and to rule on the validity under regional law of national legislation affecting internal trade in goods.

Nontariff trade barriers (NTBs) are frequently the subject of intense negotiation and remain the most troublesome feature of the customs union. Some progress has been made. For example, various directives have reduced NTBs in the auto industry, e.g., safety plate glass standards, minimum axle strength, etc. Automobiles meeting these standards can be freely sold. Progress in other areas has been less visible and endless national rules on safety, health, the environment, standards, taxation and the like continue to inhibit a completely free trade of goods.

Exceptions to Free Movement

While not intended to promote or justify NTBs, the free movement of goods within the Common Market is qualified by the Treaty of Rome. National prohibitions or restrictions on imports and exports may be justified on grounds of public morality, public policy or public security, including: health and safety laws, measures to safeguard national treasures, and industrial and commercial property protection laws. However, such prohibitions or restrictions may not "constitute a means of arbitrary discrimination or a disguised restriction on trade between member states." The public health "escape clause" has attracted headlines in some culturally symbolic litigation. Germany sought to invoke it to keep out beer from other member states that did not meet its "pure" standards. Likewise, Italy tried to block trade in impure pasta (pasta not made with durum wheat). The European Court had relatively little trouble in rejecting these arguments. Free internal trade prevailed.

INTELLECTUAL PROPERTY

The Court of Justice has frequently issued significant opinions concerning industrial and intellectual property rights. Such rights are territorially based.

Thus, traditionally, a U.S. manufacturer will typically hold a basket of national patent, copyright and trademark rights in the Common Market. However, it is now possible to obtain an EU trademark. The territoriality of IP rights threatens free trade within the Common Market because manufacturers can often sue for infringement and other relief in the national courts whenever goods to which those rights apply cross borders. However, the Court has in most cases eliminated this possibility in favor of greater "intrabrand" trade and competition.

Exhaustion Doctrine

Patented, copyrighted and trademarked goods, once sold in the Common Market with authorization, are said to "exhaust" the intellectual property rights with which they are associated. In the Court's view, blocking parallel imports through infringement actions was not intended to be part of the package of essential rights given by national laws. Even if so intended (as seems likely), the Court has ruled that the exercise of these rights would often amount to a means of arbitrary discrimination or disguised restrictions on trade. Thus, existing legal rights have been modified by the Court to promote the goal of Common Market integration.

A good example of this result is *Centrafarm v. Sterling Drug* case, Eur. Comm. Rep. 1147 (1974). A New York pharmaceutical company, Sterling Drug, held patent rights for several of its products throughout Europe. The products were produced under license by subsidiaries in Britain and Germany but not Holland. In Holland, an exclusive distributorship for Sterling Drug products was established. A Dutch importer (not the exclusive distributor) purchased certain of these drugs from UK and German third party suppliers at about half the price in the Netherlands. Sterling Drug sued the importer for infringement of its Dutch patent and trademark rights. Employing the preliminary ruling procedure, the Dutch High Court (Hoge Raad) sought the opinion of the European Court on the use of clearly existing legal rights to block trade in pharmaceuticals. The Court ruled that Sterling Drug's intellectual property rights had been exhausted upon sale of the goods in the UK and Germany. The rights existed as a matter of Dutch law, but they could not be exercised as a matter of European law. To allow them to be exercised would have the practical effect of giving to Sterling Drug the power to divide upon the Common Market.

COMPUTER SOFTWARE, DATABASES AND DATA PRIVACY

Two areas of technology law of particular interest to U.S. firms have been legislated amidst controversy and a blitz of American lobbying. Council Directive 91/250 requires member states to protect computer programs by copyright, something not all EU jurisdictions did. However, its rules on "decompilation" (reverse engineering) for purposes of interoperability with an independently created program are liberal by U.S. standards. There is a specific right to "observe, study or test the functioning of the program in order to determine the ideas and principles that underlie any element of the program." However, decompilation may not be used for the development, production and marketing of a substantially similar computer program. The directive takes no position on the patentability of computer software. Directive 96/9 protects databases. It creates exclusive rights to databases not otherwise copyrightable.

Council Directive 95/46 concerns data privacy. It details extensive rights for individuals concerning the processing of personal data, including website registrations. Individuals have broad rights to be informed of proposed usages, deny disclosure, require corrections, and, particularly, to object to "direct marketing" use of their data. Violation of these rights can result in public prosecutions and private actions by e-commerce consumers in their country of residence. The directive prohibits the transfer of personal data to non-EU countries unless they ensure "an adequate level of protection" of EU-sourced data. The adequacy of United States protection has been hotly debated. By agreement in 2000, U.S. companies processing EU data may seek "safe harbor" from the directive by submitting to U.S. Federal Trade Commission jurisdiction over approved self-regulating U.S.-based privacy organizations (e.g. BBB Online). A goodly number of firms, including Microsoft, have done so.

FREE MOVEMENT OF WORKERS

The Treaty of Rome distinguishes the "free movement of workers" (blue collar workers and artisans) from the "right of establishment" and "freedom to provide services." Regarding workers, the Treaty prohibits any discrimination based on nationality between workers of the member states as regards employment, remuneration and other conditions of work and employment. This is subject to limitations justified upon grounds of public policy, security or health, and *excludes* the public service. In general, the exceptions to the right of free movement of workers have been limited strictly by the Court of Justice. Restraints based on prior convictions, for example, cannot justify exclusion of a worker unless there is an immediate threat of criminal behavior.

A Council regulation clarifies the rights of workers' families. It provides that workers from other member states must enjoy the same social and tax advantages, the same access to vocational schools and training centers, and the same right to join labor unions and to receive housing as do citizens of the host member state. Social security and pension rights have also been safeguarded by Council regulation. As a result, workers may move freely from job to job within the region and then retire with full pension benefits in their home country.

It is illegal for a member state, despite a pledge to maintain full employment for its citizens, to institute quotas or work permit requirements for incoming citizens of other member states. The existence of such a prohibition may well intensify job restrictions upon migrants from non-member states, e.g., the large numbers of Turks in Germany or Algerians and Moroccans in France. There are also Council directives dealing with unemployment and safeguarding the rights of employees when businesses are transferred. The extensive provision for European workers' rights has no counterpart in NAFTA.

RIGHT OF ESTABLISHMENT

Free movement of self-employed persons and of services across member state boundaries is aided by the right of establishment. The freedom of establishment includes the right to take up and pursue business activities throughout the Common Market under the same conditions laid down for nationals. It includes the right of self-employed persons to set-up and manage undertakings, branches, agencies or subsidiaries. Differences in company law have, to some degree, inhibited exercise of the right of establishment. To remove these inhibitions, the Council and Commission have embarked on a program of directives intended to harmonize the company laws of member states. This effort, insofar as it applies to the self-employed, has had mixed results. The right of establishment is perhaps most evidently exercised by restaurant owners who have opened for business in other states. It has also been invoked by professionals moving within Europe.

FREEDOM TO PROVIDE SERVICES

Restrictions on the freedom to provide services across borders without local establishment are being abolished progressively, and the Treaty of Rome contains a grant of authority to extend the relevant provisions to non-member state nationals. Removal of restrictions has been relatively simple where the subject activity is much the same in each member state. For example, the Council has adopted directives about freedom to supply services in the case of travel agents, tour operators, air brokers, freight forwarders, ship brokers, air cargo agents, shipping agents, and hairdressers. Similarly, it has been relatively easy to deal with those professions (e.g., medicine and accounting) in which diplomas and other evidence of formal qualifications relate to equivalent competence in the same skill. It did, however, take 17 years to negotiate the directive on free movement of veterinarians. And litigation over the implementation of these directives continues. It took a Commission prosecution to remove the French requirement that doctors and dentists give up their home country professional registrations before being licensed in France.

Legal Profession

Where the profession is concerned with matters like law, considerable difficulty has been encountered in lifting restrictions within member states on the freedom to provide services. For example, within the legal profession there may be only a small amount of training or required knowledge held in common by a "lawyer" from a civil law jurisdiction (e.g., an avocat from France), and by a "lawyer" from a common law jurisdiction (e.g., a solicitor from England). As a result, the directive relating to lawyers' services takes a delicate approach to the question of freedom to provide legal services. The directive allows a lawyer from one member state, under that lawyer's national title (e.g., rechtsanwalt, barrister), to provide services in other member states. This has given rise to lawyer identity cards issued under the auspices of *Commission Consultative des Barreaux Europeens* (C.C.B.E.).

Admission to the practice of law is still governed by the rules of the legal profession of each member state. However, several European Court judgments have upheld the right of lawyer applicants to be free from discrimination on grounds of nationality, residence or retention of the right to practice in home jurisdictions. By joining the bar in another country, lawyers acquire the right to establish themselves in more than one nation. This right is now generally secured by a directive providing for the mutual recognition of all diplomas after three years of study. However, host country competence tests and additional training in the law of that country may still be required. In 1997, the long-awaited right of establishment directive was adopted. It mirrors much of the prior law, but makes it easier to join local bars after three years of sustained practice in the local state.

The multinational law firm, pioneered by Baker and McKenzie in the United States, has only a few regional counterparts in the practice of European law. Slowly, however, attorneys from member states are establishing affiliations and sometimes partnerships which reflect and service the economic and social integration of Europe. Ironically, one of the most rapidly integrating forces is the emergence throughout Europe of multinational accounting firms as providers and employers of legal services. Such growth is hampered in the United States by rules against unauthorized practice of law. "European law firms" often compete with existing branches of U.S. multinational firms for the lucrative practice of Common Market law.

BROADCASTING

The broadcasting directive provides that "when practicable," broadcasters (many of which are government-owned) should reserve a majority of their time for programs of European origin. Europeans refer to this language as a "political commitment," not a binding rule of law. Either way, it is more restrictive than meets the eye because broadcast time devoted to news, sports events, games, advertising and teletext services is excluded when measuring compliance. Moreover, no member state may reduce the percentage of broadcast time allotted to European works from that which existed in 1988.

The rules of origin for television programs focus on producer citizenship and production costs, not cultural content. A work is "European" if it is made by producers in a member state, supervised and actually controlled by producers there or the contribution of European co-producers to the cost is "preponderant." Many U.S. firms have moved quickly into co-productions intended to qualify as European under the broadcasting directive. This directive, when first proposed, contained an absolute requirement of more than 50 percent European broadcasting content. Intense lobbying by the United States, a major exporter of films and TV shows to Europe, introduced the "when practicable" limitation. Nevertheless, the long-term goal of broadcasting European television productions at least half the time is clearly stated and is being actively pursued.

FREE MOVEMENT OF CAPITAL

The Treaty of Rome requires the removal of national restrictions on the free movement of capital belonging to persons of member states to the extent necessary to insure the proper functioning of the Common Market. However, member states were initially just required to be "as liberal as possible" in granting authorizations under national exchange controls for capital transfers. The free movement of personal and investment capital should be distinguished from the free movement of payments necessary to trade. Current payments are, as a rule, treated more liberally and indeed are essential to the free movement of goods and services in the Common Market.

The free movement of capital goals of the Treaty of Rome were much delayed. It was not until the implementation of the Europe without internal frontiers campaign that new legislative acts firmly entrenched the right of individuals and companies to move capital across borders without substantial limitation. Short term monetary and exchange rate national safeguards are preserved, but subject to Commission controls. Capital movements to and from Europe as a whole are expected to be similarly liberalized. This capital movements legislation, when combined with the various banking reforms, promises to bring forth a remarkable new financial sector.

Late in 1991 an historic agreement was reached at the Maastricht Summit to establish a common currency governed by a European central bank. To participate, member states had to meet relatively strict economic criteria. The common currency (the EURO) took effect in 1999 for eleven nations. Britain, Denmark and Sweden negotiated special rights to participate only when and if they wish. Greece, Malta, Slovenia and Cyprus subsequently qualified for the "EURO zone".

COMMON TRANSPORT POLICY

The Common Transport Policy envisioned by the Treaty of Rome has taken a long time to materialize. The European Court of Justice ruled in 1985 that the state of the overall transport policy amounted to a "failure to act" by Council in violation of the Treaty. This ruling was sought by the European Parliament and promised greater development in the future.

A major issue is when transport may be operated within a member state by a national of another member state. The Commission has considered a general policy covering all aspects of transport (including ships and airlines), but a piece-meal approach has proved more practicable. Progress has been by small steps, representing difficult negotiations and compromises within the Council. By the end of 1992, for example, truckers were able to move freely without quotas. Directives have been issued to abolish discriminations arising from different road transport rates and from conditions applied to like goods in like circumstances. Directives deal also with common rules for international road carriage, restrictions upon drivers' hours, and installation of tachygraphs that record such hours. Differences among the member states about road taxes, and truck weights and dimensions have been mostly resolved. Considerable progress has also been made on liberalizing air, rail and sea transport.

COMMON AGRICULTURAL POLICY

The special place of agriculture within the Common Market has led to the creation of the controversial Common Agricultural Policy (CAP). The objectives of the CAP stated in the Treaty of Rome include the increase of productivity, the maintenance of a fair standard of living for the agricultural community, the stabilization of markets and the provision of consumer goods at reasonable prices. In practice, the CAP has heavily subsidized production and exports of agricultural goods, and it consumes about two-thirds of the regional budget (which is largely financed by the common customs tariff, agricultural levies and value-added tax revenues). Target prices for many commodities (e.g., grain) are established periodically and maintained through market purchases and "variable import levies." These levies are periodically changed to ensure that imports do not disrupt the CAP. They are of enormous consequence to U.S. agricultural exporters.

Equally significant are "export refunds" on agricultural commodities, refunds that affect the opportunities of U.S. exporters in other parts of the world. The United States has consistently argued that these refunds violate the GATT rules on subsidies. The results have been mixed and agricultural trade wars between the U.S. and the EU frequent. Indeed, agriculture (more than any other topic) explains why the Uruguay Round of GATT negotiations failed to reach closure on time at the end of 1990. Europeans were simply unwilling to substantially alter the CAP.

In most years, the net effect of the CAP is to substantially raise European food prices above world price levels. The CAP has also generated a significant amount of fraud to obtain subsidy payments. Despite its costs, the CAP is one of the political cornerstones of the European Union.

France and Italy might not have joined without it, the new Central European states eagerly look forward to it, and Germany (joined to a lesser extent by the UK) continues to pay heavily for it. On the other hand, Germany is the major beneficiary of industrial free trade in the Common Market.

Like the United States, Europe seems unable to effectively control the level of its agricultural subsidies, resulting in overproduction ("butter mountains", "wine lakes") and frequent commodity trade wars. More recently, the Europeans adopted rules designed ultimately to reduce agricultural expenditures by linking total expenditures to the rates of economic growth, establishing automatic price cuts when production ceilings are reached, and creating land set-aside and early retirement programs for farmers. These rules are reinforced by the 1994 WTO Agreement on Agriculture and the reality of the need to reform the CAP prior to full integration of Poland, Hungary and other new member states.

ENVIRONMENTAL POLICY

For many years, environmental law was a stepchild of European integration. The Treaty of Rome of 1957 did not expressly authorize or anticipate such a policy. Clearly, however, differing national standards on the environment can have a substantial impact on the functioning of the Common Market. As environmental politics (remember the Green Party) and consciousness came of age in Western Europe, initial environmental efforts rested on Article 94 (harmonization) and Article 308, the Treaty's "necessary and proper" powers clause. The first Environmental Action Program commenced in 1973. Europe is now embarked on its sixth such program covering 2001–2010. Hundreds of environmental legislative acts have been adopted, including a 2003 decision to use criminal law sanctions in the environmental arena. The Commission has noted at length, however, that there are serious problems with national implementation (or the lack thereof) of regional environmental law.

TAXATION

The Treaty of Rome deals with many other areas of economic and social life in member states. These include taxation, which must neither be discriminatory nor protective as between products of different member states. With considerable effort the Europeans have adopted a common tax system—*value-added taxation*. But different revenue needs and tax policies cause different levels of VAT to apply to like items in the various member states. In the UK, for example, VAT had generally been collected at one "egalitarian" rate. In France, on the other hand, different levels of VAT apply to basic goods, middle level items and luxuries. Negotiations to harmonize VAT levels and agreements on the goods and services to which they should apply have progressed slowly.

Many consider the ability of Europe to achieve a consensus as to the proper levels of VAT and excise taxation, or at least to reduce the degree of differences in such taxation among the member states, to be the litmus test of the campaign for a fully integrated market. The Council has agreed to the gradual alignment of VAT rates around a standard rate band. At this point Denmark and Sweden have the highest 25 percent VAT rates with Luxembourg the lowest at 15 percent. VAT is now collected on the Internet sales and services, including digital downloads. The tax frontiers have been eliminated by imposing VAT reporting and collection duties on importers and exporters using the destination principle on VAT rates. The excise tax frontier has been eliminated by moving to a system of interlinked bonded warehouses between which goods can move easily. As with the VAT, excise taxation follows the destination principle. The Commission would prefer taxation on the basis of origin principles.

TRADE RELATIONS

The Treaty of Rome requires member states to coordinate and implement a *common commercial policy* toward non-member states. This policy is based upon uniform principles regarding tariff and trade agreements, fishing rights, export policy and other matters of external concern. The EU, for example, regularly negotiates as a bloc within the GATT and WTO and subscribes to various GATT Codes (e.g., the Dumping and Subsidies Codes) and GATT programs (e.g., the generalized system of tariff preferences for developing countries).

The European Union has established special tariff and commodity support preferences for third world nations (mostly former colonies) participating in the Lomé/Cotonou Conventions. These Conventions establish innovative commodity export earnings protection programs known as STABEX and MINEX. The Union also has negotiated preferential trade treaties with Mediterranean basin nations, much as the United States has done in the Caribbean basin. Europe's trade relations can create duty free import opportunities for goods originating in favored nations.

The Commission generally negotiates common external commercial policies, subject to a mandate from and ultimate control by the Council. Throughout 1986, for example, Europe and the United States vigorously disputed the amount of trade compensation that the U.S. was entitled to under the GATT as a result of the expansion of the Common Market to include Spain and Portugal. After a series of threats and counterthreats to increase tariffs, this dispute was finally resolved mainly by preserving substantial U.S. agricultural exports to Spain. United States officials dealt primarily with Commissioners and staff in reaching this accord. Similar negotiations were replayed in 1995 when Austria, Finland and Sweden joined the Union, and again with the 12 member states acceding in 2004/2007.

JURISDICTION AND ENFORCEMENT OF JUDGMENTS

The European Union has adopted a convention of considerable importance to international traders: the Convention on Jurisdiction and Enforcement of Judgments in Civil and Commercial Matters (1968). The Enforcement of Judgments Convention is an extremely detailed agreement generally allowing enforcement of civil and commercial judgments of the courts of the member states in the courts of other member states. Under the Lugano Convention, its scope now reaches Switzerland and other non-members.

The Judgments Convention *denies* enforcement by European domiciliaries against European domiciliaries of certain judgments deemed to be based on "extraordinary jurisdiction" (e.g., French jurisdiction based solely on French citizenship of the plaintiff). But, in a discriminatory measure of importance, it permits European domiciliaries to enforce judgments based on extraordinary jurisdiction against non-European domiciliaries e.g., U.S. companies. The Enforcement of Judgments Convention has been extensively construed by the European Court of Justice, and is now embodied in an EU regulation.

BUSINESS ORGANIZATIONS LAW

The cumulative effect which European Union law has had upon persons doing business with or within member states is very substantial. Special attention should be paid to the Common Market rules on competition ("antitrust") outlined in the *International Business Transactions in a Nutshell*. This section briefly surveys company and securities law.

Several important directives have been adopted in the securities field. These concern admission of securities to stock exchange listings, the issuance of a prospectus, regular information disclosures by publicly traded firms, market abuses and insider trading. This directive prohibits trading on the basis of inside information by primary and secondary insiders. Inside information is defined as non-public information which if made public would be "likely to have a significant effect on the price" of securities. Many perceive that the insider trading directive closely parallels U.S. securities' law principles.

The Council has adopted a number of non-controversial directives advancing company law. The first sets out requirements for standardization of liability (including pre-incorporation liability) of companies and publication of particulars. The second deals with the classification, subscription and maintenance of capital of public and large companies. The third concerns the internal merger of public companies. The sixth directive governs sales of assets of public companies, including certain shareholder, creditor and workers' rights. The fourth standardizes the treatment of annual accounts of public and large companies (e.g., in presentation, content, valuation and publication). In this directive, there is a permissive provision relating to inflation or current cost accounting. Accounts are to show a "true and fair view" of the enterprise. There is some doubt about the degree of relation to similar requirements of, for example, the United Kingdom accounting bodies or "generally accepted accounting practices" of the United States. The fourth directive is followed by the seventh concerning requirements for accounts of groups of companies. The eighth provides certain minimum standards and qualifications for auditors of company accounts. A much debated "Works Councils" directive requires large firms to regularly meet with and disclose critical information to employee representatives.

Other less controversial directives are also planned. The ninth directive concerns liability on the part of parent companies for the debts of subsidiaries they effectively control. The tenth directive deals with cross-border company mergers. The eleventh (adopted in 1989) involves disclosure by branches operating in other EU states, and the twelfth (also adopted in 1989) affects single member private limited liability companies. Hostile takeovers, a sensitive area, are the subject of the thirteenth company law directive. This directive requires equal treatment of shareholders and specify permissible defensive measures. It was denied in 2001 by a tie vote in Parliament, but adopted at a later stage.

Innovative EU company law includes a European Company Statute (SE) and a European Economic Interest Grouping (EEIG). The former is intended to create a corporate entity, overcoming the transnational problems associated with existing methods of incorporation and mergers among member states. The EEIG is a vehicle with legal capacity formed in the manner of an international partnership of member state companies. The EEIG is prohibited from offering proprietary interests to the public and is a nonprofit enterprise. Limited liability is not obtained. The EEIG is intended for small or medium sized research and development or marketing ventures.

SOCIAL POLICY

The Treaty of Rome is dominated by economic affairs. Nevertheless, Europe has always sought to provide for some of the concerns of the human beings who are impacted by the winds of economic change. The Treaty of Rome seeks to improve working conditions and standards of living on a harmonized basis. The right of nationals to move freely to take up employment has previously been discussed. Europe's social policy builds upon this basic right. Article 144, for example, led to the enactment of social security legislation to insure coverage for those who exercise their right to move freely to work.

A major impetus came in 1987 with the addition of Article 138 by the Single European Act. This article focuses on health and safety in the working environment. Acting by a qualified majority vote, the Council in cooperation with the Parliament is empowered to issue directives establishing minimum requirements in this field. It has done so, for example, on visual display units, heavy load handling and exposure to biological agents and carcinogens. More generally, Council directives now establish minimum safety and health requirements for most workplaces, equipment used by workers, and protective devices.

The single market campaign has a social dimension. Labor unions have been especially concerned about the prospect of "social dumping," the relocation of companies to states with weaker unions and lower wages. There is no regional legislation on minimum wages and none is expected in the near future. One response to these concerns led to the Charter of Fundamental Social Rights For Workers, adopted in 1989 by 11 member states less Britain through the European Council. The Charter proclaims the following fundamental social rights for workers:

- freedom of movement and choice of occupations;

- fair remuneration (sufficient to have a decent standard of living);

- improved living and working conditions (e.g., paid leave);

- adequate social security benefits;

- free association in unions, including the right not to join, and the right to strike;

- nondiscriminatory access to vocational training;
- equal treatment for women and men;
- development of rights to access to information, and rights of consultation and participation;
- satisfactory health and safety conditions at work;
- for the young, a minimum employment age of 15, substantial limitations on night work for those under 18, and start-up vocational training rights;
- for retirees, the right to assistance "as needed" and a decent standard of living; and
- for the disabled, assistance to integrate socially and professionally.

The Charter was to be implemented immediately by the member states in "accordance with national practices." In addition, for each item listed above, regional legislation was anticipated.

Adoption of this legislation was slow chiefly because Britain held a veto power in the Council over employment matters under the Single European Act. The Commission, however, drafted a number of Social Action Program legislative measures. One such measure guaranteeing minimum maternity leave benefits of 14 weeks at statutory sick pay rates was adopted by the Council in 1992. A woman's employment cannot be terminated because she is pregnant. In addition, pregnant women are entitled to switch from night work, exempted from work detrimental to their health, and entitled to take paid leave for pre-natal check-ups. This directive required substantial improvements to existing legislation in Ireland, Portugal and the United Kingdom. Unpaid parental leave rights are detailed in Directive 96/34.

Despite its repeated opposition to development of a "social dimension," the United Kingdom under Conservative rule adopted or implemented over half of the measures noted in the Social Charter. What the Conservatives consistently objected to were rules relating directly to the employee-employer relationship, not worker benefits such as pregnancy leave or health or safety measures. Nevertheless, the Court of Justice repeatedly ruled against Britain in litigation challenging the adequacy of its implementation of worker-related directives (e.g., on collective redundancies (mass layoffs) and transfers of enterprises). And, in a major decision, the Court ruled over vehement objection that the "working time" directive (No. 93/104) was properly adopted by qualified majority vote on the basis of Article 138's authorization of worker health and safety law. This ruling had the practical effect of avoiding Britain's opt out rights. The directive creates, inter alia, a minimum right to four weeks of paid vacation.

EQUAL PAY AND EQUAL TREATMENT

Article 141 is a prominent element in European social policy. It is derived from International Labor

Organization Convention No. 100 which three states, including France, had adopted by 1957. The French were rightfully proud of this tradition of nondiscrimination between the sexes on pay. They also appreciated that gender-based inequality in pay in other member states could harm the ability of their companies to compete. Article 141 thus enshrines the principle that men and women shall receive equal pay for equal work.

Council Directive 75/117 (now Directive 2006/54) complements Article 141. It makes the principle of equal pay apply to work of equal value (to the employer), a principle now expressly incorporated in Article 141 since 1999. This mandates establishment of nondiscriminatory job classifications to measure the comparable worth of one job with another. The Commission successfully enforced Directive 75/117 in a prosecution before the European Court of Justice against the United Kingdom. The Sex Discrimination Act of 1975, adopted expressly to fulfill Article 141 obligations, did not meet European standards because employers could block the introduction of job classification systems. Danish law's failure to cover nonunionized workers also breached the equal pay directive. But its implementation under German law, notably by constitutional provisions, sufficed to meet regional standards.

The principle of equal pay for equal work has been extended to equal treatment regarding access to employment, vocational training and promotion, and working conditions (e.g., retirement deadlines). This directive (now also 2006/54) prohibits discrimination based upon sex, family or marital status and extends to the self-employed. Equal treatment is limited by three exceptions. Member states may distinguish between men and women if: (1) sex is a determining factor in ability to perform the work; (2) the provision protects women; or (3) the provision promotes equal opportunity for men and women. Discrimination is also permitted in "occupational activities" for which workers of only one sex are appropriate.

A TIMELINE OF EUROPEAN INTEGRATION

1948 — Benelux Customs Union Treaty

1949 — COMECON Treaty (Eastern Europe, Soviet Union)

1951 — European Coal and Steel Communiy ("Treaty of Paris")

1957 — European Economic Community (EE) ("Treaty of Rome") European Atomic Energy Community Treaty (EURATOM)

1959 — European Free Trade Area Treaty (EFTA)

1968 — EC Customs Union fully operative

1973 — Britain and Denmark switch from EFTA to EC; Ireland joins EEC; Norway rejects membership; remaining EFTA states sign industrial free trade treaties with EEC

1979 — Direct elections to European Parliament

1981 — Greece joins EC

1983 — Greenland "withdraw" from EC

1986 — Spain and Portugal join EC, Portugal leaves EFTA

1987 — Single European Act amends Treaty of Rome to initiate campaign for a Community without internal frontiers by 1993

1990 — East Germany merged into Community via reunification process

1991 — COMECON defunct; trade relations with Central Europe develop rapidly

1993 — Maastricht Treaty on European Union (TEU) ratified and operational, EC officially becomes EC

1994 — European Monetary Institute established

1995 — Austria, Finland, and Sweden join EU, Norway votes no again

1999 — Amsterdam Treaty ratified and operational

1999 — Common currency (EURO) managed by European Central Bank commences with 11 members

2003 — Treaty of Nice ratified and operational, draft Constitution for Europe released

2004 — Cyprus, Estonia, Slovenia, Poland, Hungary, the Czech Republic, Slovakia, Latvia, Lithuania, Malta join EU

2005 — Constitution for Europe overwhelmingly defeated in France, Netherlands

2007 — Accession of Bulgaria and Romania, Reform Treaty of Lisbon proposed

2008 — Irish voters reject Reform Treaty

2009 — Projected ratification of Reform Treaty

CHAPTER SEVEN

NAFTA AND FREE TRADE IN THE AMERICAS[1]

The evolutionary character of the free trade agreements of the United States is readily apparent. The second with Canada in 1989 was nothing less than path breaking; the most sophisticated free trade agreement in the world. This agreement provided the matrix for negotiating NAFTA, much as NAFTA creates the bulk of the framework for negotiating the Free Trade Area of the Americas (FTAA) and bilateral U.S. NAFTA–Plus agreements. Yet, for full understanding, each agreement must be viewed in its own geopolitical and economic context.

CANADA–U.S. FREE TRADE

The United States and Canada have the largest bilateral trading relationship in the world. As early as 1854, the Elgin–Marcy Treaty concluded a free trade agreement covering agriculture, resource and other primary products between the U.S. and Canadian provinces. Termination of this treaty in 1866 led to adoption of protectionist national trade policy in Canada. Canada made repeated (1891, 1896,

[1]. For much more extensive coverage, see Folsom's *NAFTA and FREE TRADE IN THE AMERICAS in a Nutshell*.

1911) unsuccessful attempts to negotiate bilateral trade agreements of various kinds with the United States. In the post World War II era, Canada was an early participant in the GATT. The GATT proved successful in expanding U.S. and Canadian trade, but by the 1980s the pace of GATT had slowed and the significance of access to the U.S. market required attention.

Prior to the Canada–U.S. Free Trade Area Agreement (CUSFTA), about 70 percent of the trade between the two nations was already duty free. Tariffs on the remaining products averaged about five percent when entering the United States and about 10 percent when entering Canada. Annual trade between the two countries was valued at more than $200 billion U.S. dollars. This is more than three times U.S.–Japan trade. Roughly one-third of all Canada–U.S. trading concerns automotive goods, an industry still largely dominated by U.S.-based companies. Canada has continued to maintain a healthy trade surplus with the United States. Free trade between the United States and Canada is based upon reciprocity and can be terminated by either party with six months notice.

THE CUSFTA AGREEMENT IN OUTLINE

Trade in Goods

The Canada–United States Free Trade Agreement covered manufactured and agricultural goods. It was generally oriented around the principle of national treatment and the Article III GATT rule to that effect was specifically incorporated in Chapter 1. Although the parties affirmed their existing trade agreements (including the GATT), if there was an inconsistency between CUSFTA and most of these agreements, it was agreed that the CUSFTA will prevail. The Provinces of Canada and the States of the U.S. must accord most-favored-treatment to goods that qualify under the CUSFTA. At Canadian insistence, "cultural industries" were specially treated, subject to a right in the other party to take measures of equivalent commercial effect in response to actions that would otherwise be inconsistent with the CUSFTA. Essentially, there was free trade in these goods, but ownership of them may be reserved to nationals and preservation of their Canadian character secured. Cultural industries are defined to include the publication, sale, distribution or exhibition of books, magazines, newspapers, films, videos, music recordings, and radio, television and cable dissemination. This exemption continues under NAFTA.

The CUSFTA did not repeal or directly amend the longstanding U.S.–Canadian Automotive Agreement (1965) under which the large majority of trading in autos and original equipment auto parts is undertaken duty free. However, a tougher 50 percent CUSFTA content rule was established for autos entering the U.S. Canada agreed to phase out its embargo on used autos by 1994. Government procurement contracts for $25,000 or more were opened to firms from both countries, but their goods must have at least a 50 percent U.S.–Canadian content. The CUSFTA expanded upon the GATT Procurement Code by creating common rules of origin, mandating an effective bid challenge system and improving the transparency of the bid process. Canada has created a Procurement Review Board before whom bid challenges based upon the CUSFTA may be made. An analysis of the decisions of this Board suggests that it provides open and effective relief.

The CUSFTA tariff removals were phased in over ten years through 1998. The most sensitive tariff reductions occurred later in the decade and these included duties on plastics, rubber, wood products, most metals, precision instruments, textiles, alcoholic beverages, consumer appliances, and agricultural and fish products. There was a petitioning procedure which permits private parties on either side of the border to seek to accelerate duty free entry in advance of 1999. This petitioning procedure was invoked to a significant degree, resulting in increased duty free trade between the United States and Canada. The CUSFTA terminated customs user fees and duty drawback programs by 1994, and duty waivers linked to performance requirements by 1988 (excepting the Auto Agreement). All quotas on imports and exports were removed unless allowed by the GATT or grandfathered by the CUSFTA.

The GATT Code on Technical Standards (1979) was reaffirmed by mutual pledges not to use product standards (health, safety and environment) as trade barriers. National treatment and mutual recognition of testing laboratories and certification bodies was required, and general commitments to harmonize federal standards as much as possible were made. A mandatory 60–day notice and comment period on proposed standards' regulations operated at all levels of government. Canada challenged the 1991 upgrading of Puerto Rico's milk standards to existing federal requirements as a violation of CUSFTA. The practical effect of this upgrading was to end Puerto Rican imports of long-life milk from Canada.

On agriculture, the CUSFTA eventually eliminated most bilateral tariffs and export subsidies, and selectively limited or removed quotas (including quotas on sugar, poultry, eggs and meat imports). The Canadians agreed to terminate import licenses for wheat, oats and barley whenever U.S. price supports for those commodities were equal or less than those in Canada. Wine and distilled spirits (but not beer) were generally opened to free and nondiscriminatory trade. Import and export restraints on energy products, including minimum export prices, were prohibited. Petroleum, natural gas, coal, electricity, uranium and nuclear fuels were covered. In short supply conditions, export quotas must be applied so as to proportionately share energy resources. There was permission to export 50,000 barrels per day of Alaskan oil to Canada, and a lengthy list of specific regulatory changes by both sides.

Rules of Origin

Either nation could invoke escape clause proceedings if there was a surge of imports resulting in injury to a domestic industry. Bilateral escape clause proceedings were eliminated after 1998. A "global" agreement altered traditional third party escape clause criteria to allow relief against CUSFTA goods only when these imports were substantial (over 10 percent of total) and contributed importantly to serious domestic injury or the threat thereof. Escape clause decisions were ultimately referred to binding arbitration if consultation between the United States and Canada did not result in a settlement.

The innovative rules of origin applicable under the Canadian–U.S. Agreement were established in Chapter 3. There were general and product-specific rules of origin. Ordinarily, goods must be either wholly-produced in the United States or Canada or (if they contain materials or components from other countries) must have undergone a transformation sufficient to result in a new designation under the Harmonized Tariff Classification System employed by both countries. This was treated as the equivalent of "substantial transformation."

In addition, regarding certain assembled products, at least 50 percent of the cost of manufacturing the goods must be attributable to U.S. or Canadian material or the direct cost of processing in the United States or Canada. Note that these rules focus on production costs. The costs of advertising, sales, profit and overhead were excluded for purposes of determining Canadian or U.S. origin. The 50 percent local content test also served as a residual rule of origin applicable whenever the required change in tariff classification was absent in certain cases (notably textiles). The Canadian–U.S. rules of origin are found in Section 202 of the United States–Canada Free Trade Area Agreement Implementation Act. Special U.S.–Canada Free Trade Agreement Certificates of Origin must be completed by exporters seeking duty free entry. United States law requires the retention of records, including these certificates, supporting CUSFTA preferential treatment for five years.

Services and Investment

Apart from reductions in tariffs, one notable feature of the Canadian–U.S. Free Trade Area Agreement was its application to services and investment. Many provisions of the Agreement sought to liberalize trade in services and investment capital flows between the two nations. In Chapter 16, traditional Canadian controls over foreign investment were substantially reduced for United States investors. In 1973 Canada enacted a restrictive investment law, the Foreign Investment Review Act (FIRA), and created a Foreign Investment Review Agency to pass upon new investment and acquisitions in Canada. The law was not as restrictive as those in the developing nations, but it did require substantial review. Joint ventures were not mandated, although the review agency often extracted local content promises before it approved new investment. That practice was condemned by the GATT after a request for review was submitted by the United States. The GATT based its decision on Article III:4 national treatment requirements.

Canada replaced the FIRA with the Investment Canada Act in 1985. This Act continues the practice of reviewing proposed investment, but review is reserved for large investments. The Act is more investment encouraging and simplifies procedures. The CUSFTA changed the extensiveness of the restrictions that are placed on U.S. investment. Canada ended review of indirect acquisitions (U.S. firms buying U.S. firms with Canadian subsidiaries), but could still require divestiture of cultural subsidiaries to Canadian owners. For direct acquisitions, thresholds were increased, time for review shortened and procedures made easier. A general rule of national treatment in establishing, acquiring, selling and conducting businesses within CUSFTA was created. Transportation investments were notably excluded from this general rule. Most investment performance requirements were banned, and profits and earnings are freely transferable.

Not all services could be freely provided across the Canadian–U.S. border under the CUSFTA. A lengthy listing of covered services is found in Annex 1408 to Chapter 14 of the Agreement. These include agriculture and forestry, mining, construction, distribution, insurance, real estate, and various commercial and professional services. Engineering and accounting services were included but transportation, legal and most medical services were not. Covered services had to be accorded national treatment and a right of establishment, except as differences were required for prudential, fiduciary, health and safety and consumer protection reasons. State, provincial and local governments must grant most favored treatment to service providers. In addition, the U.S. and Canada agreed that their licensing and certification procedures not be applied on a discriminatory basis and be based upon assessments of competence.

A general "standstill" on trade restraints applicable to services was agreed. This had the effect of grandfathering most existing restraints or discrimination. Special rules permitting temporary entry for business persons in either country supported free movement in services. Individual rules for architecture, tourism, computer services and telecommunications network services were detailed in separate annexes to the CUSFTA. Professionals, investors, traders, business visitors and executives also benefitted from a newly created temporary entry CUSFTA visa agreement.

Financial services were covered in Chapter 17 of the CUSFTA. Each side made specific commitment to alter or apply its regulatory regimes for the benefit of the other's financial services' companies. For example, the U.S. promised not to apply less favorable treatment to Canadian banks than that in effect on Oct. 4, 1987 and to grant them the same treatment accorded U.S. banks if and when the Glass–Steagall Act was amended. The continuation of multi-state branches of Canadian banks was guaranteed. Canada, for its part, removed various statutory restraints on foreign ownership of financial institutions (including insurance and trust companies) and assets' controls over foreign bank subsidiaries. Applications for entry into the Canadian financial market were treated on the same basis as Canadian applications, and U.S. banks could underwrite and deal in Canadian debt securities. All of these commitments were continued under NAFTA. Financial services' disputes are subject to formal consultation between the U.S. Treasury Department and the Canadian Department of Finance.

DISPUTE SETTLEMENT UNDER CUSFTA

Disputes under CUSFTA were handled in one of two ways. Disputes of a general nature were taken up under the GATT (now WTO) or addressed under Chapter 18, first by consultation and then by a binding arbitration panel of five independent experts. Each side chose two experts and those experts chose a fifth. Panels were formed in 1989 on salmon and herring and in 1990 on lobsters. Other trade disputes of special note focused on the allegedly low level of Canada's "stumpage fees" for timber (treated as a subsidy by the U.S.), mutual recriminations about trade restraints in beer and a ruling of the U.S. Customs Service regarding the Canadian–U.S. content of Hondas manufactured in Canada. This ruling had the effect of disqualifying these automobiles from CUSFTA tariff treatment.

Antidumping and Subsidy Disputes

Special, unique dispute settlement rules applied to antidumping and countervailing duty tariffs under Chapter 19. Basically, both nations agree to allow a binational panel to solve disputes of this kind, the governing law changing according to which is the importing country. The panels were drawn from a roster of 50 Canadian and United States citizens, a majority of whom were lawyers. Any final determination at the national level could be appealed by private or governmental parties to this panel using pleadings similar to those used in judicial proceedings. Binational panels replaced traditional judicial review of antidumping and countervailing duty orders.

The only appeal from a binational panel decision in countervailing duty and antidumping cases was to the so-called "Extraordinary Challenge Committee." This Committee was composed of ten judges or former judges from the United States and Canada. Three of these judges were chosen to hear extraordinary challenges. These could be raised only if the panel was guilty of gross misconduct, made errors in procedure, or exceeded its authority. Numerous antidumping or countervailing duty determinations had been reviewed under Chapter 19 by the end of 1994 and the arrival of NAFTA. Most of these panel decisions were unanimous.

Extraordinary Challenges

The first Extraordinary Challenge Committee decision involved U.S. countervailing duties on Canadian exports of pork. These duties and the underlying subsidy law decisions by United States agencies were challenged before a binational panel. The panel's first decision found that the International Trade Commission's domestic injury determination was based upon questionable evidence. The panel remanded the matter to the ITC for reconsideration. Upon reconsideration, the ITC again found a threat of material injury to the U.S. domestic pork industry. A second binational panel decision held that the ITC had exceeded its own notice of remand proceedings. The second panel gave a number of specific evidentiary instructions to the ITC and again remanded the proceeding. In its second remand proceeding, the ITC found no threat of material injury expressly and only because of the binding nature of the Canadian–U.S. Free Trade Area Agreement. The ITC's second remand decision bitterly denounced the binational panel's second review decision. The ITC asserted that the panel's decision violated fundamental principles of the Agreement and contained egregious errors of U.S. law.

The USTR sought review by an Extraordinary Challenge Committee. The Committee ultimately ruled that the panel's decisions did not contain gross error. The Committee therefore declared itself jurisdictionally ineligible to hear the dispute. Specifically, there was no gross error even if some of the panel's rulings might not follow U.S. rules of evidence, but cautioned the panel not to rely on extra-record evidence. There were two additional extraordinary challenges to CUSFTA Chapter 19 panel decisions. Both were raised by the United States, and in both Canada prevailed. One challenge concerned Canadian live swine exports, and the other Canadian softwood lumber exports. In the latter case, a blistering dissent by a U.S. judge serving on the ECC asserted panelist conflicts of interest and egregious errors in applying U.S. law.

NORTH AMERICAN FREE TRADE

The economic integration of Canada and the United States was a certainty. The blueprint was already there. For most Canadians and Americans, revising the design to include Mexico required considerably more effort and discomfort. The discomfort came from years of observing protectionist Mexican trade policies, uncontrolled national debt, corruption, and the sense, somehow, that Mexico just did not "fit." In the end, these perspectives were overcome.

Mexico under Presidents de la Madrid, Salinas, Zedillo, Fox and Calderon has been breaking down its trade barriers and reducing the role of government in its economy. Over half of the enterprises owned by the Mexican government a decade ago have been sold to private investors, and more are on the auction block. Tariffs have been slashed below WTO bindings and import licensing requirements widely removed. Export promotion, not import substitution, has become the highest priority. Like the U.S. and Canada, Mexico (since 1986) participates in the General Agreement on Tariffs and Trade (GATT) and World Trade Organization (WTO). This brought it into the mainstream of the world trading community on a wide range of fronts, including participation in nearly the full range of the WTO agreements.

Mexican debt, assisted by the Brady Plan with its emphasis on loan forgiveness, has become a manageable problem, although the collapse of the peso in December of 1994 and Mexico's ensuing financial crisis brought back painful memories. One party rule has ended, with signs of an increasingly pluralistic democracy on the horizon. Admittedly, political and economic corruption runs deep in Mexico, but the winds of change are blowing. Major prosecutions of leading police, union and business leaders have been undertaken. Perhaps most significantly, the rapid privatization of the state-owned sector of the economy combined with increasing tolerance of international competition has reduced not only the need for government subsidies but also the opportunity for personal enrichment by public officials.

Fast Track Negotiations

Presidents Bush and Salinas, and Prime Minister Mulroney, pushed hard in 1991 to open "fast track" negotiations (discussed in Chapter 2) for a free trade agreement. In 1992, these efforts reached fruition when a NAFTA agreement was signed by Canada, the United States and Mexico with a scheduled effective date of Jan. 1, 1994. President Bush submitted the agreement to Congress in December

1992. President Clinton supported NAFTA generally, but initiated negotiations upon taking office for supplemental agreements on the environment and labor. This delayed consideration of the NAFTA agreement in Congress until the Fall of 1993.

Ratification was considered under fast track procedures which essentially gave Congress 90 session days to either ratify or reject NAFTA without amendments. After a bruising national debate that fractured both Democrats and Republicans with each party doing its best to avoid Ross Perot's strident anti-NAFTA attacks, ratification was achieved in mid-November, just weeks before NAFTA's effective date. During this same period, Canada's Conservative Party suffered a devastating defeat at the polls. This defeat was partly a rejection by the Canadian people of the earlier ratification of NAFTA under Prime Minister Mulroney.

The United States is Mexico's largest trading partner, accounting for nearly 70 percent of all Mexican trade and more than 60 percent of its foreign direct investment. In contrast, trade with Mexico totaled only seven percent of all U.S. international trade. Those facts help explain why Mexico is the major beneficiary of the NAFTA accord.

THE NAFTA AGREEMENT IN OUTLINE

Although each partner affirms its rights and obligations under the General Agreement on Tariffs and Trade (GATT), NAFTA generally takes priority over other international agreements in the event of conflict. Certain exceptions to this general rule of supremacy apply; the trade provisions of the international agreements on endangered species, ozone-depletion and hazardous wastes notably take precedence over NAFTA (subject to a duty to minimize conflicts). Unlike the GATT, NAFTA makes a general duty of national treatment binding on all states, provinces and local governments of the three countries.

TRADE IN GOODS

Prior to NAFTA, Mexican tariffs on U.S. goods averaged about 10 percent; U.S. tariffs on Mexican imports averaged about five percent. Under NAFTA, Mexican tariffs were eliminated on all U.S. exports within 10 years except for corn and beans which were subject to a fifteen-year transition. United States tariffs on peanuts, sugar and orange juice from Mexico also lasted 15 years. Immediate Mexican tariff removals under the "A" list covered about half the industrial products exported from the United States. Further tariff eliminations occurred for the "B" list after five years and the "C" list when the treaty matured in 10 years. The existing Canada–U.S. tariff reduction schedule remained in place.

Import and export quotas, licenses and other restrictions have been eliminated under NAFTA subject to limited rights to restrain trade, e.g. to protect human, animal or plant health, or to protect the environment. Customs user fees on internal

NAFTA trade were terminated in 1999 and tariff drawback refunds or waivers removed by 2001. These changes, it is thought, discourage the creation of "export platforms" in one NAFTA country to serve markets in the other member states by insuring that non-NAFTA components and materials are tariffed. NAFTA essentially phased out maquiladora tariff preferences over seven years, notably disadvantaging producers who source heavily outside North America.

Export taxes and new waivers of customs duties are banned with few exceptions. Once goods are freely traded under NAFTA, they are subject to nondiscriminatory national treatment, including at the provincial and state levels of government. Goods sent to another NAFTA country for repair or alteration may return duty free.

Rules of Origin

NAFTA trade is subject to important "rules of origin" that determine which goods qualify for its tariff preferences. These include goods wholly originating in the free trade area. A general waiver of the NAFTA rules of origin requirements is granted if their non-regional value consists of no more than seven percent of the price or total cost of the goods. Goods containing non-regional materials are considered North American if those materials are sufficiently transformed so as to undergo a specific change in tariff classification. Some goods, like autos and light trucks, must also have a specified North American content. For example, 62.50 percent of the value of such vehicles must be North American in origin. A 60 percent regional content rule applies to other vehicles and auto parts. Starting in 2004, U.S. auto producers no longer needed to manufacture in Mexico in order to sell there.

Regional value content may be calculated in most cases either by a "transaction value" or a "net cost" method. The former avoids costly accountings and requires 60% North American content for free trade access. The latter, a 50% NAFTA content rule, is based upon the total cost of the goods less royalties, sales promotion, packing and shipping, and allowable interest. Either requires manufacturers to trace the source of non-NAFTA components and maintain source records. The net cost method must be used for regional value calculations concerning automotive goods. Uniformity of tariff classification and origin decisions is promoted by NAFTA regulations, a common Certificate of Origin, and a trilateral working group.

Special rules of origin apply to free trade in textiles and apparel under NAFTA. For most products, a "yarn forward" rule applies. This means that the goods must be produced from yarn made in a NAFTA country. A similar "fiber forward" rule applies to cotton and man-made fiber yarns. Silk, linen and certain other fabrics in short supply within NAFTA are treated preferentially, as are yarns, fabrics and apparel covered by special tariff rate quotas. Safeguard import quotas and tariffs could be imposed during the transition period if a rise in textile and apparel trade caused serious damage.

Other special rules of origin were created for electronics. For example, if the circuit board (motherboard) is made in North America and transformed in the region so as to change a tariff classification, the resulting computer may be freely traded.

Energy

Distinct rules govern energy and petrochemical products. Perhaps most notably, Mexico reserves to its state (as its Constitution provides) the oil, gas, refining, basic petrochemical, nuclear and electricity sectors. A limited range of new investment opportunities are created for non-basic petrochemicals, proprietary electricity facilities, co-generation and independent power production. As under the GATT, minimum or maximum import or export price controls are prohibited on energy products, but licensing systems may be used. Trade quotas or other restraints are permissible only in limited circumstances, e.g. short supply conditions, and a general duty of national treatment applies. Mexico, unlike Canada, has not committed itself to energy sharing during times of shortage.

Food Products

A second set of distinct rules apply to agricultural trade. These are undertaken principally through separate bilateral agreements between the U.S. and Mexico and Canada and Mexico. The United States–Mexico agreement converts all nontariff trade barriers to tariffs or tariff rate quotas. These were phased out over a maximum of 15 years. Roughly half of the bilateral trade in agriculture was made duty-free immediately. Under special rules, trade in sugar was gradually liberalized with all restraints removed over 15 years after a major dispute before the WTO. All three countries agreed to combat agricultural export subsidies, including consultation and what amounts to joint action against third-country subsidies affecting any one of their markets. Special rules of origin apply in the agricultural sector and standards on pesticide residues and inspections are being harmonized.

Another food-related issue is sanitary and phytosanitary measures against health, diseases, contaminants or additives (collectively known as SPS protection). Each country retains the right to establish its own SPS levels of protection provided they are based upon scientific principles and a risk assessment, apply only as needed and do not result in unfair discrimination or disguised restrictions on trade. Each NAFTA nation is committed to accepting the SPS measures of the others as equivalent to its own provided the exporting country demonstrates that its measures achieve the importing country's chosen level of protection. This is facilitated by procedural transparency rules requiring public notice of any SPS measure that may affect NAFTA trade. A committee on SPS measures strives to facilitate all of these principles and to resolve disputes.

Product Standards

Technical standards and certification procedures for products are classic nontariff trade barriers. The

NAFTA reaffirms each country's commitment to the GATT Agreement on Technical Barriers to Trade (1979). In addition, each must provide national treatment and most favored nation treatment. As in the food products area, international standards will be used whenever possible, but each country may have more stringent requirements and scientific justification is not mandatory. Procedural transparency rules and a committee on standards are also created. One innovation of note allows companies and other interested parties to participate directly in the development of new standards anywhere within NAFTA. All three countries agreed not to lower existing environmental, health and safety standards and to attempt to "upwardly harmonize" them.

Safeguards (Escape Clause Proceedings)

Escape clause rules and procedures are generally applicable to United States–Mexico trade under the NAFTA. These permit temporary trade relief against import surges subject to a right of compensation in the exporting nation. During a ten year transition period, escape clause relief could be undertaken as a result of NAFTA tariff reductions only once per product for a maximum in most cases of three years. The relief was the "snap-back" to pre-NAFTA tariffs. After the transition period, escape clause measures may only be undertaken by mutual consent.

If a global escape clause proceeding is pursued by one NAFTA partner, the others must be excluded unless their exports account for a substantial share of the imports in question (top five suppliers) and contribute importantly to the serious injury or threat thereof (rate of growth of NAFTA imports must not be appreciably lower than total imports). Exclusion of NAFTA partners from global escape clause remedies has been ruled invalid by the WTO Appellate Body.

Procurement

There are a variety of other areas of law impacted by the NAFTA accord. Government procurement, apart from defense and national security needs, generally follows nondiscriminatory principles on the supply of goods and services (including construction services) to federal governments. The threshold for the application of the NAFTA to such procurement is $50,000 U.S. for goods and services, and $6.5 million U.S. for construction services. When state enterprises (e.g. PEMEX and CFE), not agencies, are the buyers, thresholds of $250,000 U.S. and $8 million U.S. respectively apply. The use of offsets or other requirements for local purchases or suppliers are prohibited. Independent bid challenge mechanisms must be created by each member state and transparency in the bidding process promoted by timely release of information. These provisions are particularly important because Mexico, unlike Canada, is not a signatory to the GATT Procurement Code. They do not apply to state and local procurement.

TRADE IN SERVICES

Cross-border trade in services is subject to national treatment, including no less favorable treatment than that most favorably given at federal, state or local levels. No member state may require that a service provider establish or maintain a residence, local office or branch in its country as a condition to cross-border provision of services. However, a general standstill on existing discriminatory or limiting laws affecting cross-border services was adopted. Mutual recognition of professional licenses is encouraged (notably for legal consultants and engineers), but not made automatic. All citizenship or permanent residency requirements for professional licensing were eliminated.

Additionally, a NAFTA country may deny the benefits of the rules on cross-border provision of services if their source is in reality a third country without substantial business activities within the free trade area. For transport services, these benefits may be denied if the services are provided with equipment that is not registered within a NAFTA nation. Most air, maritime, basic telecommunications and social services are not covered by these rules, nor are those that are subject to special treatment elsewhere in the NAFTA (e.g. procurement, financing and energy). Even so, the NAFTA considerably broadens the types of services covered by free trade principles: accounting, advertising, architecture, broadcasting, commercial education, construction, consulting, enhanced telecommunications, engineering, environmental science, health care, land transport, legal, publishing and tourism. Whereas the CUSFTA allowed free trade in services only for those sectors that were positively listed in the agreement, the NAFTA adopts a broader "negative listing" approach. All services sectors are subject to free trade principles unless the NAFTA specifies otherwise.

Transport

Unlike CUSFTA, NAFTA created a timetable for the removal of barriers to cross-border land transport services and the establishment of compatible technical, environmental and safety standards. This extends to bus, trucking, port and rail services. It should eliminate the historic need to switch trailers to local transporters at the border. Cross-border truck deliveries in the border states were supposed to come on line late in 1995, but U.S. concerns about the standards of Mexican carriers and (one suspects) Teamsters Union influence have repeatedly delayed this result. After six years, truckers were supposed to be able to move freely anywhere within NAFTA. Mexico eventually won a Chapter 20 arbitration against U.S. cross-border trucking restraints, which finally at this writing appear ready to disappear. Bus services should have been totally free within three years, but got caught up in the trucking dispute. One hundred percent investment in Mexican truck and bus companies should now be possible. Investment in port services was immediately open. However, national restraints upon domestic cargo carriage (cabotage) may be retained.

Telecommunications

Public telecommunications networks and services must be opened on reasonable and nondiscriminatory terms for firms and individuals who need the networks to conduct business, such as intracorporate communications or so-called enhanced telecommunications and information services. The "reasonableness" of Telmex connection fees was hotly contested in the United States, a dispute successfully taken to the WTO. Cellular phone, data transmission, earth stations, fax, electronic mail, overlay networks and paging systems are open to Canadian and American investors, many of whom have entered the Mexican market, not always succeeding against Telmex's near monopoly power. Each NAFTA country must ensure reasonable access and use of leased private lines, terminal equipment attachments, private circuit interconnects, switching, signaling and processing functions and user-choice of operating protocols.

Conditions on access and use may only be imposed to safeguard the public responsibilities of network operators or to protect technical network integrity. Rates for public telecommunications transport services should reflect economic costs and flat-rate pricing is required for leased circuits. However, cross-subsidization between public transport services is not prohibited, nor are monopoly providers of public networks or services. Such monopolies may not engage in anticompetitive conduct outside their monopoly areas with adverse affects on NAFTA nationals. Various rights of access to information on public networks and services are established, and the NAFTA limits the types of technical standards that can be imposed on the attachment of equipment to public networks.

CROSS–BORDER INVESTMENT AND INVESTOR–STATE ARBITRATIONS

Investment in the industrial and services sectors of the NAFTA nations is promoted through rules against nondiscriminatory and minimum standards of treatment that even benefit non-NAFTA investors with substantial business operations in a NAFTA nation. For example, an Asian or European subsidiary incorporated with substantial business operations in Canada will be treated as a Canadian investor for purposes of NAFTA. Investment, for these purposes, is broadly defined to cover virtually all forms of ownership and activity, including real estate, stocks, bonds, contracts and technologies.

Investor Rights

National and most favored treatment rights apply at the federal, state and local levels of government, and to state-owned enterprises (e.g. PEMEX, Canadian National Railway Corporation). Furthermore, each country is to treat NAFTA investors in accordance with "international law," including fair and equitable treatment and full protection and security. This is known as the "minimum standard" of treatment. Performance requirements, e.g. specific export levels, minimum domestic content, domestic source preferences, trade balancing, technology transfer and product mandates are disallowed in all areas except government procurement, export promotion and foreign aid. Senior management positions may not be reserved by nationality, but NAFTA states may require that a majority of the board of directors or committees thereof be of a designated nationality or residence provided this does not impair the foreign investor's ability to exercise control. Joint ventures with local partners (common in Mexico) are no longer mandatory.

A general right to convert and transfer local currency at prevailing market rates for earnings, sale proceeds, loan repayments and other investment transactions has been established. But this right does not prevent good faith and nondiscriminatory restraints upon monetary transfers arising out of bankruptcy, insolvency, securities dealings, crimes, satisfaction of judgments and currency reporting duties. Direct and indirect expropriations (and government measures "tantamount to" expropriation) of investments by NAFTA investors are precluded except for public purposes and if done on a nondiscriminatory basis following due process of law. A right of compensation without delay at fair market value plus interest is created.

Investor–State Arbitrations

In the event of a dispute, a NAFTA investor may (and quite a few have) elect as between monetary (but not punitive) damages through binding arbitration under the ICSID[2] Convention if both nations are parties (not possible presently), the Additional Facility Rules of the ICSID if only one nation is a party to the Convention (most commonly used) or the UNCITRAL arbitration rules. An arbitration tribunal for investment disputes will be established by the Secretary–General of ICSID if the parties are unable to select a panel by choosing one arbitrator each and collaborating on or having those arbitrators choose a third. However, there are no time limits for the arbitration and either side may appeal the award to the courts of the arbitration's situs, typically chosen with a view towards neutrality by the arbitrators. Alternatively, the investor may pursue judicial remedies in courts of the host state.

The number of investor-state arbitrations under Chapter 11 of NAFTA has exploded. Many of these proceedings challenge federal, state or local regulatory actions, such as Mexican rules for hazardous waste plants, Canadian and California controls over gasoline additives, and Mississippi punitive damages and appeal bond requirements. Mexico, after losing a court appeal of an award against it, was the first to pay an investor under Chapter 11 procedures. Other arbitrations have settled favorably for NAFTA investors, provoking outcries from governments,

[2]. International Center for Settlement of Investment Disputes (Washington, D.C.).

NGOs and especially environmentalists that the entire process is skewed too heavily in favor of the interests of business. The three governments, collectively in defense, have issued a controversial restrictive interpretation of the "minimum standard" of treatment afforded cross-border investors under NAFTA.

Exclusions

The NAFTA investment code does not apply to Mexican constitutionally-reserved sectors (e.g. energy, railroads and boundary and coastal real estate) nor Canada's cultural industries. It did, however, remove Mexican foreign investment controls for U.S. and Canadian investors below an initial $25 million U.S. threshold phased-up to $150 million U.S. in 2004, and opened new Mexican mining ventures to NAFTA investors after 1998. Canadian review of direct U.S. investments in excess of $150 million U.S. and indirect investments in excess of $450 million (indexed for inflation from Jan. 1, 1993) will continue. Maritime, airline, broadcasting, fishing, nuclear, basic telecommunications, and government-sponsored technology consortia are exempt from the NAFTA investment rules. All of the NAFTA countries agreed not to lower environmental standards to attract investment and permit (as Mexico requires) environmental impact statements for foreign investments. However, apart from consultations, there was no remedy in this area prior to the environmental side agreement discussed below.

FINANCIAL SERVICES

Financial services provided by banking, insurance, securities and other firms are separately covered under the NAFTA. Trade in such services is generally subject to specific liberalization commitments and transition periods. Financial service providers, including non-NAFTA providers operating through subsidiaries in a NAFTA country, are entitled to establish themselves anywhere within NAFTA and service customers there (the right of "commercial presence"). Existing cross-border restraints on the provision of financial services were frozen and no new restraints may be imposed (subject to designated exceptions). Providers of financial services in each NAFTA nation receive both national and most favored nation treatment. This includes equality of competitive opportunity, which is defined as avoidance of measures that disadvantage foreign providers relative to domestic providers. Various procedural transparency rules are established to facilitate the entry and equal opportunity of NAFTA providers of financial services. The host nation may legislate reasonable prudential requirements for such companies and, under limited circumstances, protect their balance of payments in ways which restrain financial providers.

National Commitments

The following are some of the more notable country-specific commitments on financial service made in the NAFTA:

United States—A grace period allowed Mexican banks already operating a securities firm in the U.S. to continue to do so until July of 1997.

Canada—The exemption granted U.S. companies under the Canada–U.S. FTA to hold more than 25 percent of the shares of a federally regulated Canadian financial institution was extended to Mexican firms, as was the suspension of Canada's 12 percent asset ceiling rules. Multiple branches may be opened in Canada without Ministry of Finance approval.

Mexico—Banking, securities and insurance companies from the U.S. and Canada are able to enter the Mexican market through subsidiaries and joint ventures (but not branches) subject to market share limits during a transition period that ended in the year 2000 (insurance) or 2004 (banking and securities). Finance companies are able to establish separate subsidiaries in Mexico to provide consumer, commercial, mortgage lending or credit card services, subject to a three percent aggregate asset limitation (which does not apply to lending by affiliates of automotive companies). Existing U.S. and Canadian insurers could expand their ownership rights to 100 percent after 1996. No equity or market share requirements apply for warehousing and bonding, foreign exchange and mutual fund management enterprises.

INTELLECTUAL PROPERTY

The NAFTA mandates adequate and effective intellectual property rights in all countries, including national treatment and effective internal and external enforcement rights. Specific commitments are made for virtually all types of intellectual property, including patents, copyrights, trademarks, plant breeds, industrial designs, trade secrets, semiconductor chips (directly and in goods incorporating them) and geographical indicators. NAFTA's coverage of trade secrets was a "first" internationally and was replicated in the WTO Trade–Related Intellectual Property Rights Agreement (TRIPs).

For copyright, the NAFTA obligates protection for computer programs, databases, computer program and sound recording rentals, and a 50 year term of protection for sound recordings. For patents, the NAFTA mandates a minimum 20 years of coverage (from date of filing) of nearly all products and processes including pharmaceuticals and agricultural chemicals. It also requires removal of any special or discriminatory patent regimes or availability of rights. Compulsory licensing is limited. Service marks are treated equally with trademarks. Satellite signal poaching is illegal and trade secrets are generally protected (including from disclosure by governments). The NAFTA details member states' duties to provide damages, injunctive, antipiracy and general due process remedies in the intellectual property field. This has, for example, required major changes in Mexican law.

OTHER NAFTA PROVISIONS

Business Visas

The provisions on temporary entry visas for business persons found in the CUSFTA are extended under the NAFTA. These entry rights cover business persons, traders, investors, intra-company transferees and 63 designated professionals. Installers, after-sales repair and maintenance staff and managers performing services under a warranty or other service contract incidental to the sale of equipment or machinery are included, as are sales representatives, buyers, market researchers and financial service providers. White collar business persons only need proof of citizenship and documentation of business purpose to work in another NAFTA country for up to five years. Many Canadians have taken advantage of NAFTA's special entry rights, particularly professionals obtaining TN visas. Apart from these provisions, no common market for the free movement of labor is undertaken.

State Monopolies and Antitrust

The NAFTA embraces a competition policy principally aimed at state enterprises and governmentally sanctioned monopolies, mostly found in Mexico. State owned or controlled businesses, at all levels of government, are required to act consistently with the NAFTA when exercising regulatory, administrative or governmental authority (e.g. when granting licenses). Governmentally-owned and privately-owned state-designated monopolies are obliged to follow commercial considerations in their transactions and avoid discrimination against goods or services of other NAFTA nations. Furthermore, each country must ensure that such monopolies do not use their positions to engage in anticompetitive practices in non-monopoly markets. Since each NAFTA nation must adopt laws against anticompetitive business practices and cooperate in their enforcement, Mexico has revived its historically weak "antitrust" laws. A consultative Trade and Competition Committee reviews competition policy issues under the NAFTA.

Miscellaneous Provisions

Other notable provisions in the NAFTA include a general duty of legal transparency, fairness and due process regarding all laws affecting traders and investors with independent administrative or judicial review of government action. Generalized exceptions to the agreement cover action to protect national security and national interests such as public morals, health, national treasures, natural resources, or to enforce laws against deceptive or anticompetitive practices, short of arbitrary discriminations or disguised restraints on trade. Balance of payments trade restraints are governed by the rules of the International Monetary Fund. Taxation issues are subject to bilateral double taxation treaties, including a new one between Mexico and the United States. The "cultural industry" reservations secured by the CUSFTA now cover Canada and Mexico, but are not extended to Mexican–U.S. trade. A right of compensatory retaliation through measures of equivalent commercial effect is granted when invocation of these reservations would have violated the Canada–U.S. FTA but for the cultural industries proviso.

Right of Withdrawal

The NAFTA is not forever. Any country may withdraw on six months notice. Other countries or groups of countries may be admitted to the NAFTA if Canada, Mexico and the United States agree and domestic ratification follows. In December of 1994, Chile was invited to become the next member of the NAFTA. Negotiations stalled for want of U.S. Congressional fast track negotiating authority. By 2004, Chile had bilateral free trade agreements with Canada, Mexico and the United States.

DISPUTE SETTLEMENT UNDER NAFTA

The institutional dispute settlement arrangements accompanying the NAFTA are minimal. A trilateral Trade Commission (with Secretariat) comprised of ministerial or cabinet-level officials meets at least annually to ensure effective joint management of the NAFTA is established. The various intergovernmental committees established for specific areas of coverage of the NAFTA (e.g. competition policy) to oversee much of the work of making the free trade area function. These committees operate on the basis of consensus, referring contentious issues to the Trade Commission.

Forum Selection: NAFTA or WTO

Investment, dumping and subsidy, financial services, environmental-investment and standards disputes are subject to special dispute resolution procedures. A general NAFTA dispute settlement procedure is also established (Chapter 20). A right of consultation exists when one country's rights are thought to be affected. If consultations do not resolve the issue within 45 days, the complainant may convene a meeting of the Trade Commission. The Commission must seek to promptly settle the dispute and may use its good offices, mediation, conciliation or any other alternative means. Absent resolution, the complaining country or countries ordinarily commence proceedings under the GATT/WTO or the NAFTA. Once selected, the chosen forum becomes exclusive. However, if the dispute concerns environmental, safety, health or conservation standards, or arises under specific environmental agreements, the responding nation may elect to have the dispute heard by a NAFTA panel.

Chapter 20

Dispute settlement procedures under Chapter 20 involve nonbinding arbitration by five persons chosen in most cases from a trilaterally agreed roster of experts (not limited to NAFTA citizens), with a special roster established for disputes about financial services. A "reverse selection" process is used. The chair of the panel is first chosen by agreement or, failing agreement, by designation of one side selected by lot. The chair cannot be a citizen of the selecting side but must be a NAFTA national. Each side then selects two additional arbitrators who are citizens of the country or countries on the *other* side. The Commission has approved rules of procedure including the opportunity for written submissions, rebuttals and at least one oral hearing. Expert advice on environmental and scientific matters may be given by special procedures accessing science boards. Strict time limits are created so as to keep the panel on track to a prompt resolution. Within 90 days an initial confidential report must be circulated, followed by 14 days for comment by the parties and 16 days for the final panel report to the Commission.

Early NAFTA Chapter 20 arbitrations have concerned Canadian tariffication of agricultural quotas (upheld), U.S. escape clause relief from Mexican corn broom exports (rejected) and a Mexican challenge of the U.S. failure to implement cross-border trucking (upheld). Once the Trade Commission receives a final arbitration panel report, the NAFTA requires the disputing nations to agree within 30 days on a resolution (normally by conforming to the panel's recommendations). If a mutually agreed resolution does not occur at this stage, the complaining country may retaliate by suspending the application of equivalent benefits under the NAFTA. Any NAFTA country may invoke the arbitration panel process if it perceives that this retaliation is excessive.

When NAFTA interpretational issues are disputed before domestic tribunals or courts, the Trade

Commission (if it can agree) can submit an interpretation to that body. In the absence of agreement within the Commission, any NAFTA country may intervene and submit its views as to the proper interpretation or application of the NAFTA to the national court or tribunal.

Antidumping or Subsidy Disputes

The independent binational review panel mechanism established in the CUSFTA for dumping and subsidy duties was carried over into NAFTA, along with the extraordinary challenge procedure to deal with allegations about the integrity of the panel review process. Chapter 19 panels are substituted for traditional judicial review at the national level of administrative dumping and countervailing duty orders. Mexico has undertaken major improvements to its law in this area. The procedures and rules for such panels generally follow those found in the CUSFTA. They are limited to issues of the consistency of the national decisions with domestic law, and once again have been numerous.

In addition, a special committee may be requested by any country believing that another's domestic law has prevented the establishment, final decision or implementation of the decision by such a panel. A special committee may also be invoked if the opportunity for independent judicial review on a dumping or subsidy determination has been denied (a concern focused especially on Mexico). This committee's findings, if affirmative, will result in member state consultations. Absent resolution, the complainant may suspend the panel system or benefits under the NAFTA agreement.

THE SIDE AGREEMENTS ON LABOR AND THE ENVIRONMENT

The NAFTA side agreements on labor (NAALC) and the environment (NAAEC) do not create additional substantive regional rules. Rather the side agreements basically create law enforcement mechanisms. The side agreements commit each country to creation of environmental and labor bodies that monitor compliance with the adequacy and the enforcement of *domestic* law. The Commission for Environmental Cooperation (CEC)(Montreal) and three National Administrative Offices (NAO) concerning labor matters are empowered to receive complaints. Negotiations to resolve complaints first ensue.

Environmental Disputes

In the absence of a negotiated solution, the NAAEC establishes five environmental dispute settlement mechanisms. *First*, the CEC Secretariat may report on almost any environmental matter. *Second*, the Secretariat may develop a factual record in trade-related law enforcement disputes. *Third*, the CEC Council can release that record to the public. *Fourth*, if there is a persistent pattern of failure to enforce environmental law, the Council will mediate and conciliate. *Fifth*, if such efforts fail, the Council can send the matter to arbitration and awards can be enforced by monetary penalties. To date, no NAAEC disputes have gotten beyond the second Factual Record stage, and few have made it that far.

Labor Disputes

The NAALC labor law enforcement system is a calibrated four-tier series of dispute resolution mechanisms. *First*, the NAOs may review and report on eleven designated labor law enforcement matters that correspond to the NAALC Labor Principles. *Second*, ministerial consultations may follow when recommended by the NAO. *Third*, an Evaluation Committee of Experts can report on trade-related mutually recognized labor law enforcement patterns of practice concerning eight of the NAALC Labor Principles (excluding strikes, union organizing and collective bargaining). *Fourth*, persistent patterns of failure to enforce occupational health and safety, child labor or minimum wage laws can be arbitrated and awards enforced by monetary penalties. To date, no NAALC disputes have gone beyond the second Ministerial Consultations stage.

The NAAEC and NAALC law enforcement mechanisms have been invoked more frequently than many expected. Quite a few labor law enforcement complaints have focused on the organization of "independent" unions in Mexico. A major study explored pregnancy discrimination in the Mexican workplace. United States plant closings and treatment of immigrant workers have also been reviewed. Regarding the environment, a wide range of complaints have been filed asserting inadequate Canadian, Mexican and U.S. law enforcement. Nevertheless, in terms of enhancing environmental and labor law enforcement, the NAEEC and NAALC seem marginally relevant.

COMPARISON WITH THE EUROPEAN UNION

Some of the most revealing aspects of the NAFTA agreement are found in what it does *not* provide. By comparison with the European Union, the NAFTA is politically, legislatively and judicially streamlined. There is no NAFTA Court of Justice, no NAFTA Parliament, nor a NAFTA Council of Ministers. The trilateral Trade Commission's powers pale in significance to those of the European Commission. Substantively, the most dramatic differences are the absence of any free movement rights for workers or the citizenry at large, the lack of a common external tariff and a common international trade policy, the complete omission of any single currency and economic convergence goals, and the right of member state withdrawal upon six months notice. Nor are there common NAFTA defense, foreign, internal affairs, regional development, research, technology transfer, education, taxation, company law, antitrust and social policies (to name only some of the areas in which the EU is quite active).

In short, when compared with European integration, the NAFTA is strikingly limited in its goals and techniques. This conclusion has a variety of implications for the future of North America. It suggests, on the one hand, that North America's limited trade and investment-oriented goals ought to be more obtainable than the grand panorama of European economic, social and political union undertaken in a treaty of unlimited duration. On the other hand, the European experience suggests that once commenced the process of integration in North America will gradually and inevitably advance to greater and greater degrees.

FREE TRADE AND THE AMERICAS

The United States "Enterprise for the Americas Initiative" (EAI) under President George H. W. Bush raised hopes of economic integration throughout the Americas against a background of competitive regionalism in trade relations, especially between the European Union and North America. At the Americas Summit in Miami, President Clinton and 33 Latin American heads of state (only Fidel Castro was absent) renewed this hope by agreeing to commence negotiations on a Free Trade Area of the Americas (FTAA). Formal FTAA negotiations were delayed several times, particularly because of differences between Brazil-led MERCOSUR and U.S.-led NAFTA. The year 2005 was targeted at the Miami Summit for creation of the FTAA, a target that was not met.

FTAA preparatory working groups have regularly met since 1995 to discuss the following topics: (1) Market Access; (2) Customs Procedures and Rules of Origin; (3) Investment; (4) Standards and Technical Barriers to Trade; (5) Sanitary and Phytosanitary Measures; (6) Subsidies, Antidumping and Countervailing Duties; (7) Smaller Economies; (8) Government Procurement; (9) Intellectual Property Rights; (10) Services; (11) Competition Policy; and (12) Dispute Settlement. It is expected that each of these areas will be covered in any FTAA agreement.

Fast Track Delayed

The absence of "fast track" authority (see Chapter 2) and the general perception that political support for free trade in the United States was waning under the Clinton administration clearly slowed FTAA developments. MERCOSUR and Brazil in particular seized the opportunity to accelerate South American free trade and generate a better position to negotiate FTAA terms and conditions with the NAFTA nations. To that end, Bolivia, Peru and Chile are MERCOSUR free trade associates and negotiations with virtually all South American countries are in progress. Venezuela is actively seeking MERCOSUR membership, and has a socialist-style Trade Treaty for the Peoples with Cuba and Bolivia. Late in 2003, MERCOSUR and the ANDEAN COMMMUNITY (ANCOM: Ecuador, Peru, Colombia, Venezuela, Bolivia) signed a free trade deal. Indeed, MERCOSUR is even negotiating along the same lines with Canada, Mexico, the Central American states, and the European Union.

Fast Track Arrives

In 2002, a bipartisan Congress authorized President George W. Bush to negotiate free trade agreements on a fast track basis. This authorization was valid until July of 2007. President Bush, following the pattern established by Canada and Mexico, rapidly concluded a bilateral U.S. free trade agreement with Chile, including coverage of the environment and labor.

The 2002 Congressional authorization of fast track free trade negotiations covers the FTAA. President George W. Bush sought such an agreement, while simultaneously concluding U.S. free trade deals with five Central American states and the Dominican Republic (2004), Peru (2007), Colombia (pending) and Panama (pending). Such a "divide and conquer" strategy undermines Brazil's hopes for a united South American trade negotiating front. It also reflects the reality of the United States playing catch up with Canada (which has free trade agreements with Chile, Peru and Costa Rica) and Mexico (which has numerous Latin American free trade agreements). See Chapter 5.

Divisions were particularly evident during the November 2003 FTAA ministerial meeting in Miami. Lowered expectations, known as FTAA–Lite, reflect U.S. refusal to budge on agricultural protection and trade remedies, and Brazilian refusal to fully embrace investment, intellectual property, services and procurement "free trade." Absent successful resolution of these issues in the WTO Doha Round negotiations, an unlikely prospect at this writing, even FTAA–Lite with different levels of country commitments seems unlikely.

U.S. Free Trade Agreements—NAFTA Plus

United States free trade agreements since NAFTA have evolved substantively under a policy known as "competitive liberalization." For example, coverage of labor law has been narrowed to core ILO principles: The rights of association, organization and collective bargaining; acceptable work conditions regarding minimum wages, hours and occupational health and safety; minimum ages for employment of children and elimination of the worst forms of child labor; and a ban on forced or compulsory labor. Coverage of labor and environmental law enforcement is folded into the trade agreement (compare NAFTA's side agreements) and all remedies are intergovernmental (compare private and NGO "remedies" in the side agreements).

Other NAFTA-plus provisions have emerged. These are most evident regarding foreign investment and intellectual property. Regarding investor-state claims, for example, post-NAFTA U.S. free trade agreements insert the word "customary" before international law in defining the minimum standard of treatment to which foreign investors are entitled. This insertion tracks the official Interpretation issued in that regard under NAFTA. In addition, the contested terms "fair and equitable treatment" and "full protection and security" are defined for the first time:

"fair and equitable treatment" includes the obligation not to deny justice in criminal, civil, or administrative adjudicatory proceedings in accordance with the principle of due process embodied in the principal legal systems of the world; and

"full protection and security" requires each Party to provide the level of police protection required under customary international law.

More significantly perhaps, starting with the U.S.–Chile FTA, these agreements contain an Annex restricting the scope of "indirect expropriation" claims:

> Except in rare circumstances, nondiscriminatory regulatory actions by a Party that are designed and applied to protect legitimate public welfare objectives, such as public health, safety, and the environment, do not constitute indirect expropriations.

Hence the potential for succeeding with "regulatory takings" investor-state claims has been reduced. Morever, the CAFTA–DR agreement anticipates creating an appellate body of some sort for investor-state arbitration decisions.

Regarding intellectual property, NAFTA-plus has moved into the Internet age. Protection of domain names, and adherence to the WIPO Internet treaties, are stipulated. E-commerce and free trade in digital products are embraced, copyrights extended to rights-management (encryption) and anti-circumvention (hacking) technology, protection against web music file sharing enhanced, and potential liability of Internet Service Providers detailed.

Less visibly, pharmaceutical patent owners obtain extensions of their patents to compensate for delays in the approval process, and greater control over their test data, making it harder for generic competition to emerge. They also gain "linkage," meaning local drug regulators must make sure generics are not patent-infringing before their release. In addition, adherence to the Patent Law Treaty (2000) and the Trademark Law Treaty (1994) is agreed. Anti-counterfeiting laws are tightened, particularly regarding destruction of counterfeit goods.

Other NAFTA-plus changes push further along the path of free trade in services and comprehensive customs law administration rules. Antidumping and countervailing duty laws remain applicable, but appeals from administrative determinations are taken in national courts, not binational panels. Except for limited provisions in the Chile–U.S. agreement, business visas drop completely out of U.S. free trade agreements, a NAFTA-minus development.

In sum, the United States has generally used its leverage with smaller trade partners in the Americas to obtain more preferential treatment and expanded protection for its goods, services, technology and investors. It has given up relatively little in return, for example a modest increase in agricultural market openings. The net results substantively suggest that the NAFTA/MERCOSUR divide is deepening.

Quebec and NAFTA

The Canadian Constitution of 1982 was adopted by an Act of the British Parliament. As such, the

Act and Constitution of 1982 are thought to bind all Canadian provinces including Quebec. That province, however, has never formally ratified the Constitution of Canada. Since 1982 a series of negotiations have attempted to secure Quebec's ratification, and all have failed miserably.

In 1987, for example, the "Meech Lake Accord" was reached. This agreement recognized Quebec as a "distinct society" in Canada. What the practical consequences of this recognition would have been will never be known. Quebec's adherence to the Meech Lake Accord was nullified when Manitoba, New Brunswick and ultimately Newfoundland failed to ratify the Accord. A second set of negotiations led in 1992 to the Charlottetown Accord which also acknowledged Quebec as a distinct society with its French language, unique culture and Civil Law tradition. This time a national referendum was held and its defeat was overwhelming. Quebec, five English-speaking Canadian provinces, and the Yukon territory voted against the Charlottetown Accord.

The failure of these Accords moved Quebec towards separation from Canada. In 1994, the Parti Quebecois came to power. It held a provincial referendum on separation in 1995. By the narrowest of margins, the people of Quebec rejected separation from Canada. Just exactly what "separation" would have meant was never entirely clear during the debate, perhaps deliberately so.

In 1998, Canada's Supreme Court ruled that Quebec could not "under the Constitution" withdraw unilaterally. To secede, Quebec would need to negotiate a constitutional amendment with the rest of Canada. The rest of Canada would, likewise, be obliged to enter into such negotiations if a "clear majority" of Quebec's voters approved a "clear question" on secession in a referendum. Subsequently, the Canadian Parliament legislated rules which will make it difficult for Quebec to separate, should it ever wish to do so. That prospect now seems more remote, particularly because the Parti Quebecois lost power in 2003.

If Quebec ever separates from Canada this will raise fundamental issues about Quebec and NAFTA. Would Quebec be forced to negotiate for membership in NAFTA? If so, would English-speaking Canada veto its application? Might Quebec's relationship to Canada continue in some limited manner (such as for defense and international trade purposes) such that NAFTA is not an issue at all? Might Quebec automatically "succeed" to the NAFTA treaty, thus becoming a member without application? Customary international practice maintains existing treaties when nations sub-divide. This practice was applied to the Czech Republic, Slovakia, and various states of the former Yugoslavia. Thus custom suggests that fears in Quebec about losing NAFTA benefits are exaggerated.

Conclusion

The future of free trade in the Americas remains uncertain. NAFTA's expansion is permanently stalled, and the FTAA proposal seems dead in the water. Canada, Chile, Mexico, MERCOSUR and others seized the opportunity to advance their trade relations while Congress deliberated fast track between 1994 and 2002. With the United States back in the free trade game between 2002 and July 2007, bilateral agreements have been the wave. Once again, however, the absence of U.S. fast track negotiating authority seems likely to freeze future developments. Brazil, Venezuela and MERCOSUR are no doubt smiling.

A NAFTA/Free Trade in the Americas Timeline

1986	Canada–U.S. free trade negotiations commence. Mexico joins the GATT. Uruguay Round of GATT negotiations launched.
1989	CFTA enters into effect.
1991	Congress extends fast track authority to NAFTA and Uruguay Round.
1992	NAFTA signed by Presidents Bush and Salinas, Prime Minister Mulroney.
1993 (August)	Side agreements on North American Labor and Environmental Cooperation concluded under President Clinton.
1993 (October)	Vice President Gore "defeats" Ross Perot in nationally televised NAFTA debate.
1993 (November)	U.S. Congress ratifies NAFTA and sides agreements.
1993 (December)	Uruguay Round agreements concluded.
1994	NAFTA enters into effect.
1994 (December)	Miami Summit supports creation by 2005 of a Free Trade Area of the Americas (FTAA).

1994–95	Mexican peso crashes, U.S. organizes rescue package.
1995	Uruguay Round agreements enter into effect. WTO created. Negotiations commence for Chile to join NAFTA. Quebec voters barely reject separation from Canada.
1997	Canada and Chile agree on free trade with side agreements. Mexico revises its free trade agreement with Chile.
1995–2002	Congress refuses to authorize fast track negotiations. Mexico agrees to free trade with Colombia, Venezuela, Costa Rica, Bolivia, Nicaragua, Guatemala, Honduras, El Salvador, Peru and Uruguay. Canada agrees to free trade with Costa Rica.
2002	Congress authorizes bilateral and FTAA fast track negotiations.
2003	U.S.–Chile agree on free trade.
2004	U.S.–CAFTA agree on free trade.
2005	FTAA deadline is not met, CAFTA–DR agreement passes House of Representative by two votes.
2006/2007	Panama, Peru and Colombia agree on free trade with the U.S. Venezuela applies for MERCOSUR membership, signs Peoples' Trade Treaty with Cuba and Bolivia.
2007 (July)	U.S. fast track authority expires.
2007 (October)	Costa Rican people barely approve CAFTA.
2008 (Jan)	U.S.-Peru and Canada–Peru FTAs take effect

INDEX

References are to Pages

AMERICAS, FREE TRADE, 186–188, 310–314

ANTIDUMPING, see Dumping, this index

ASIA, see ASEAN
East Asian integration, 199
Trade patterns, 18–19

ASSOCIATION OF SOUTHEAST ASIAN NATIONS (ASEAN)
Background, 188–191
Complementation schemes, 196–199
Industrial projects, 192
Joint Ventures, 197–199
Trade rules, 192–195

BOYCOTTS
Antiboycott of Israel, U.S. law, 166–168
Cuba, 164
U.S. provisions, 164

CUSFTA (Canada–U.S. Free Trade Area)
Dispute settlement, 277–280
Origins, 268
Outline, 269–277

COMMON MARKET
See European Union

COUNTERVAILING DUTIES
CUSFTA, dispute settlement under, 277–279
Imports, 135–137
NAFTA, dispute settlement under, 305
U.S. law, 139–143
WTO Code, 137–139

COURT OF INTERNATIONAL TRADE, 150

CUSTOMS
Africa Growth and Opportunity Act, 105
Andean Trade Preference Act, 104
Caribbean Basin Economic Recovery Act, 103–105
Customs classification, 96–98
Customs Valuation Code, 98
Duty free access to U.S., 107
Generalized System of Preferences, 100–103
Harmonized Tariff Schedule, 96–98
Rules of origin, 99
Section 9802.00.80, 106–107
Tariff Schedule of the U.S., 89–93

DUMPING
Antidumping, generally, 124–128
CUSFTA, dispute settlement under, 279
NAFTA, dispute settlement under, 305
U.S. antidumping law, 128–135
WTO Code, 131–135

ECONOMIC INTEGRATION
Africa, 183–185
Americas, 186–188
Association of Southeast Asian Nations, this index
Developing world, 182
East Asia, 199
GATS, 181
GATT Article 24, 179–181
Islamic world, 185

ENVIRONMENT
EU policy, 253
NAFTA, and, 306

ESCAPE CLAUSES (SAFEGUARDS)
Adjustment assistance, 146
NAFTA, 288
U.S. law, 143–147
WTO Code, 147–149

EUROPEAN COMMUNITY, see EUROPEAN UNION

EUROPEAN UNION, see Chapter 6
Agricultural policy, 251–253
Amsterdam Treaty, 209
Broadcasting, 248
Business organization law, 257–260

EUROPEAN UNION, see Chapter 6—Cont'd
Capital, free movement of, 249
Commission, 217–220
Constitution, defeat of, 212
Council of Ministers, 215–217
Court of First Instance, 228
Court of Justice, 224–229
Directly effective law, 230–233
Environmental policy, 253
Equal pay and treatment, 263
Establishment, right of, 245
Euro zone, 83–84
European Parliament, 220–224
Free movement, 205–208
Goods, 205, 237–240
History, 200–204
Intellectual property rights, 240–242
Languages, 204
Law enforcement, 234–237
Legislative process, 215–224
Reform Treaty, proposed, 213–215
Services, freedom to provide, 246–248
Social policy, 260–263
Supremacy doctrine, 225
Taxation, 254
Technology law, 242–243
Timeline, 265
Trade relations, 255
Transport policy, 251
Treaty of Nice, 210–212
Treaty on European Union, 208
Workers, 244

EXPORTS
Boycotts, this index
Bureau of Industry and Security (BAS), 157
COCOM controls, 158
Controls, Chapter 4, 9–12
Export Administration Act and Regulations, 156–163
    Sanctions for violations, 163
Foreign Corrupt Practices Act, 168–171
Section 301 and Super 301, 171–176
U.S. policy, 154–156
Wassenaar Arrangement, 159

FAST TRACK, 42, 281, 310

INDEX
References are to Pages

FOREIGN CORRUPT PRACTICES ACT, 168–171

FREE TRADE AGREEMENTS, see AMERICAS, ASEAN, NAFTA,
generally Chapter 5
Africa, 183–185
Americas, 186–188, 309–318
Canada–U.S. free trade, 268–280
East Asia, 199
Islamic world, 185
NAFTA, this index
U.S. agreements, 42, 310–314

GENERAL AGREEMENT ON TARIFFS AND TRADE (GATT)
See also WTO
Countervailing Duties, this index
Dumping, this index
GATT 1947, 34–38
GATT 1994, 42–44
Import restrictions, 36–38
MFN treatment under, 36–37
Negotiating rounds, 39–40
Quantitative import restrictions under, 37–38
Trade agreements, 179–181

IMPORTS
Africa Growth and Opportunity Act, 105
Agriculture, 51–53
Andean Trade Preference Act, 104
Antidumping, 124–135
Buy American Act of 1933, 114–116
Caribbean Basin Economic Recovery Act, 104
Competition, responses to, 122–124
Countervailing duties and unfair subsidies, this index
Court of International Trade, this index
Customs, this index
Dumping, this index
Duty free, 107
Escape Clauses, this index
Foreign trade zones, 95
GATT, this index
Generalized system of preferences, 100–103
Harmonized Tariff Schedule implemented, 96–98
NAFTA, this index
Nontariff trade barriers, 117–122
Procurement, 111–116

IMPORTS—Cont'd
Product standards, 117–122
Quotas, 108–110
Restrictions, Chapter 3
Section 201 proceedings, see Escape Clauses
Section 9802.00.80, 106–107
Tariff Act of 1930, 87–89
United States restrictions, see generally Chapter 3, 4–6
U.S. tariffs, 87–93
WTO, this index

INTERNATIONAL MONETARY FUND, 78–84

LABOR, North American cooperation, 307

MULTINATIONAL ENTERPRISES
    Generally, Chapter 1
Corporate counsel, 28–31
Transfer pricing, 25–27

NAFTA, see Chapter 7
    See also Free Trade Agreements
Antidumping and countervailing duty disputes, binational panels
        for resolution of, 305
Business visas, 300
Dispute settlement, 302
Energy, 286
Environment, side agreement on, 306
EU, comparison with, 308
Fast track, 281
Financial services trade, 297
Food products, 286
Goods, 283
Intellectual property rights, 299
Investment, rules, 293
Investor-state arbitrations, 295
Labor, side agreement on, 307
Origins, 280
Outline of agreement, 282
Procurement, 289
Product standards, 287
Quebec, and, 314
Rules of origin, 284
Safeguards, 288
Services, trade in, 290
Telecommunications, 292

References are to Pages

NAFTA, see Chapter 7—Cont'd
Timeline, 317
Transport, 291

NONTARIFF BARRIERS, 19–20, 117–122
See also specific subject matter headings

PROCUREMENT, 111–116, 289

SAFEGUARDS, see Escape Clauses, this index

SUBSIDIES, see Countervailing Duties, this index

TRADE LAWS
See specific subject matter headings
Incentives, 20–21
Legal framework, 21–22
Services trade, 17–18
United States trade laws, generally, 85–90

UNITED STATES TRADE REPRESENTATIVE, 42–43

WORLD TRADE
Generally, Chapters 1 and 2
See WTO, this index

WORLD TRADE ORGANIZATION (WTO)
See also GATT, see generally Chapter 2
Admission, 58
Agreement on Agriculture, 51–53
Agreement Establishing the World Trade Organization, 44–46
Agreement on Subsidies and Countervailing Measures, 137–139
Antidumping Agreement, 131–135
Decision-making, 55–59
Dispute settlement, 59–72
General Agreement on Trade in Services (GATS), 53–55
Nontariff trade barrier codes, 48–51
Procurement Code, 113–116
U.S. laws, and, 46, 73–78

†